Advance Praise for
Understanding Loss and Grief for Women

"This impressive book is an excellent addition to the existing literature on critical issues facing women who are dealing with loss and grief. This book is extremely helpful in assisting women in transition through their grief to find resolution, peace, and growth through a very difficult time in their lives."

—*Bill Richardson, MA, Diplomat and Special Envoy, former U.S. Ambassador to the United Nations, former U.S. Secretary of Energy, former two-time Governor of New Mexico, four-time Nobel Peace Prize nominee*

"Buckingham and Howard's book provides an important contribution to the study of bereavement, with an insightful gender-specific perspective on coping with loss and grief. Because of the position women hold in society and their social responsibility, the way they experience loss is unique. By looking at grief through this gendered prism, we have more clarity on how to support women and the people they support. I recommend this book to all who have suffered a loss and those who are close to them."

—*Michelle A. Williams, ScD, Dean of Faculty, Harvard T.H. Chan School of Public Health*

"Modern western societies have only recently been willing to talk openly about death and dying, loss of loved ones, palliative care and grieving. This book by Buckingham and Howard offers insights within the historical and gender context as to why this has been so challenging and why it is time to rethink our societal and personal acceptance of death, dying and grief. This is not only important reading for women suffering or facing the loss of a loved one but also for the people around them. The more men that read this book the greater will be their own understanding of the women close to them and the issues they face not only in the sharpened context of grief but also in life generally."

—*Michael Moore, President, World Federation of Public Health Associations; CEO, Public Health Association of Australia; four-term Minister of Health and Community Care; Adjunct Professor, University of Canberra*

"There are many mediators of the mourning process, of which gender is an important one. Gender responses to loss are fashioned and shaped both by culture and history. In this book, Buckingham and Howard lead the reader to think about women's grief and how gender affects their response to loss, not only by death but also to other life losses such as divorce, health changes, and retirement.

This book provides a perspective for both men and women to understand how women integrate loss into their lives as we emerge into a postmodern age."

—*J. William Worden, PhD, ABPP, clinical psychologist, author of* Grief Counseling & Grief Therapy: A Handbook for the Mental Health Practitioner

"Robert Buckingham and Peggy Howard have written an important book that informs our understanding of women's loss and grief, and points to proactive approaches to healing."

—*Peter MacKinnon, QC, Order of Canada; Past President, University of Saskatchewan, Past Interim President, Athabasca University*

"As one of the founders of Hospice in the United States, Dr. Buckingham, along with his co-author, Dr. Peggy Howard, bring a fresh and needed perspective to the literature, which broadens the reader's understanding of the universal experience of loss and grief. The attention given to the social construction of grief viewed from a cultural perspective gives an insightful lens through which to view changing roles of women today and differing responses to loss and grief of significant relationships and social identities. The case studies presented illustrate well the journey of grief. A must read for health professionals and all of us who inevitably travel this road."

—*Suzanne Selig, PhD, MPH, MSW, Director, Public Health and Health Sciences, University of Michigan, Flint*

"Grief has many aspects and many faces. The inconsolable loss of a loved one casts a very long shadow on the life of those left behind. While grief does cover the gamut of the human experience, there are some gender-specific reactions and needs that are often overlooked. *Understanding Loss and Grief for Women: A New Perspective* is a fresh look at understanding the impact of loss and grief of women in our culture. While grief is complicated for everyone, the unique role women have in dealing with their own losses, as well as those of their loved ones, puts additional pressures on women to cope quickly and to help others in need. I recommend this book without hesitation. As a clinician who has been working with grief and loss for many years, this book is a must."

—*Donald Schumacher, PsyD, President and CEO, National Hospice and Palliative Care Organization, United States*

"To be human is to experience loss, which occurs in many forms. For women responding to or preparing for loss, and for anyone desiring to support others coping with loss, this thoughtful book will help the reader understand women's individual responses to grief, appreciate their personal resiliency and have hope for eventual recovery. Buckingham and Howard compellingly present the grieving process for women as a healthy, transformational opportunity. From the earliest days of Hospice care in the US, Robert Buckingham has effectively addressed the most difficult topics in thanatology. Now, he and co-author Peggy Howard bring to light a long-neglected aspect of the discussion in this engaging and important book."

—*William G. Faraclas, DrPH, Professor of Public Health, Department of Public Health, Southern Connecticut State University*

"Public Health has to recognize and study all the subjects which can affect the well-being of vulnerable communities. If we better understand loss and grief for women, we will be better equipped to help them. The authors' analysis is undoubtedly a precious contribution."

—*Laurent Chambeau, MD, Dean, EHESP French School of Public Health, France*

"'Everyone hugs you when your husband dies. Very few hug you when you get a divorce,' says a bereaved woman. Yet, undeniably, both are experiences of loss that may lead to profound grief. Robert Buckingham and Peggy Howard have written an eloquent and thoughtful text that gives surprising insights into the history, psychology, and social complexities of women's experiences of various kinds of grief. While loss is levitas that lessens life, grief is gravitas that makes it heavier. Buckingham and Howard show how loss, and the grief it causes, may seriously unsettle but they also may deepen and strengthen us as we open to the fullness of our personal being."

—*Max Van Manen, PhD, EdD (Hon.), Professor Emeritus, University of Alberta, Adjunct Professor, University of Victoria*

"The authors have deftly tackled a complex but very important subject. Should be required reading for all primary and palliative care doctors."

—*Robert S. Weiner, MD, Medical Director, Kauai Hospice*

"This book is relevant to women and men alike in that it details the historical and socio-structural account of our post-modern societies. The key message, that grief is largely determined by cultural and gender specific norms, offers a broader understanding of the complexity and individuality of grief and mourning, as well as the intergenerational effects of grief suppression. The authors offer advice for healthy grieving as a way to accept a new life resulting from loss."

—*Ulrich Laaser, Dr. Med, DTM&H, MPH, Past President of the World Federation of Public Health Associations, the Association of Schools of Public Health in the European Region, and the German Association for Health Sciences and Public Health*

"*Understanding Loss and Grief for Women: A New Perspective on Their Pain and Healing* makes a timely and important contribution to our ways of understanding and engaging grief. Unpacking social constructs and expectations of women and grief is critical to deepening our abilities to engage grief, our own and/or of those we work with. Through deconstructing our current knowledge and providing interventions, Drs. Buckingham and Howard have developed an excellent tool to assist women with moving through our grief more wholly, increasing the possibilities for healing and growth."

—Susan Borrego, PhD, Chancellor, University of Michigan, Flint

"This is a 'must-read' for people wanting an excellent guide to understanding women, loss, and grief. Buckingham and Howard have created an important resource describing the unique nature of loss and grief as experienced by women through the examination of sociocultural constructs of women's roles juxtaposed with society's approach to grief. The reader will garner a greater understanding of the impact of loss and clearer insights and tools to support women and their mindfulness of the distinctive character of their own grieving."

—Lori J. Miller, Executive Director, Kaua'i Hospice, Inc.

Understanding Loss and Grief for Women

Understanding Loss and Grief for Women

A New Perspective on Their Pain and Healing

Robert W. Buckingham, DrPH, and
Peggy A. Howard, PhD

PRAEGER™

An Imprint of ABC-CLIO, LLC
Santa Barbara, California • Denver, Colorado

Library of Congress Cataloging in Publication Control Number: 2017005735

ISBN: 978-1-4408-5782-9
EISBN: 978-1-4408-5783-6

21 20 19 18 17 1 2 3 4 5

This book is also available as an eBook.

Praeger
An Imprint of ABC-CLIO, LLC

ABC-CLIO, LLC
130 Cremona Drive, P.O. Box 1911
Santa Barbara, California 93116-1911
www.abc-clio.com

This book is printed on acid-free paper ∞

Manufactured in the United States of America

We dedicate this book to our grandchildren—the people who hold our hopes and dreams. They are our treasures and our legacy.

From Robert W. Buckingham to
Bronté Buckingham
Boden Buckingham
From Peggy Ann Howard to
Willis McLennan

Contents

Preface

This book is written to help women, and the people who support them, better understand why women experience loss and grief as they do. With understanding, we believe, comes empowerment and strength to deal with loss and grief, however tragic and unplanned these life events may be.

Grief is an intense emotion, resulting from sudden or anticipated death of a spouse or partner or child but also from loss of a relationship with a significant other and from more common occurrences such as loss of a career. We acknowledge that there are many other situations that occasion grief, but we have chosen these four types because of their universality and their increasing prominence in an aging population, particularly among that group of people labeled "Baby Boomers" living in North America.

In this book we look at the social construction of women's roles and how that has influenced, and continues to influence, women's experiences of loss and grief. As well, we situate the women's experience within the field of grief as it has evolved over time. These two foundations (sociocultural influence on women's roles, and how grief has been conceptualized and addressed over time) create a backdrop for women to situate their own experiences of loss, and help them to make sense of their grieving process. Insights drawn from that base can allow women to address the dissonance between what they may feel emotionally and what cultural or societal norms dictate as acceptable grief response.

Lack of acknowledgment of grief, and suppression of grief, can have significant health impacts on women—physically, mentally, socially, and spiritually. It is our intent to enhance understanding of loss and grief to support women in reenvisioning, repurposing, and recreating their lives after significant loss.

This book is borne from our research and collective personal and professional experiences of loss and grief—not only in North America but worldwide. We have also drawn on our skills, both individually as a pioneer of the hospice movement in North America, and a former Dean of a School of Public Health, and collectively as academic researchers. We include vignettes and case studies drawn from women's personal experiences. The women's names have been changed to protect their privacy, but their stories and what they have learned from their experiences are shared to help women worldwide.

Acknowledgments

We are grateful to the women who shared their stories of loss and grief. We appreciate their openness and willingness to disclose very personal emotions and details of their lives in a way that has helped us to make the loss and grief experience accessible to others.

We also express our gratitude to the many graduate students who, over the years, have inspired the need for this work.

We wish to thank the many friends and colleagues who have supported the creation of this book, in particular the individuals from around the world who have so generously endorsed it: New Mexico Governor Bill Richardson (USA), Dr. Michelle Williams (USA), Dr. Michael Moore (Australia), Dr. J. William Worden (USA), Peter MacKinnon (Canada), Dr. Suzanne Selig (USA), Dr. Donald Schumacher (USA), Dr. William Faraclas (USA), Dr. Laurent Chambeau (France), Dr. Max Van Manen (Canada), Dr. Robert Weiner (USA), Dr. Ulrich Laaser (Germany), Dr. Susan Borrego (USA), and Lori J. Miller (USA). Your words confirm that understanding women's loss and grief is important, not just for women and the professionals who support them but to men and women worldwide.

We wish to express our gratitude to the following people:

Dr. Selig (Director, Public Health and Health Sciences, University of Michigan–Flint) for continued support for Dr. Buckingham's research, scholarship, and vision for the globalization of public health.

Teresa Bladon, MA, for her first-rate research support.

Patti Ruhala, Administrative Assistant, Public Health & Health Sciences, University of Michigan–Flint for her administrative and technical support.

The team at Praeger who recognized the importance of this work, in particular to Debbie Carvalko, Senior Acquisitions Editor, the design and marketing team, and Jennifer Hartmann, Editorial Operations Assistant.

Introduction

In our death-denying society (Kübler-Ross, 1969), death is not a comfortable subject. For most of us we experience discomfort and trepidation at confronting even the idea of death. This is not surprising given that in American society mass media focuses on and glorifies youth. One's "golden years" are not a time that anyone looks forward to. Aging and death are things to be worried about later. We don't like to talk about death or dying, and in fact, we don't like to think about them much either.

From a social standpoint, loss is something that is acknowledged, but often only in a marginal way. Death is something to be dealt with, let go of, and gotten over quickly. However, for women, the real problem with the societal denial of loss (including death) is that women don't know very much about grief, or the grieving process. Women feel overcome with intense, heart-stripping emotion, and they feel every agonizing breath and sometimes even wish that they could trade places with the dead. But beyond those moments of excruciating pain, women carry on. Their role is to survive and continue to nurture those around them. Grief is to be lived through. It is unfamiliar for sure; it is almost always troublesome; and worse, sometimes it lingers.

Hardwired to endure, women generally deal with grief in ways that seem socially acceptable—in other words, according to their gender role and culture. Grief is such an intense emotion that it cannot be hidden or ignored. And that is the purpose of this book.

In a society marked by constant change, and in a world where everything is transitory, where social structures change rapidly and affect our lives, loss and people's reactions to loss are becoming a social and medical problem that needs to be addressed. Grief, and the emotional suffering following loss, is a powerfully disruptive force that affects all of us, particularly women, as it is our natural role to nurture—sometimes others more than ourselves.

Why and how women are affected by grief, and to what extent it disrupts their lives, has much to do with the woman's position within the socioeconomic structure in which she lives and the degree to which her identity and self-esteem are bound up in that position. Because of past socialization practices, for women in particular, incidences of loss can have devastating effects on a woman's health and wellbeing. Unresolved grief is cumulative and cumulatively negative (James and Friedman, 2009). These impacts are relative to each woman's self-concept and identification with her gender role, which has undergone significant change over the past few decades. Old social patterns are falling away, and new ones are emerging. The woman must define and redefine herself, and this redefinition will affect the way a woman experiences grief. By realizing her perception of her role in society and how her relationship with the person she has lost also affect that role, she can aid herself in dealing with loss. How well she knows herself, or comes to know herself, is critical in order to fully come to terms with the loss of someone she loves (or the thing that she has loved).

This book focuses on women and the way women experience grief according to the woman's alignment with different gender role classifications, as it is the role of women that is undergoing the most intense modification in terms of worldview and development of self. (We acknowledge that men's roles are undergoing modification as well, but the change is less readily apparent with men than women from a sociocultural perspective.) These gender role classifications are social constructions themselves and reflect behavioral characteristics commonly labeled as "masculine" or "feminine" (characteristics that traditionally have been associated with an individual's biological sex). In the past, that which was feminine and associated with women was universally devalued. Contemporary thinking argues for an integration of the masculine and feminine within each of us, and for an equal valuing of each one. We acknowledge that that which has been labeled feminine is not necessarily present only within women, and that which has been labeled masculine is not only present in men. We all share these characteristics, and the suppression of the masculine that occurs in traditionally socialized women and the suppression of the feminine that occurs in traditionally socialized men is not healthy and leads us to live sort of half-lives, suppressing an essential part of our being. Ancient philosophies such as Taoism argue that "the opposition, alternation, and interaction of these two forces give rise to all phenomena of the universe" (Ortner, 1974), and one force is not possible without the other. The female principle, the yin, and the male principle,[1] yang, are a part of us all, and neither part has greater value. One part is not possible without the other. The complexity of the question as to why the feminine principle has been so universally devalued does not allow for its being addressed here, but particularly in dealing with grief there is a need to recognize the value of both feminine and masculine. If the emotions, traditionally considered a feminine quality, are suppressed by individuals who are trying to overcome loss, this suppression may affect the rest of their lives—with devastating outcomes. A woman, for example, who appears to have resolved her grief as defined within the accepted societal parameters may actually be suppressing her emotions. Often this suppressed grief is only recognized years later, hidden under a veil of alcoholism, drug dependence, clinical depression, or physical ailments. With the cultural acceptance of both the masculine and feminine as having equal value, we could all lead fuller, healthier lives and be better equipped to deal with loss and grief, which is an inevitable and necessary part of life.

Note to Readers

With respect to the terms used in this book, bereavement refers to a state of loss, to be robbed or deprived of someone or something (Doka and Martin, 2010). Loss signals a life change from losing or changing an attachment relationship, a prior lifestyle, or a behavior pattern (McCoyd and Walter, 2016). Although we acknowledge that one of the most devastating losses involves the death of a family member or significant other, grief can also arise from separation or divorce, loss of social standing or economic security, and career change. Grief,[2] or grieving, is a person's reaction or response to loss that disrupts one's life (Attig, 2011). Grief typically involves an emotional response, but it may also have physical, cognitive, behavioral, social, and philosophical dimensions (James and Friedman, 2009). Grieving is a social process (Durkheim, 1947) that is expected following loss (Walter, 1999).

Attempting to generalize women's role categories is an assumptive endeavor that will apply to individual women differently, and which will be accurate in some ways and not applicable in others. Take what applies to your individual situation and understand that role classifications allow for fluctuation between roles. The purpose of the role classifications is to help define and clarify the psycho-sociocultural impression a woman has of herself and how this may affect her response to loss and grief.

Notes

1. The Male Principle is a philosophical concept described in sex and character as early as 1903 by Austrian philosopher Otto Weininger; it speaks to issues

of gender, race, cultural identity, the roots of Nazism, and the intellectual history of modernism and modern European culture. The diagram of the yin and yang has been used to graphically represent the philosophy whereby neither sex is completely masculine or feminine. The Female Principle also reflects traditional and rigid culturally defined gender roles, but Jung and others have helped to promote the notion that a fully integrated individual is a unique and balanced expression of both masculine and feminine traits. The earlier concept of the Feminine Principle was that of a nature-based, interconnected existence for all creation (stemming from "Mother Nature"). Aristotle's notion of female inferiority (both scientific and social) promoted the idea that the active male gives form and spirit or movement to the passive, shapeless matter of the female. According to Carol Winters (2006), church fathers marketed Mary Magdalene as the epitome of "feminine" virtues—voiceless, sexless, and submissive. More recent interpretations acknowledge that *female* refers to a person's sex, whereas *feminine* is an attribute that either gender may integrate.

2. Grief, from Latin *gravis*, means "to bear" (Hollis, 2005).

CHAPTER ONE

The Social Construction of Women's Roles (Traditional, Transitional, Modern/Postmodern)

Historical Time Frame

In this text, we refer to traditional societies as those prior to 1900 and ending with the conclusion of World War I (1918). Modern societies essentially dominated the whole of the 20th century[1] and the period between approximately 1920 through to the early 1960s. This transitional period marked a significant shift in the traditional role of women through the feminist movement of the 1960s and 1970s,[2] which focused on dismantling workplace inequality and providing access to better jobs and salaries, ushering in another major shift in the role of women—that of the modern woman.

We refer to the period from the 1970s to present day as postmodern (Walter, 2007). Postmodernity, made popular by Jean-Francois Lyotard, represents a shift to a plurality of knowledge claims and an unpredictable future in which science does not have a privileged place. Both the scope and pace of change are rapid, and nothing can be known with certainty because all preexisting foundations of epistemology (ways of knowing) have been shown to be unreliable. Globalization influences worldwide social relations, and new political and social agendas abound, with prominence of ecological concerns and new social movements (Giddens, 1990).

We begin our goal to better understand women's experiences of grief by looking through the socially constructed lenses of traditional, transitional, and modern/postmodern frames, in which women's roles and their experiences of loss and grief are embedded.

Culture Shaping of the Traditional Role of Women

The period prior to the 1900s, ending with WWI, marks the time of traditional societies. This time coincides with what is commonly referred to as the Victorian era of British history during the reign of Queen Victoria (from 1837 until her death in 1901). This period enjoyed peace, prosperity, refined sensibilities, and national self-confidence for Britain, and the entire Western world felt its influence.

A woman's life and role were essentially defined by, and in accordance with, a prescribed patriarchal tradition, in which life choices are limited, and the primary role is one of caretaker and caregiver—unfortunately, to the extent of the woman's own self-negation. The traditional woman's energies are directed toward others rather than herself. Her focus is family and home, which subsume her individuality. The traditional woman has no identity that is uniquely hers, as her primary function and purpose in life is being a wife and mother, and serving her husband and family.

A woman's success within the traditional role depends on her ability to please and gain approval from parents, husband, family, and church. Approval is gained only if she remains within the rigid confines of her role and lives her life solely in service to others. This rigid gender classification creates boundaries that clearly delineate "women's work" from men's. Generally speaking, from the traditional perspective, men are privileged and honored for doing the "more important things."

Culturally, a traditional role for women is not a new concept. Since before ancient Greece, women were not allowed to walk about in public. They were confined strictly to the "women's quarters," where their primary function was to spin wool for cloth. Men's activities were assigned a higher value, and women's work was continually derided and seen as secondary, if not humiliating (Keuls, 1985). This assignment of cultural value led to the devaluation of women and suppression of the feminine.

Simone de Beauvoir (1949) was one of the first female authors to address the issue in her pioneering book *The Second Sex*.

> What peculiarly signalizes the situation of woman is that she—a free and autonomous being like all human creatures—nevertheless finds herself

> living in a world where men compel her to assume the status of the Other. . . . She is defined and differentiated with reference to man and not he with reference to her; she is the incidental, the inessential as opposed to the essential. He is the Subject, he is the Absolute—she is the Other. ("Beginnings," p. 44)

Influences of Religion, Socioeconomic Status, and Ethnicity on the Traditional Role

Religion

Religion enforces a strong sense of community as a nuclear culture with its own standards for governing actions and choices, and is therefore instrumental in shaping women's roles.

Many of the predominant religious sects today still relegate women to a secondary status and encourage women (overtly or indirectly) to accept a traditional role. If a woman sees her purpose as caregiver and her role as one that is reinforced by the Word of God, it is difficult for her to question her role in the family, and indeed within the community, as anything but that of a vital and necessary caregiver.

Within the community, social affairs are organized in conjunction with religious celebrations so that people with similar beliefs and values spend time together reinforcing age-old doctrines and traditions. This kind of adherence maintains stability and safeguards against outside interference. Those community members who do question the beliefs or actions of the church (oftentimes due to the influence of education or non-church affiliations) are generally shunned for associating with sinners or nonbelievers who have not yet seen "the Light."

Being a "good Christian" requires following church doctrine, and although this applies both to men and women, those doctrines and values affect the traditional woman most, particularly with respect to her gender role. The manifestations of early Christian beliefs that women were evil because of their sexuality can still be seen in traditional family life. The Catholic Church, for example, does not condone divorce or the use of birth control. A woman is expected to marry for life and have a large family to whom she is dedicated for the rest of her life. But sexuality creates a double standard for the traditional woman. On one hand, she is valued and respected for being able to bring more children into the world—children that will perpetuate church doctrine. On the other hand, as a sexual being whose urge to be sexually active is an innate biological tendency, as it is in men, she must deny her natural urge in observation of church doctrine. Only for the purposes of procreation is a women's sexuality condoned, and because of Church resistance to birth control, a woman must be perpetually pregnant or celibate. Taught that her body is evil, a woman can only redeem herself through the saving virtues of motherhood. The virgin/whore dichotomy has had a devastating impact on women's lives, and this traditional view of sexuality works as a powerful mechanism to keep women subordinate to men. As well, because of this view of sex as sinful, women who accept the traditional gender role may never learn to enjoy sex. The traditional woman may see herself only as an entity to reproduce or as a sexual object to please her husband. Her sexual experience may be unfulfilling, and she may not consider that sex can be pleasurable or an act of lovemaking in which she can take an active part (Sklansky and Algazi, 1981). Further, if the traditional women finds herself living into old age within a contemporary society where a good deal of emphasis is placed on sexuality and each individual's ability to find fulfillment through it (the opposite extreme to traditional religious views), a traditional woman's perception of herself may be greatly confused by the contradictory messages she receives.

Socioeconomic Status

In many cases, the lower the social class and economic status of a woman, the more likely her life reflects a traditional gender role. Unfortunately, in our materially oriented society, social class is a direct reflection of income. When a woman is poor, and basic survival is of primary concern, she has fewer opportunities for education and travel, both of which allow her to see and perhaps experience ways of life that are different from her own. There is limited opportunity to explore alternate ideologies about what life can be for a woman; what is right, fair, or just.

A traditionally socialized woman will almost certainly have children and because the primary responsibility to support and care for them falls to her, opportunities to envision a different life are limited. This situation is exacerbated when a traditional woman divorces and is forced to support herself and her children with only marginally marketable skills.

Ethnicity

Generally speaking, on a global scale women whose role is traditional are more typically found is less technologically advanced societies, as small and isolated communities are more slowly affected by the ides of social change. There are still many cultures that encourage women to remain in a traditional role, but even in strictly sex-segregated cultures such as those in the Middle East, some change is evident. Within the last generation, several women's universities have opened, signaling a break in the rigid cast of oppression for mid-Eastern women.

Changing Status, Blurred Boundaries, and Choice

With its philosophical, religious, and historical basis, women's secondary status has been both culturally learned and imposed, and it is basic to having built the foundation of the traditional woman's identity as one of caregiver. That identity is derived not from her essential self, but rather from duty and service to others. Compliance and fear of rejection, harsh censure, and alienation from family and community have served to keep the traditional woman in her place, and this cultural phenomenon has persisted well into the mid-twentieth century in the Western world. Only because of the courage of women who dared to act against social pressure (such as those active in the "women's movement") were the traditional gender role boundaries loosened, and the secondary status of women questioned.

Today, women who continue to define themselves and their lives as "traditional" are generally over 40 years of age. They were raised in male-dominated households where the lower status of women was not questioned. (Incidentally, men today who regard women as being secondary also tend also to be over age 40.) Increased public awareness of the subtleties of sexual discrimination and the devaluation of women, along with the implementation of Women's Studies courses into mainstream university curricula, have done much to educate both women and men as to the limitations of the traditional gender role and its influence on women's self-concept and worth.

Carol: A "Traditional" Woman Looks at Her Role

The following case study is of Carol. She is a self-described traditional woman, whose life reflects some key elements described in the previous section, but other aspects of her life demonstrate that she has moved beyond the boundaries of that role.

> There is no doubt that I fit the definition of the traditional woman. I am a caretaker and a caregiver whose arena for over 40 years has been my family and my home, except for one brief period. I have not worked for wages since my marriage. However, I do not feel that my role as homemaker has led to self-negation or that I have had no identity outside this role. Perhaps it is because I married late at age 31 and had traveled, taught school, done graduate work, and various things for 10 years after college. Perhaps it is also

because, luckily, I have been married to a "modern" man who did not feel threatened by the blurring of sex roles and who did not feel that housekeeping and child care were solely a wife's responsibility.

From the beginning, we cooked together, grocery shopped together, changed diapers together, hung out the wash together, attended PTA meetings together, and so on. My husband was, of course, the breadwinner, so I was the one most directly involved with the day-to-day life of the household. Admittedly, often I did feel confined, but I never felt that I had lost my identity as a person.

Because housework was not for me an end in itself, but a shared responsibility with the rest of the family, I have always been able to devote some of my energies to unpaid volunteer work of various kinds. For many years, this has given me a strong sense of identity within a traditional relationship. So although I feel that I am a traditional woman, I do not feel that I am restricted by that label. Perhaps this is because of the way I have reacted to my own upbringing.

I was raised by a mother who was very much a traditional woman. She felt the lack of an identity that was uniquely hers, and she was vigorously unhappy with her lot in life. She, like me, married late, having taught school for some years before her marriage. But early on she had to give up her great ambition to become a lawyer. She had attended law school for one semester but had to drop out because her tuition money was needed to send her brother to law school. From the beginning, she rebelled against her role as "just a housewife." I was determined never to do that, and at the same time I looked forward to being married and I was happy giving up whatever career I had embarked upon. So, from that perspective my role has been partly traditional and partly not. I think that applies to my daughters as well.

I have two daughters, just a couple of years apart. One was married at age 19, divorced seven years later, and is now remarried with a husband and a three-year-old to care for. She has a PhD in cell and molecular biology and a full-time career running a cancer research lab at a university.

My other daughter taught school briefly before marriage but now is a full-time wife and mother of two little girls—very much a traditional woman, devoting almost all of her energies toward others, her family, Girl Scouts, PTA, and her church.

So, while I categorize myself as largely a traditional woman, and one of my daughters as a traditional woman, it's apparently not entirely a question of age, but of individual attitudes and choices. My mother, a frustrated traditional woman born in 1879, raised me, a happy traditional woman, who has in turn raised two very different daughters—only one of them traditional. Each of us seems to be coping well within our chosen sphere.

As Carol's case study indicates, the most important factor in her role classification may be the element of choice. Different people are meant to do different things, and the rigid role construction, which existed at the time Carol's mother lived, was clearly a situation that denied individual choice. Since the time of Carol's mother (late 19th century/early 20th century), societal norms have changed somewhat, allowing greater flexibility in gender-role expectations and greater individual choice. Even as in Carol's immediate family, the traditional role reflects the realities of one daughter's life, but not the other's, sharing of once clearly defined roles and responsibilities has somewhat blurred the lines of the traditional role. Societal norms also reflect an increasing valuing of what has been historically considered a strictly feminine/traditional role.

Culture Shaping of the Transitional Role of Women

The period from the 1960s onward is referred to as "modern," in that society was marked by diversity in lifestyle, choice, and a focus on individual rights (Walter, 2007). While many women held jobs outside the home during this time (either on a part- or full-time basis), the traditional orientation of the average American family was for women to focus their priorities on the family unit. This orientation persisted throughout the first half of the 20th century, when women were neither expected, nor encouraged, to pursue a career outside the home as unwaveringly as were men. Even with the exodus of women from the kitchen to industry to fill positions previously held by men who had gone off to war, (WWII), it was assumed that when the men returned, women would resume their domestic duties.

However, the war effort afforded women a taste of a different lifestyle, independence in decision-making, and an opportunity to question their importance and contribution to society. For these women, identity was no longer strictly associated with that of homemaker—even if that is what the woman preferred. Her identity reflected a choice between traditional and modern roles, and she was called upon to navigate between these two polarities.

The transitional woman exists somewhere between the independence of taking responsibility for her self-definition, and having others define her place, how she should act, and who she should be. The degree to which the woman is influenced by the thoughts and beliefs of those around her, and the strength with which she expresses and lives according to her own ideas and direction, determines the ease of her transition. Some transitional women find themselves moving with ease and comfort between traditional and modern roles. Others experience feelings of discord, inner turmoil, conflict, anger, frustration, and uncertainty about which role best suits them. Typically, this is not a decision or choice a woman needs to make until she matures. Interestingly, this choice and the decisions related to it are not something men typically have to make. Historically, males have been taught to be independent and forge their own way, and women have been taught to listen and conform to what others tell them.

A woman who has experienced traditional socialization will find it even more difficult to resist others' opinions and societal influences. The views of her parents, peer group, or mainstream society matter to her, but so too do her own thoughts and feelings. Reconciliation to whatever predominant role the transitional woman chooses depends on her level of awareness of options available to her and her level of introspective ability to evaluate the situation independently to decide what feels right for her. Essentially, she must decide the degree to which others will define her identity and the degree to which she will be self-determining. The decision is not simply one of choosing between a traditional or modern role. There are many factors that influence the decision. For example, the degree to which the woman herself is aware and conscious of not only the factors influencing her decision, but also the beliefs and social mores underlying the factors themselves, together provide a framework for the transitional woman to define herself against and within. A decision is never a clear decision unless the decision-maker is aware of the subtleties involved in multiple sides of the issue, including those that are often not clearly defined or evident. Coming to a clear decision about what role she will play can lead to a kind of identity crisis or, minimally, at least inner conflict and confusion that over time can fester and hold her in a sort of stasis or inability to act.

Some of the key factors that impinge upon the woman's decision about her role are addressed below.

Factors Influencing Role Definition and Choice

Family and/or Career

Raising a family and dedicating one's self to home and family reflects traditional family values by which many American families have been raised. The transitional woman, however, may experience disappointment or frustration in terms of struggling to achieve self-reliance in the face of dedicating herself to home and family while wanting more stimulation in her life. Women who choose to focus on a career reflect a more contemporary approach to establishing priorities. In this case, the transitional woman, because of her socialization, may feel a void in choosing not to follow the traditional blueprint of marriage and children. The current societal emphasis is on women having both successful careers and successful home lives, including a stable, fulfilling, and healthy relationship with a husband, as well as a loving and productive relationship with children. Women are now encouraged to make the most of themselves and participate in a career, recognizing there is still pressure to marry and have a family. Most women feel they can do this with little problem. However, the tremendous commitment and responsibility that each requires may be harder to attain than most women think, especially if the stigma remains that everything to do with domestic activity is a woman's responsibility. It is here that the husband and his attitudes become critical, especially if the woman is ambivalent about what her role as a transitional woman is.

A common source of conflict for the transitional woman who works is the experience of guilt about not spending enough time with her children. Current studies on the children of working mothers show that children do not suffer unless the home is a stressful place. This fact, however, does not change old social attitudes, which communicated directly or indirectly that mothers should be at home when children return from school to listen to them and give advice and comfort (Paloma, 1972). The source of the guilt or anxiety the mother may feel is probably the vestige of former socialization patterns such as those discussed in relation to the traditional role. A woman who believes that the caregiver role is something she must fulfill will experience angst if she perceives herself as neglecting this duty.

There are options for a woman as far as arranging to have time for both her career and family, but of course she must compromise somewhere. The more liberal and willing the father is to assume responsibility for caregiving and domestic duties determines how well this duality can work for the transitional woman. It is here that the dissolution of traditional societal mandate seems necessary: if both parents work, they should share equally in domestic responsibilities. It is, of course, possible for the father to stay home while the mother works, if she has a more profitable job and if he desires to do so. Either way, the greater the transitional woman's earning power, the more likely she is to lean toward an acceptance of a modern role.[3]

Influence of the Male's Perspective

The views of the men that transitional women choose to be with are influential on transitional women's perceptions of their roles. The transitional woman may choose a partner in part because of his affinity to a certain view of the world and both his and her place in it. His view is influential on her decision because, unlike the modern woman, she is still affected by the traditionally "feminine" desire to please him and gain his approval. His opinion, whether supportive or discouraging, has an effect on her.

A man with a "traditional" view of the world, for example, expects his wife to attend to his needs. He assumes an innate superiority in terms of social position because he is the one who "provides," and operates under certain unconscious assumptions that negate the intrinsic value of the woman, whose value is rated according to how well she can fulfill the man's needs and how happy she can make him. The transitional woman who marries a man with these values will find herself trapped in a marriage situation very similar to that of her parents. The male's reaction to the traditional woman's desire to work is usually something like, "Why do you need to do that? I will take care of everything. You stay with the children. They need you." He tends to regard her interest in a career as being an amusement or hobby to him, as her true purpose is fulfilled in the domestic sphere.

A man with a "neo-traditional" view of the world could be called the male equivalent of the transitional woman because he operates somewhere between the strictly traditional role and a more contemporary one. The difference between this man and the transitional woman is that she is the one who is initiating the change in values. He is more of an idle observer, slowly modifying his standards along with the rest of the population. He offers conditional support for his wife's extrafamilial interests. He is tolerant of her work and even claims to support it as long as she will come home on time to prepare his meals and not question the fact that the children take priority over her work. He does realize that her interest in a profession is a serious one that functions to fulfill her needs for a life outside the home, but his understanding of this may be superficial and he may only pay lip service to equality.

Finally, a man with a more "modern" view of the world supports the transitional woman's decision to gain self-identity and self-sufficiency. The modern man is comfortable with the fact that women are equal and participate outside the home to a similar degree to men. He assumes that a woman's need to work is equivalent to his need and that there is no reason why he should not be equally responsible for sharing domestic work and raising the children. This man tends to be from a younger generation, a generation that was raised with values other than traditional ones. This is not to say that it is impossible for someone raised with traditional values to wholeheartedly accept the more modern ideology, but this does occur less frequently.

Woman's Intellectual Capacity

Traditional socialization practices reflect a view that women are less intelligent and therefore inferior to men. Within the traditional view of the world, males typically make decisions on behalf of their wives and children, and if a woman is intelligent, she typically chooses to remain quiet or "play dumb" (Komarovsky, 1946). In either case, historically, negation or suppression of intelligence occurred in deference to male superiority and to maintain a type of stasis within the family unit.

However, there is a difference between a woman who consciously hangs back and does not reveal her intelligence because she has decided to mask it, and a woman who has been indoctrinated with the "should be seen and not heard" principle. In the latter case, the woman is suppressing her intelligence even to herself because she has been taught that whatever she says cannot possibly be important. She has been devalued and invalidated by a traditional attitude that denies the possibility of her intelligence. This attitude was so prevalent that many traditional women, even extremely intelligent ones, regarded women as a group intellectually inferior to men (Goldberg, 1968). Condescension and denial of women's intelligence was, and in some cases still is, perpetuated in expressions such as (however playfully expressed) "Don't worry your pretty little head over it."

In some cases, there is evidence that transitional women have leaned toward the traditional role in suppressing their own intelligence and capabilities by not discussing their jobs or even not accepting a promotion because of perceived competition with the male in the family. One female attorney, for example, expressed that she never spoke of her work in front of her children for fear that they would think her job was more important than her husband's (Rapoport and Rapoport, 1972).

Economic Status

Economic dependence on a spouse was one of the key factors influencing the oppression of women and it was/is a common characteristic of the life of a traditional woman. The more comfortable a woman is financially, the more likely she is to be independent. As society became more tolerant of women working outside the home for wages, women began to contribute financially to the care and support of the family. Further, once a woman's children grew to school age or moved out of the house altogether, women were able to return to the workforce, which they did particularly after the death of their spouse or a divorce. In these cases, the transitional woman took on an increasingly independent identity from that of her spouse.

The Influences of Time—Natural Transitions of Age and Maturity

There are times in a woman's life that challenge her identity more than others (Scarf, 1980). These times force the woman to reconsider her commitment to the role she has chosen, or they may encourage her to strengthen her conviction to her chosen role. Life circumstances, such as the death of a loved one, loss through dissolution of a marriage, or simply a woman's stage of life, create opportunities for women to reevaluate their roles and, in a larger sense, to reassess their fit within their chosen social group. People tend to gravitate toward the sector of society that most readily accepts or accommodates the roles they think best suit them. A brief look at the process of maturation and its affect on women's role development is useful here.

Childhood to Adolescence—As in childhood, the adolescent girl is still relatively dependent on her parents to define her role. She is vulnerable to external influences and is not yet at the point of making conscious role decisions on her own. She is still reliant on her parents, but as she becomes more aware of and influenced by the opinions of peers, the adolescent girl tries to assimilate both parental and peer input in creating a blueprint of her future role.

Adolescence to Young Adulthood—Exiting the teen years and entering adulthood is a critical decision-making time for a young woman. She decides what school to attend; whether she wants a career; whether she wants a partner with whom to raise a family (or not); whether she wants to independently support herself (or not). It is a time of making key decisions, and revisiting and reevaluating the influences of childhood and adolescence, particularly if a traditional upbringing formed part of her past. The young adult woman may be faced with the realization that she does not agree with same values that were instilled in her, and may make a conscious effort to do right what her parents did wrong. For the first time, this woman is free of parental influence and for the most part in the position of making decisions about how she will organize her life. It is at this time that she will essentially confront the question of her role by acting on her collective life experiences and personality.

Middle Age—This is the time at which women who have prioritized their husbands and children over a career or other interests face a significant reassessment and oftentimes difficult realization that as their children begin to leave home, a kind of void is created in their lives (commonly referred to by psychiatrists and sociologists as the "empty rest syndrome"). These women may perceive themselves as having lost their importance and not knowing what to do with their time and what remains of their lives.

Middle age is also the time when approximately three-quarters of women become widowed (half of them in their mid-50s), and what women in this age group fear most about widowhood is having to make decisions on their own (Paloma, 1972). Further, with a middle-age glimpse toward the end of their own lives (widowed or not) as both imminent and unavoidable, and a hard look at the role of their own mothers (whom they may not have liked very much), as well as a look at the much different lives that their own daughters likely enjoy (Kalish and Reynolds, 1976), middle age becomes the looking glass that looks backward and forward at the same time. It is not the easiest of times for women.

Older Age—The older a woman becomes, the more accepting or resigned she becomes to the role she has played out in her life. She has little time to change the way she sees herself now, and may speak fondly, or with varying degrees of regret, of how she has lived her life—and often that has been through her children. Some of her children and her spouse may already have predeceased her. If widowed late in life, the elderly widow loses not only key elements of her identity but also someone she loved deeply, her primary source of companionship and ties to her past. For many elderly women, old age is another role to be assumed—one for which she is often unprepared.

Transition then, through a woman's life, is constant, and the roles she assumes at each stage of that life may be in flux. These are important considerations in addition to those that have to do with loss and grief. Collectively, they form a personal and social context around the woman and how she functions within the confines of her life and the role(s) she has chosen for herself—consciously or unconsciously.

Ruth: A Tough (But Worth It) Transition—a View from the Middle

Ruth is a self-described "transitional woman," whose life reflects some key elements described in the previous section on the transitional role, although the life she lives at the present time fits more closely with the description of the "modern/postmodern" woman. She is an important administrator at a major Southwestern American hospital and lives happily alone in a house she bought herself. Ruth maintains an active community and social life along with a close and productive relationship with her two daughters, who are both in their 20s. Divorce initiated Ruth's transition from a woman with very low self-esteem, who limited her potential so she could best serve others, to a woman who has a powerful sense of herself, the world around her, and her position in it.

> I would categorize myself as a transitional woman because I received traditional imprinting growing up, but now I live the independent life of the modern woman. But my emotional reactions as well as my value systems vacillate a lot. In a way, I envy the less complex role of the traditional woman.

Although I could never live that way again, it seems so simple for both men and women. The roles are clear-cut and complementary; the rules are definite. In the modern situation, if equality exists, the ideal is for each partner to do that which he or she does best. But much time must be spent negotiating who takes what responsibility so that everything is attended to. It is never simple.

Unconsciousness and rationalization have always played a big role in my feelings about my position as a woman. I can remember thinking as I was about to be married in the mid-1960s that I was in an equal relationship. I based this on the fact that we both had the same education and both had professional jobs. I saw my relationship as more important than my career, but so, I thought, did he. After marriage, it didn't really bother me to cook or clean because he stayed busy with the cars and outside chores, so if pressed to define our roles, I would have said we had separate but equal responsibilities. From there, it was an easy step to add responsibility for the children and, of course, our social life largely to me.

The women's movement did add a certain conscious perception of my situation, and I remember becoming furious when he would "help" me around the house. What I hated was that I took all the responsibility for things getting done even while he and the kids were doing parts of it. They would all sort of report to me, so it was clear I retained the ultimate responsibility. I didn't know how to get out of it. I explained my feelings repeatedly, but when nothing changed, I felt I had to jump in again and again so that tasks would not be neglected. Why I thought I was responsible for all these people, I don't know. I can only put it to conditioning that led me to believe whatever my husband told me, and a distinct lack of asserting my own identity.

By the early 1980s, I was working full-time, running the house, and going to graduate school full-time. I became aware that what I had given up in doing all of this was forming any concept of myself as a person apart from my many roles and responsibilities at home. I had been too busy doing all this to even notice. Now the kids were teenagers, and I started paying some attention to me. I realized that any self-esteem I had managed to salvage came primarily from professional endeavors, graduate success, and my own admiration that I could juggle all these roles and survive. I had uprooted a particularly successful career situation to follow my husband's employment more than once, and I was proud of my ability to accommodate.

All of a sudden, though, I realized the reason I could accommodate so easily was that I hadn't done much to define myself. At age 40, I was still holding myself back so that I could go in any direction that my man needed me to go in. I remembered becoming aware of my need for this at age 23, when I could have married vastly different people. But I chose to remain uncommitted so that I would have the flexibility to go off in any direction with a husband. Then, to leave the boundaries loose enough not to limit the options seemed normal and desirable. At age 40, that whole idea seemed hideous to me. And so my age-old midlife search for meaning began in earnest at age 40.

My search was accelerated because so little time in the child-rearing/professional years had been spent on me. I knew there was a "me," apart from all my roles and achievements, but I had no idea what that looked like. I got more excited about life than I had ever been. It was not easy, though, because it involved leaving a 20-year marriage and accepting my existential alone-ness. I very quickly found myself on a spiritual path involving whole worlds I never knew existed. In mere months, I made up for lost years and found myself, rather simply I think, emerging from the years of put-down and limitation with my ex-husband. It was no less than the proverbial rebirth.

I'm not sure I can ever or would ever want to join the ranks of the thoroughly modern woman. I can't negate my traditional conditioning, nor do I want to, for it is a part of me. I now have a clear picture of self that transcends these categories. But it does mean that I can grow in any way I choose. You see, I still retain that flexibility and tentativeness to be able to go off in any direction. The only difference is that now the direction I choose will be determined by my own essence and will not be Other-directed. This gives me the freedom to be the "modern" woman with both male and female mind fully integrated. It gives me freedom and choice whether I am in a significant male–female relationship or alone. As, in Jung's writings, something larger has arisen on the horizon that makes these details of life seem less important.

I have come to understand that individual choice, apart from prescribed roles, is terribly important. I'm glad that society has evolved to give my daughters more choices than I had. As we continue to upgrade the role of the intuitive, the listening, the feminine, all people—men and women—will become more adept at receiving guidance and then be able to act following their own individual routes. During the time we learn to trust this feminine aspect of ourselves, society itself will be in transition. But the feeling of certainty that what we are doing is right for us, will produce individuals with confidence in the actions we take. And ultimately, we will be responsible first for ourselves and then, lovingly, for each other as we learn and come to accept our oneness.

Culture Shaping of the Modern/Postmodern Woman

Modern societies are characterized by urbanization, geographic mobility, rationality and science, and much more complex social circles than those in traditional cultures. Postmodernity entails forming new forms of social relationships in an increasingly globalized world (Walter, 2007).

Modern feminism saw its origin in the political ideas of 18th-century Enlightenment and the French Revolution (1789), which saw lists of grievances expressing women's demands presented to the Estates General. Unfortunately, though, French feminists made less progress than their colleagues in Britain or America (Pugh, 1993). In England, the groundbreaking efforts of Mary Wollstonecraft, who has been called the "first feminist" or "mother of feminism," led to publishing a book-length essay on women's rights and women's education (*A Vindication of the Rights of Women*) in 1792 (Pugh, 1993). Emily Bronte's Catherine Earnshaw in *Wuthering Heights* (1847), Kate Chopin's Edna in *The Awakening* (1899), and Edith Wharton's Lily Bart in *House of Mirth* (1905) provide some striking examples of literary heroines striving to develop themselves as human beings despite societal dictates that relegated their status to that of domestic servants and baby machines.

The women's movement had reached the end of its first cycle by the 1950s, but it was resurrected with authors such as Virginia Woolf, who devoted her life to advancing women's causes and suffered "madness" as a result of her efforts, eventually committing suicide. Simone de Beauvoir, whose book *The Second Self* (written in 1949) was widely read by women, exposed the pervasiveness and intensity of women's oppression. (Interestingly, de Beauvoir's book was banned by the Vatican for its radical views on the role of women.) Similarly, Betty Friedan (1997), whose book *The Feminine Mystique* was first published in1963, is credited with giving voice to "the problem with no name" and through those efforts furthering the feminist movement in all of America.

In fact, in the Western world, feminism is marked by three waves: the first involving suffrage and political equality of women; the second aimed at addressing further social and cultural inequalities (e.g., reproductive rights, domestic violence, maternity leave, equal pay, sexual harassment, and violence); and the third, which continues to address financial, social, and cultural inequalities, including support for greater influence of women in politics and the media. So if one were to view modernism with its Enlightenment-humanist legacy as an opening of the discussion about women's rights and roles in the first place, and postmodernism as deconstructing the meta-narratives of the very structures and ideologies of the modern legacy itself, then contemporary feminism can be seen as "one of the most influential and radical movements of the second half of the twentieth century" (Hekman, 1990, p. 1) as both postmodernism and feminism challenge the epistemological foundations of Western thought, specifically its rationalism and dualisms (e.g., male–female gender biases and the masculine definition of truth claims). Hekman refers to feminism as postmodernism's ally in interrogating the basis of the gender argument, but she also emphasizes that it extends the postmodern critique of rationalism by "revealing its gendered character." Yet, a postmodern feminist, while rejecting a masculine bias of rationalism, would not replace it with a feminist bias either. Rather, a postmodern feminist would support many truths, none privileged along gendered lines (Hekman, 1990).[4]

One might think that this discussion has little to do with women's roles, but in fact, it is central to it, as feminism challenges not only the social arrangements of the society in which women live but the very foundations of Western thought and social structure (Hekman, 1990), and this turmoil—or at least shifting landscape—has and does affect the role of the modern and postmodern woman.[5] In brief, despite changing ideologies underpinning our social institutions, and reconsideration of traditions, practices, and scriptures from a feminist perspective, the effects of centuries of inequality persist even at one of the most basic levels: that of integration of women into the workforce, which is one of the principal characteristics of the modern role of women.

Today, more women are completing graduate and postgraduate degrees, and more women are in professional-level positions than ever before. Yet, even in academe there is still a strong disproportion of women occupying top-level positions. Granted, there has been some change in social attitudes about what women "should" do with their lives, and it is no longer expected that women will primarily devote their lives to raising a family, although if a young woman expresses that she does not wish to have children, the common reaction by members of both sexes is that the woman will change her mind when she gets older. It is a common assumption that women will develop a career of their own but that they will also raise a family. This expectation causes obvious conflicts in women's lives, as both career and family can be considered full-time positions. And unfortunately, those women who have resorted to adopting the traditional male role of aggression, competitiveness, and self-interest to help them compete with men in the corporate environment, also find themselves in a catch-22 situation whereby they continue to contribute to the universal and age-old devaluation of the feminine, which true equality would eliminate.

The modern/postmodern woman, then, often finds herself in an ongoing struggle to achieve equality and liberation in a fundamental sense, and although today's societal framework offers less rigid guidelines for behavior and a more equal distribution of choices and opportunities for women compared to men, some 'traditional' structures and ideologies persist.

Gender Roles: The Integration of Masculine and Feminine Principles

In the initial struggle for equality, it may have appeared that the easiest way to obtain equality was for woman to reject her identity as a woman in the traditional sense and adopt the traditional male gender role. This would involve the rejection of anything considered "feminine," including the expression of emotion that has historically been considered "womanish." The suppression of the feminine, though, was also a problem for men (remember the expression "Real men don't cry"). Part of the financial success of women seemed to result from their donning an iron mask and being strong and unemotional—in other words, "in control." In her illuminating book *The Pregnant Virgin*, psychologist Marion Woodman (1985) relates a case study of a woman masculinized this way.

> Martha, like other woman of her type, can be an enigma to men. Functioning without a strong feminine ego, she nevertheless gives an appearance of being, as she says "some kind of iron lady who can take anything, and take it alone," but behind it all "there's a black rock in the heart." (Woodman, 1985)

Because emotions are a part of being human, not just feminine in nature, their suppression leads to a "black rock in the heart." Once the feminine is not culturally devalued, people will no longer see this suppression as necessary to success. Because all of us have both feminine and masculine characteristics, both emotions and reason, an integration of the two will allow us to function more fully. In dealing with grief, integration is of the highest necessity.

Raegan: A Modern Woman's Experience of Suppressing the Feminine

Many women today, when in their 20s or 30s, experienced contradictory messages in terms of their socialization. A society in transition is not going to be certain about where it stands, and its members have to struggle to define themselves against or between these conflicting messages. One of the most powerful messages of the 1960s and 1970s was that for women to be successful, they needed to act like men and adopt traditionally male characteristics—at the expense of anything feminine. This denial of self has led to much confusion among women. The personal narrative that follows explicates one woman's experience of this contradictory socialization and the problematic nature of defining her role in a modern/postmodern society.

THIS IS RAEGAN'S STORY:

I was born in 1964, when the Women's Movement was still in its developmental stages. By the early 1970s, when I was most influenced by cultural trends, I had somehow picked up that I could be successful as long as I didn't act like a girl. I'm not sure exactly where I got this from, probably from a variety of sources. My father had wanted a boy, and I was a first child, and after he didn't get one, he decided to make do with what he got, so I was raised doing basically "male" activities such as chopping wood and hunting deer.

I did very well in school, and personal achievement was always strongly encouraged, both by family and teachers, and even at an early age I had an unconscious sense that in order to succeed, I had to "beat the boys." Girls were not even a consideration.

Inside the classroom, it seemed especially important that I do better than the boys. It was the same at recess. I was always challenging the boys to races and was particularly exhilarated (and they were particularly humiliated) when I won. I didn't understand why. I just felt it. As long as I can remember, my confrontations were with males. There just didn't seem to be a need to compete with females.

I learned early that showing emotions was something women did. My father was abusive, both physically and especially verbally. He was always saying and doing things that made my mother crumple up in the corner crying. I can remember saying things to her like, "Why don't you get a divorce?" (How I even knew what divorce was back then, I don't know.) Seeing her just cry and cry and then hearing her say that she "loved him" . . . well, I hated her for being what I perceived as weak, and I vowed never to act like she did. I told myself I would never love and would never cry in front of others. I became particularly obsessed with wanting to be a boy and always dressed like one. When my breasts began to grow around age 12, I was horrified and wrapped scotch tape around my chest as tightly as I could to keep them from growing. When my mother discovered this a month later, I didn't understand why she seemed so upset.

Antagonism between the sexes was actually promoted in school (or so it seemed to me). In the sixth grade, we had a history teacher who used to devote a class period a week to having a spelling bee—boys against the girls. Two kids sat on chairs in the back of the room (one girl and one boy), with the blackboard at the front of the class. A member of each team took turns sitting in the chairs, and when the teacher would read off the question, the two participants would race to the board, write down an answer, and then race back to the chairs. If both answers were right, the one who got back first would get the points. If one was wrong, the right answer got the check. I enjoyed this game more than any other activity in all my grade school years, and I was almost militaristic in my attitude against the boys. It was only much later on that I realized just why it seemed so important to me that we beat the boys.

Not long after that, I started to worry about other people liking me, and I noticed that the girls that most people liked were the pretty ones. So I stopped trying to be like a boy and tried to act like a girl. I started wearing makeup and curling my hair, and because I was reasonably pretty, I got a lot of attention this way—much more than I had ever gotten as a tomboy.

I knew people thought I was a bright girl because I was always good in school, so when we moved to a different state, I decided to try to cover up my intelligence. I never let people see what grades I got, and I started talking to football players in class rather than listening to the teachers. All of this got me the approval I wanted. I was a cheerleader, on student council, and had many, many friends. Why I was so unhappy, I didn't know.

I was particularly good at athletics, so that gave me a balance for the "female" things I kept doing (against my better judgment). I was a cheerleader in high school even though I hated it because I thought I had to date in order to be "popular." I took athletics very seriously, and because I showed particular talent, the coaches let me work out with the boys (I was a long-distance runner). It was always that way. Any girl who was better than the others would have the privilege of working out with the boys. I was looked at differently and taken more seriously because of this. The other girls were seen as "just doing it for fun." I was given a certain respect they didn't have. This made me very contemptuous of the girl's team, and I wouldn't have anything to do with them.

All of my friends were male, and they kind of looked at me as being one of them—sort of. The thing that probably made me happiest during that time was when there was an article written in the local paper whose headline proclaimed me as "one of the guys." I thought the girls were stupid and lazy, and so I stayed as far away from them as possible. I identified myself both with socially approved activities, such as cheerleading, and with the approval I got from being "one of the guys" and a serious and successful athletic competitor. I dimly understood that I was doing things that were mutually exclusive, but I didn't understand until much later that I was trying to adopt both gender roles, both the feminine and the masculine. People saw me as kind of an enigma, and I certainly saw myself that way too.

I began to reject any feminine activities or tendencies within myself. I completely based my identity solely on athletics and the approval that my success in this field brought me. I didn't realize that this desperate need for approval was part of a woman's socialization. I was trying to get male approval for participating in what had previously been male territory—the physical arena.

The complications and contradictions implicit in this I didn't understand at all because I didn't see myself as being female. If anyone ever referred to my "fe-maleness" I became furious and insisted that I not be compared to those trivial and meaningless persons (women) whom I was nothing like and with whom I had nothing in common. I was unwittingly more misogynistic than any of my male acquaintances. Not seeing myself as female and succeeding at primarily male activities, I did not recognize any of the dynamics going on. When I heard people speak of inequality between the sexes, I contemptuously denied that it existed, saying that I certainly had never seen it and that such talk was just someone blowing hot air. The men to whom I addressed this agreed.

It wasn't until college that I became aware of anything resembling inequality, or of my violent suppression of the feminine within myself. I still denied acting like a man; lifted weights, competing with men; and articulated myself as aggressively as possible. I made sure everyone listened to what I had to say, and often found myself attacking others verbally in order to get them to listen. I drove myself so hard physically and was so confused emotionally that finally my body just broke down. I developed "mixed connective tissue disease," which, when active, brought 105°F temperatures to my body and caused such a painful stiffening in the joints that I couldn't lift a brush to my own hair. I was told I had to stop competing and live as stress-free a life as possible.

It wasn't until a few years later that I began to realize what the primary source of this stress was. Having lost my identity as an athlete, I was left with the tremendous task of constructing a new self. I turned to the closest thing and threw all my energy into academic endeavors. Luckily it was through this that I began to find some self-understanding in some of the literature and eventually women's studies courses that I took. Slowly, I became aware of my incredible denial and self-division and began to understand part of the source of my unhappiness and many failed relationships.

I am still uneasy with my feminine tendencies and with the fact that I am a woman. I was always trying to prove to the world that I wasn't what I was—a woman. I could not see myself as being worthless and trivial and silly as our culture made me understand women were. I took myself very seriously and wanted to be looked at that way. In a culture where a human being's value is determined by her success in established fields, fields that often subtly deny access to women, it was hard to see any value in being a woman. Crippled with my sense of female valueless-ness, the self-hatred that I have always felt is something I am only now beginning to come to terms with. In order to come to like and enjoy myself, I have come to like women—to really like them, not just accede them a certain credence when they succeed at male endeavors, just as I have to really like myself, not just feel slightly validated when I succeed at something. It is time to succeed at living, at being who I am, and I am female. I am in the process of learning to value myself for that fact and not basing any sense of self-worth simply on achievements that are more recognized as success in a "man's world." It has been an ongoing struggle.

Loss and Development of Self

Many modern/postmodern women feel Raegan's conflict of self-definition. In a society where value is ascribed through a masculine lens, it is not surprising that women, particularly women who have grown up in a transitional generation, find themselves conflicted about their identities in a modern/postmodern world—not so much in knowing that they have value, but in who gets to judge that value.

For decades authors have tried to both enlighten and shed the male principle. Gilbert and Gubar (1979), for example, in their "*The Madwoman in the Attic: The Woman Writer and the Nineteenth-Century Literary Imagination*," stressed the importance of abandoning metaphors applied to woman writers and to the literary characters they created. Neither the "madwoman" nor the "monster" dichotomies were accurate then, Gilbert and Gubar contended, particularly through a very limited and limiting patriarchal view of the world. Their view has been shared by an entire Women's Movement that has fought continuously for the rights of women to be equal on every sociopolitical level possible. Those efforts continue.

What has also been highlighted through postmodernism is that women and men embody both feminine and masculine traits and characteristics, and together they form a complete human being. Self-definition, which denies or suppresses part of that being (either the masculine or feminine part), can have very negative psychological consequences as well as health impacts on the individual. As Raegan's story tells, through embracing the feminine, women (and men) can move forward without feeling a "black rock in the heart," without losing parts of themselves through the turmoil that self-denial creates, and without losing relationships that might otherwise be productive.

Notes

1. Giddens (1991) referred to modernity as models of social life or organization that emerged in Europe from about the 17th century onward and that subsequently became worldwide in their influence. However, besides a known time frame and initial geographic location, Giddens would say that the rest of modernity's characteristics were uncertain.

2. See Appendix.

3. Research indicates that in Canada, college-age women are more likely than men to obtain a college degree. However, although women make up the majority in most universities, they remain concentrated in humanities and social sciences that have weaker labor market outcomes. Among 25- to 29-year-olds, women are now obtaining higher levels of education than men (Hepburn and Simon, 2006).

4. Demographic considerations are important in order to understand cultural forces at play in the societies in which women live. In coming decades, the United States is projected to be even more diverse than at present. By 2055, it is projected that the United States will not have a single racial or ethnic majority. (This is largely driven by immigration, with new growth projected to be linked to new Asian and Hispanic immigration. Asia has replaced Latin America, including Mexico, as the biggest source of new immigrants.) Millennials (born after 1980) are expected to be the generation that differs most from their elders (more educated, more student debt, but also most hopeful about a positive financial future). Women's roles in the labor force and leadership positions are changing (in 40% of all households with children in 2011, women were the primary breadwinners, and the number of women in top leadership jobs has risen, although women still make up a small share of the U.S. political and business leaders relative to men). One in six American families are blended, converging mothers' and fathers' roles in the households. Source: D. Cohn and A. Caumont, "10 Demographic Trends That Are Shaping the U.S. and the World," Pew Research Center, March 31, 2016, http://www.Pewresearch.org/staff/dvera-cohn/.

5. Hekman, in *Gender and Knowledge: Elements of a Postmodern Feminism*, 1990, presents a thorough discussion on the various seminal critical theorists, such as Habermas, Foucault, Derrida, and Gadamer, who are critical of the instrumental reason of Enlightenment thought and the power structures it has created in the modern world.

CHAPTER TWO

The Social Construction of Grief

In the same manner as women's roles were examined from a social construction perspective in Chapter 1, this chapter examines the societal characteristics and norms that have governed grief behavior. Within each major time frame, we describe common responses to grief, experts' views on grief, and criticisms of the various conceptualizations and strategies popularized to deal with grief. Summary tables are presented throughout.

Women's experiences of grief from within the traditional, transitional, and modern/postmodern categories, in light of how grief has been conceived and addressed, are then presented in Chapter 3.

Loss and Grief in Traditional Societies

Traditional societies prior to the 1900s ended with World War I (Stroebe et al., 1992). Generally speaking, they were labeled as patriarchal societies, that is, male dominated, with women serving a minor role in all aspects of life—save child rearing. Small villages were common, life expectancy was short, and child deaths were common. Grief was essentially a private experience confined mainly to the household (parents and siblings of the deceased) and to the immediate village in which the deceased lived.

By the 1880s, a rigorous and detailed system of rules governed proper mourning practices, including appropriate dress (thanks to Queen Victoria, who wore black for the remainder of her life after the death of her husband Prince Albert). The closer the relationship to the deceased, the longer one was expected to mourn—a kind of public barometer of the strength

Table 2.1 The Social Construction of Grief in Traditional Societies—A Summary

	Social Structure within Which Grief Is Situated			Cultural Response to Grief		
	Modernity			Modernism		
	Societal Characteristics	Grief Characteristics	Grief Norms	Response to Grief	Grief Experts	Criticisms
Traditional Societies* Prior to 20th century and in the early 1900s, ending with WWI	Families generally lived in small villages where everyone knew everyone else. Living with relatives and caring for one another when ill was common. Traditional sex-role conditioning emphasized family and home. Children grew up understanding that death was a natural part of life.	A private experience shared primarily within the confines of the household. Grief entered the public realm in1865 for several decades except for between 1915 and the 1960s (Konigsberg, 2011). **Typical Death** Children **Primary Survivors** Parents and siblings, but also the entire village	Women's grief was private. Rituals and ceremonies prescribed grief practices (Rando, 1988), including dress and duration of mourning (Konigsberg, 2011). **Cultural Variations** Maintenance of ties with the deceased is supported in	**Source of Knowledge/ Authority** Patriarchal **Goal of Grief** To limit grief and mourning To decathect from the dead Grief work involved reclaiming the psychological energy once invested in the deceased	Sigmund Freud (*Mourning and Melancholia*, 1915) Carl Jung (analytical psychology)	Socially prescribed rules for mourning prevalent in the Victorian 19th century kept women in their place in a patriarchal society (therefore, women's grief must be kept private). Schlereth (1991) identified that "The Victorian way of death transformed the traditional brief, personal private grief process into a prolonged, ceremonial, public ritual.

(continued)

Table 2.1 *(continued)*

	Social Structure within Which Grief Is Situated			Cultural Response to Grief		
	Modernity			Modernism		
	Societal Characteristics	**Grief Characteristics**	**Grief Norms**	**Response to Grief**	**Grief Experts**	**Criticisms**
			Japanese culture (belief in Shinto and Buddhist religions). Hopi tradition is to actively forget the deceased as soon as possible. In Egypt, the bereaved express grief openly and widely. In Bali, no overt bonds are evident.	**Approach** Private and hidden. The woman's role was to nurture others grieving around her (Rando, 1988).		Grief became a public barometer of the strength of someone's affections and loyalty to the deceased" (Konigsberg, 2011). **Impact on Women** Women accepted their role both at home and in the grief process, typically without question.

*Adapted from T. Walter (2007), "Modern Grief, Postmodern Grief," *International Review of Sociology*, 17(1), 123–134.

of affection and loyalty to the deceased (Konisberg, 2011). These Victorian 19th-century practices transformed the traditional brief private grieving process into a prolonged, ceremonial, and public ritual. Funerals became elaborate public affairs, and burials, once private family events, now took place in large public parklike settings.

Unfortunately for women, Victorian mourning practices also served to keep women in their place, that is, as keepers of hearth and home. The woman's role was to nurture others through their grieving and at the same time, as much as possible, keep her own grief private. Rituals and ceremonies provided support and direction to families, giving the bereaved meaning, security, predictability, and control (Rando, 1988).

Loss and Grief in Modern Societies

Modern societies (considered to be from the 1960s onward) were marked by large-scale cities and urbanization; geographic mobility; and complex, fragmented, nonoverlapping social circles. Modern societies reflected a strong faith in rationality, science, expertise, progress, the future, and the young (Walter, 2007). The modern individual was typically detached from tradition, place, and kinship (Giddens, 1991).

Death in modern society was typically associated with older persons. Adult children or elderly spouses were the primary "survivors" of the deceased. With fragmented social and geographic lives, mourners became separated from both family and work colleagues, with whom they often spent most of their time. Their mourning often became private and isolated. Unfortunately for the children of these parents, it meant that they learned little about grief themselves. Death became hidden.

As a consequence of isolating grief, the 1950s and onward saw a ready market for therapists and counselors to "help" individuals resolve their grief. Grief experts and their theories sanctioned by the medical science of psychiatry governed both understanding and treatment of grief: psychiatrists such as Parkes (1964), Bowlby (1998), and Kübler-Ross (1969); and, psychologists such as Worden (2009), Stroebe and Schut (1999). Based on the work of these and other experts, the 1970s to 1990s reflected a proliferation of healing centers, individual counseling, and support groups, offered privately or through churches, hospitals, and even funeral homes. In short, the grief industry flourished during the modern era (Konigsberg, 2011).

Popularized Approaches to Grief Therapy

Experts' theories involved "stages" (Kübler-Ross, 1969), "phases" (Parkes, 1964), or "tasks" (Worden, 2009), that all led to one primary goal—that of detaching from grief, recovering from the state of intense emotionality, and returning to normal functioning and effectiveness as soon as possible (Stroebe et al., 1992) (see Table 2.2 for a summary).

About six months' time was considered normal to resolve grief and "move on."[1] According to Rando (1988), the goal of grief was recovery—that is, learning to live with the loss and adjust to one's new life accordingly. Pain was something to be "worked through" so that the mourner could once again be reconstituted as a free individual (Walter, 2007). Ultimately, one must sever bonds with the deceased (a notion dating back to Freud's theory of attachment published in 1917) in order to "let go" so that the bereaved could form attachment to a new person.

But mourners, particularly women, received contradictory messages. On the one hand, they were encouraged and told to let go, but on the other hand popular arts and literature continued to communicate undying and eternal love to the deceased (especially if a child was involved), romanticizing the notion of never letting go. The place of spiritualism was uncertain, and by some considered marginal, dangerous, or even satanic. And there were other contradictions too, particularly with respect to expression of grief. During wartime, large-scale losses called for public stoicism. As well, for a time, certain types of death were not socially sanctioned making expression of grief problematic (e.g., death of an infant, death from AIDS, gay relationships) (Rando, 1988). These situations created much dissonance for women. Not surprising that many women (and men) sought professional help to deal with their grief, and if they didn't, they struggled with it in private (Konigsberg, 2011).

Note that the following tables, though not exhaustive, identify some of the most predominant grief theories, including their criticisms, which are covered more fully in the next section, Loss and Grief in Postmodern Societies.

Loss and Grief in Postmodern Societies

Postmodern society began in the early 1970s, and some would argue, as early as early as 1966[2] (McHale, 2008) and continues to the present time. With technology, especially the Internet, the world has become a global village, facilitating the formation of different kinds of social relationships, including "virtual" relationships. People form relationships and mutual support groups based on a shared experience rather than knowing one another personally. And because individuals construct their own realities that they recognize as true for themselves, many truths exist—each within its own history and unique social context (Berger and Luckmann, 1967). First-hand experience is considered valid and credible. Diversity in all its forms is celebrated, with minimal boundaries restricting inclusion.

Table 2.2 Predominant Stage/Phase Theories and Models

Theorist	Model	Common Patterns	Medicalization	A Healing Process
Erich Lindemann (1944) Psychiatrist who coined the phrase *grief work* (1944).	**Three Stages** Shock and disbelief Acute mourning Resolution	There is some predictable sequence in the physical, emotional, behavioral, social, and intellectual consequences that must be endured: **First:** We are hit hard by bereavement (experience shock, disbelief, longing). **Next:** Middle phase, we experience full force of bereavement (somatic distress, intense emotions: sadness, depression, anxiety, despair, helplessness, anger, frustration, guilt), we lose motivation, become isolated, fall into purposelessness and hopelessness.	Symptomatology and management are similar to psychiatric illness.	Grieving involves "symptoms" (somatic distress, including tight throat, shortness of breath, sighing, emptiness in the abdomen, lack of muscular power, tension); crying; numbing; helplessness; preoccupation with the deceased; feelings of guilt, anger; falling into hopelessness and despair; reacting with hostility (usual pattern of behavior breakdown).

(continued)

Table 2.2 *(continued)*

Theorist	Model	Common Patterns	Medicalization	A Healing Process
John Bowlby[1] (1961)	**Three Phases** Urge to recover the lost object Disorganization and despair Reorganization **Four Stages (1998)** Numbness Separation Anxiety Despair and disorganization Acquisition of new roles/ reorganization	**Finally** Subsiding somatic effects, reduction in intense emotion; emotional equilibrium is restored, and we begin to accept what has happened, reestablish social contacts, adopt new roles/ skills; restored to daily purpose and hopefulness.	Grief is like a disease with a classic syndrome of symptoms. Grief is a healing process.	
George Engel (late 1970s) Formulation of the biopsychosocial model, a general theory of illness and healing	**Six Stages** Shock and disbelief Development of awareness Restitution Resolution of the loss Idealization Outcome		Grief is a functional psychiatric disorder of known etiology, with distinctive features and relatively predictable course. Compares grieving to recovery from a physical injury or wound. Result: healing, healing with scars, failure to heal, reopening the wound.	

Colin Murray Parkes (adaptation of Bowlby's)[2] (1964)	**Four Phases** Numbness Yearning and searching Disorganization and despair Reorganization			
Elisabeth Kübler-Ross (1969)	**Five Stages** Shock and denial Anger Bargaining Depression Acceptance			
Therese Rando (1988, 1993)	Three-phase, six-stage process: **Phase 1** Avoidance (Task 1. Recognize the loss) **Phase 2** Confrontation (Task 2. React to the separation Task 3.	The key aim is to distinguish abnormal from normal grief. Emphasis on leaving the dead behind and therapy for malfunctioning individuals. Professional help comprises 1:1 counseling for struggling individuals. Grief is placed in developmental psychology	Rando (1988) highlights types of unresolved grief as calibrated by Parkes and Weiss (1983): absent, inhibited, delayed, distorted, chronic, unanticipated, abbreviated.	Note that Silverman and Klass (1996) disagreed that grieving is abnormal or pathological. They supported continued bonds with the deceased. Two models: (1) The idea of the purpose of grief is

(continued)

Table 2.2 *(continued)*

Theorist	Model	Common Patterns	Medicalization	A Healing Process
	Recollect and reexperience the deceased and the relationship. Task 4. Relinquish the old attachments to the deceased and the old assumptive world.) **Phase 3** Accommodation (Task 5. Readjust to move adaptively into the new world without forgetting the old. Task 6. Reinvest in new relationships and roles to indicate a resolution to active grieving) Kavanaugh expanded this to seven phases: shock, disorganization, volatile emotions, guilt, loss and loneliness, relief, and reestablishment (1972). In 2003, Estlund expanded the phases to 10.	with the aim to help the individual move toward autonomy.	Calls for complicated grieving to receive clinical attention. Rando (1988) identifies grief as a potential health risk.	to sever the bonds (disengage) with the deceased in order to free the survivor to make new attachment (this notion is reflected in Frued's original theory of attachment). To avoid psychological problems associated with disengagement (Dietrich and Shabad, 1989; Horowitz, Wilener, Marmor, and Krupnick, 1980), an alternative model was based on mourner's continuing bonds with the deceased (Silverman and Klass, 1996).

Stroebe and Schut (1999)	**Dual Process Model** Back and forth between loss-oriented and restoration-oriented activities	Covered in the postmodern section.

[1] Bowlby (1969–1980) examined grieving from the perspective of psychic trauma by studying it in children rather than looking at it from Freud's Oedipal conflict perspective. He used the term *adaptation* (the child adjusting to the loss of the mother) to describe how the child adjusted to the trauma, and projected that idea to grief generally. Bowlby (1998) found a positive correlation between level of attachment of the griever to the person lost and the level of grief and mourning; the bereaved also experience an uncertain future, which may provoke anxiety and a heightened sense of vulnerability.

[2] Parkes extended Bowlby's work, and together their theory of grief reflected a preprogrammed series of behaviors cued by specific environmental stimuli. In his study of widows, Parkes understood identification with the dead as an early stage of grief left behind once the survivor took on the responsibilities once assumed by the deceased. Bowlby and Parkes outlined four phases of grief: numbness, searching and yearning, depression, and reorganization.

Table 2.3 The Social Construction of Grief in Modern Society—A Summary

	Social Structure within Which Grief Is Situated			Cultural Response to Grief		
	Modernity			Modernism		
	Societal Characteristics	**Grief Characteristics**	**Grief Norms**	**Response to Grief**	**Grief Experts**	**Criticisms**
Modern Societies* 20th-century (1960s onward)	Urbanization; geographic mobility; complex, fragmented, nonoverlapping social circles. Modern individual is detached from tradition, place, and kinship, with little overlap of membership in various groups. Emphasis is on reason and observation and faith in continuous progress. with a	19th-century Victorian rules are abandoned to reflect women's emancipation efforts and the view that expressions of grief should reflect personal feelings. Grief is a private inner emotion, inaccessible to others; therefore mourning is private and highly individualistic, which divides mourners and everyone else around them who may support them	Key tenet: individual liberty. Grief is shaped by social factors (Lofland, 1985), is socially and culturally influenced (Walter, 1999). Grievers should recover from their state of intense emotionality and return to normal functioning and effectiveness as quickly as possible (Stroebe et al, 1992).	**Source of Knowledge/ Authority** Faith in rationality, science, and expertise (medical science of psychiatry and professional expertise), the future, and the young, as reflected in 20th-century grief psychology **Goal of Grief** To detach from grief, recover, move on, let go, live with the loss, and adjust (Rando, 1988).	Freud (1917). Psychiatrists: Parkes Bowlby, Kübler-Ross. Psychologists: Worden, Stroebe, and Schut. Stages of grief: Lindemann (1944), Kübler-Ross (1969). Phases of grief: Bowlby (1961) and Parkes (1972). Tasks of grief: Worden (1982).	2008: a call to revisit stage theories to reconsider their potential clinical utility (Prigerson, 2008). A major criticism of Kübler-Ross's stage theory (embedded across the Western culture) was that it was based on terminal patients' views, not survivors'; also, its linearity.

	special emphasis on goal directedness, efficiency, and rationality. Psychology adopts a machine metaphor of human functionality (Stroebe et al., 1992).	(e.g., Britain, North America), but less so in Italy, where people live, work, play, and worship in the same community. Immediate family contacts are colleagues, friends, and neighbors who likely did not know the deceased (due to longevity of the deceased, geographically mobility, home/work separation). Decreased familiarity with death because the ill and elderly typically die in hospitals or nursing homes. Bereavement is dealt with in isolation (Rando, 1988).	Grief is to be "worked through," and breaking bonds to the deceased is integral to recovery (Stroebe et al., 1992). The "letting go" perspective was put forth by Sanders (1992) as a necessary resolution of grief work. Stroebe et al. (1992) highlighted the prevailing view of the importance of breaking bonds and the problematic implications of deeply dependent relationships.	Pain is to be worked through so that the mourner can once again be reconstituted as a free individual. **Approach** The term *grief work* is coined by psychiatrist Erich Lindemann (1944). Grief work is placed in the field of developmental psychology with the aim to help the individual move toward autonomy. Emphasis is on eaving the dead behind and therapy for malfunctioning individuals. The key aim is to distinguish	Dual Process Model: Stroebe and Schut (1999). Rando (1988) highlights types of unresolved grief as calibrated by Parkes and Weiss (1983) as absent, inhibited, delayed, distorted, chronic, unanticipated, abbreviated. Grief is identified as a public health issue (Rando, 1988).	Stage and phase models that reflect a grief work hypothesis were discredited in the 1990s by Stroebe and Stroebe (1991). Also criticized was open expression of emotion. Expressing one's grief openly does not uniformly benefit the bereaved (Bonanno, Ray, and Gross, 2007). All stage/phase theories criticized for lack of methodological soundness. Konigsberg (2011) highlighted that

(*continued*)

Table 2.3 *(continued)*

	Social Structure within Which Grief Is Situated			Cultural Response to Grief		
	Modernity			Modernism		
	Societal Characteristics	**Grief Characteristics**	**Grief Norms**	**Response to Grief**	**Grief Experts**	**Criticisms**
		Private grief meant parents kept grief to themselves, so children did not learn about grief. A mourning-avoidant culture (Wolfelt, 2007) and a death-denying society (Kübler-Ross, 1969, 1974). **Typical Death** The elderly	The concept of widows developing new identities was supported in counseling and therapy approaches (e.g., Worden, 1982). Women too socially dependent on their deceased spouses had greater adjustment problems (Lopata, 1973, 1979).	abnormal from lnormal grief. There is professional help (1:1 counseling) for struggling individuals. Rando (1988) discusses sex-role conditioning whereby men and women grieve differently and have different needs in grief. "Grief work" took time and was the only way to address loss (possibly longer than the suggested six-month time frame).		the efficacy of all the professional interventions to ameliorate grief was uncertain (despite a plethora of instruments to measure it) because of a lack of a consistent definition of grief and a way to measure and assess it.

	Primary Survivors Adult children, possibly elderly spouse **Cultural Variation** England, North America—private grief. Ireland/Japan affirm the diverse networks of relationships (social mourning where attendance at funerals/wakes is expected if you know the deceased or one or more of the chief mourners). Modern urban Japan and China—mourning rituals transform deceased into an ancestor who lives on with survivors. In	From 1950 onward—a ready market for development of strategies that therapists and counselors to help individuals with grief resolution. The 1970s–1990s saw a proliferation of healing centers, individual counseling or support groups. Grief became a process that required (usually) professional help (largely based on stage theory of Kübler-Ross) (Konigsberg, 2011). With 9/11, public expression of grief		Currier, Neimeyer, and Berman (2008) controlled study found no consistent overall preventive effect of grief counseling. Over time, everyone just got better. Forte. Pazder, and Feudtner (2004) efficacy studies produced similar results. Grief counseling helped people who suffered prolonged, complicated grief. To avoid psychological problems associated with disengagement,

(continued)

Table 2.3 *(continued)*

	Social Structure within Which Grief Is Situated			Cultural Response to Grief		
	Modernity			Modernism		
	Societal Characteristics	Grief Characteristics	Grief Norms	Response to Grief	Grief Experts	Criticisms
		Western culture, consulting with the deceased is private, and "spiritualism" is its formal ritual expression.	became commonplace (and even expected).			an alternative model was based on mourners' continuing bonds with the deceased (Silverman and Klass, 1996). **Impact on Women** Contradictory messages were given to mourners: on one hand, to let go; on the other, that love of a lost one (especially children) is eternal.

Women experienced much dissonance between what they were experiencing in loss and grief, and how they were told to respond, as well as what they were told they should be experiencing at given points in time.

---

*Adapted from T. Walter (2007), "Modern Grief, Postmodern Grief," *International Review of Sociology*, 17(1), 123–134.

Death visits all age groups, and the primary mourners are individuals in social and virtual relationships. Mourners may be separated from other family members, friends, neighborhoods, even countries and cultures. There are fewer formal funerals, and mass media enables virtual mourning to occur even though virtual mourners are typically not bereaved like close family members or incapacitated by their grief. Mutual help groups represent a radical shift from the modernist faith in professional expertise, and these groups are often resistant to knowledge experts if they have not directly shared in the experience of support group members. They are also more resistant to the language of modernist psychology with its tendency to pathologize any grief process that does not fit modernist norms (Walter, 2007).

The goal of grief is to celebrate diversity and to make relevant the grieving experience to the individual. This focus reflects a postmodern shift to deconstruct science, tradition, and heritage. How a person grieves depends on personal choice, and the community with which one chooses to identify (Neimeyer, Klass, and Dennis, 2014). Individualizing in a multicultural world reflects a celebration of various cultural, ethnic, religious, and sexual groups—in other words, an absence of normalization. Because one's assumptions about how the world works are disrupted in a postmodern world, grief requires a "psychosocial transitional state" and a reexamination of one's assumptions (Parkes, 1998)—something Attig (2001) referred to as "relearning of the world."

Note that Parkes was mentioned in the previous section, Loss and Grief in Modern Societies, and his work is mentioned again here to reflect a consistency with a postmodern approach to an evolving understanding of grief and loss. In his earlier work, Parkes focused on two psychological processes: grief, which is the painful search for a lost person or object of attachment; and transition, which is the process of changing the assumptive world in ways that ensure that nothing worthwhile need be completely lost. Out of the struggle to resolve the conflict between holding on and letting go of the old assumptions, Parkes, Laungaini, and Young (2015) suggested that there gradually emerges a new and more mature model of the world. This view is more consistent with Attig's view of relearning one's world, but perhaps based on a different worldview (as we shall examine shortly).

Relearning the world essentially means breaking down old assumptions (such as reexamining breaking bonds with the deceased) (Klass, Silverman, and Nickman, 1996; Walter, 1996). But Neimeyer (2001), for example, posits that new theories of meaning making have arisen, partially out of postmodern grief theorists' criticisms of counselors/therapists practice of "disciplining grief" to achieve conformity to existing or preexisting social norms. (Interestingly, one might wonder whether the plethora of self-help groups that have sprung up across the world may simply be creating, or recreating, yet another set of social norms.)

However, at its root, postmodern consciousness supports culturally embedded practices and curtailing the search for ideal therapeutic procedures. Postmodern's approach to grief includes growth, flexibility, and appropriateness within a cultural context (Stroebe et al., 1992). Most people will work through grief on their own without professional intervention, drawing on their own resilience (Bonanno, 2004; Bonanno et al., 2002; Bonanno, Ray, and Gross, 2007). Only in instances where the mourner suffers prolonged grief disorder or experiences disenfranchised grief (e.g., in cases such as abortion, AIDS, or when the griever is developmentally delayed) (Doka, 2002) may professional assistance be required. Maintaining continuing bonds with the deceased is supported and perhaps even encouraged (remember "holding on" was once thought disruptive to healing and recovery). In short, rather than "working through grief" (a modern tenet), "grief works through the person" (Stroebe et al., 1992).

This changed sentiment has been incorporated by researchers and grief experts Stroebe and Schut (1999) into the model they call the Dual Process Model. This model reflects mourners' oscillation between moving through grief and learning new skills to move forward with their own lives (oscillation between loss and restoration orientations). We mention the Dual Process Model in this section (postmodernism) rather than earlier (modernist) because of the inherent fluidity of the model and its acknowledgement that other models seemed inappropriate to capture the complexity of the grief experience.

"Relearning the world" (Attig, 1996, 2001) requires relearning a sense of safety and belonging in one's world, then assimilating that learning into a new way of negotiating the world for the mourner. According to Attig's model, mourners construct and reconstruct their new lives in the absence of the lost entity, thereby assimilating the multiple meanings of loss into the overarching story of their own lives (Attig, 2015). (Note that other mindfulness practices involving meditation have also emerged in the grief literature) (Cacciatore and Flint, 2012).

Why the Need for New Approaches?

"Grief work" (a phrase coined by psychiatrist Erich Lindemann in 1944) has been around a long while, but today there is less acceptance of modern society's goal directedness and focus on efficiency. Even the field of psychology, which adopted a machine metaphor of human functionality (Stroebe et al., 1992), is undergoing significant criticism when it comes to casting loss and grief into a uniform set of stages, phases, or tasks. A major criticism of Kübler-Ross's stage theory, for example (which became embedded across Western culture in the late 1960s), is that the stages were based on terminal patients' experiences of death, and not on the experiences of mourners or survivors of those deaths. Further, stage- and task-based theories inferred that if one just followed the stages in a linear progression, one would be successful in working through one's grief. All these notions were consistent with, or perhaps predicators to, the self-help movement beginning in the 1970s (Konigsberg, 2011) and, in fact, a whole grief industry. As well, denial of the concept of continuing bonds with the deceased because it did not align with Freud 's 1917's definition of successful mourning whereby one must detach from the dead in order to develop new attachments simply was not resonating with mourners, particularly women. What is more, regarding maintaining bonds with the dead as some sort of pathology further discredited the grief work hypothesis (Stroebe and Stroebe, 1991). And if one needs further evidence, Bonanno found that expressing one's grief openly (as was so popular in recent decades), does, in fact, not uniformly benefit the bereaved (Bonanno et al., 2007).

One of the major problems with stage and task theories is that they have tended to create rigid parameters for "proper" behavior, which do not match what most people experience. And because the two things don't match, doubt and suspicion arise when it appears that the person has coped quite well, that is, without much disruption to his or her life (Bonanno, 2009). Bonanno contends that most people are able to handle their grief effectively, and they simply move on with their lives. Granted they may have lingering thoughts about the relationship and the changes that the loss has brought to their lives, and are saddened for a time and perhaps even adrift, but they are not swallowed up by their grief. Sadness allows us to turn our attention inward (Bonanno, 2009) and focus, and promotes deeper and more effective reflection. By dampening our biological systems and giving us a forced time-out, sadness helps us adjust to loss. For resilient people, grieving is a process of finding comfort, regardless of what the relationship was like. Resilient people draw comfort from remembering the good parts and talking about them. Resilient people tend to have better financial resources, a higher education level, fewer ongoing life stressors to worry about, better physical health, and a broader network of friends and relatives to rely on for emotional support and helping with the demands of life (Bonanno, 2009; Bonanno et al, 2005). Resilient people tend to be more confident, and believe that they have some control over the outcome of difficult circumstances and that things will turn out alright. Being able to express or suppress emotions with flexibility is what Bonanno refers to as "coping ugly" (2009), and coping ugly appears to be a pragmatic way to deal with grief.

In their most recent text (2016), McCoyd and Walter provide a good description of the mechanistic formula of Kübler-Ross' grief stages, particularly as they have become the basis of practice for much of the helping professionals (grief counselors, therapists, self-help groups). Other problematic "recipes for grief" also continue to be put forth as linear movement through grief that one could or even should follow and use as a guide to monitor progress. In her rather scathing look at the grief industry, Konigsberg (2011) highlighted that the efficacy of all the professional interventions to ameliorate grief is actually uncertain, despite a plethora of instruments to measure it, because of a lack of a consistent definition of grief and ways to measure and assess it. Further, Currier, Neimeyer, and Berman (2008) in their controlled study found no consistent overall preventive effect of grief counseling. Grief counseling did help with people who suffered prolonged, complicated grief, but over time they found that everyone just got better. (Forte's efficacy studies [2004] produced similar results.) The takeaway point here is that the most accurate predictors of how people will handle their grief are their personality and temperament prior to the loss (Gamino, Sewall, and Easterling, 1998). The ability to rebound after loss remains the norm throughout adult life regardless of the type of severity of the loss (Bonanno, 2004).

Table 2.4. summarizes the social construction of grief in a postmodern world.

A New Way of Looking at Loss—a More Feminine Way?

Not only has the efficacy of past and current grief strategies been called into question, but so too has the pathology of grief that has largely been associated with the stereotype of feminine behavior (Silverman and Klass, 1996). Therefore, women have had to defend their reactions and responses to grief (or hide them). In a postmodern world, women are more likely to search out support groups of other individuals who have shared similar experiences of loss and grief in an effort to make meaning of the grief experience, find one's current place in a changed social context, and align with (or not) the cultural context the griever finds herself in (Neimeyer, Klass, and Dennis, 2014).

New ideas or theories of grief have necessarily developed out of what researchers regard as inadequate, inaccurate, or just plain indefensible.

Table 2.4 The Social Construction of Grief in Postmodern Societies—A Summary

	Social Structure within Which Grief Is Situated			Cultural Response to Grief		
	Modernity			Modernism		
	Societal Characteristics	**Grief Characteristics**	**Grief Norms**	**Response to Grief**	**Grief Experts**	**Criticisms**
	Postmodernity			Postmodernism**		
Postmodern Societies* 1966/1972–73 onward	Global village, new forms of social relationships, virtual relationships, increasingly globalized instant communication. Global media signal a possible reversion to "traditional mourning," where everyone knows and everyone participates. Different ethnic, religious and	Mourners join groups who share the experience, not necessarily the deceased or one another. Support groups may fragment and subdivide to address specific needs. The Internet supports mourners who may be separated from family, friends, neighborhoods, even countries and cultures. Mass media enables virtual mourning,	A deconstruction of science, tradition, and heritage reflects a radical break with the modernist faith in professional expertise and modernist psychology to pathologize anything outside the norm. Anti-establishment groups form (e.g., Mothers Against Drunk Drivers [MADD]).	**Source of Knowledge/ Authority** Based on their own experience, individuals construct their own realities that they recognize as true for them. Therefore, there are many truths—each within its own history and social setting.	Until Bonanno, therapists and psychiatrists considered the absence of grief a pathology to be feared rather than a healthy outcome. Individuals find ways to retain the dead in their lives without getting stuck in their grief (Walter, 1996). Sometimes individuals are assisted by a skilled therapist.	Whether termed *processes* (Rando, 1993) that incorporate more individuality within the various phases of the grieving processes, postmodern grief theory looks more critically at all the task- and stage-based theories (Stroebe and Stroebe, 1991) and also criticizes the big grief business that has grown out of those

	sexual groups are celebrated. Characterized by a newly developing consciousness (Stroebe et al., 1992).	where mourners are not bereaved like close family members nor incapacitated by their grief. By the 1990s, there are fewer funerals. Technological mediation and support for grievers become commonplace (Parkes, Laungani, and Young, 2015). Theories of meaning making (Neimeyer, 2001) and continuing bonds (Klass, Silverman, and Nickman, 1996) are supported.	Continuing bonds (Klass, Silverman, and Nickman, 1996) with the deceased are supported. One's assumptions about how the world works are disrupted. Grief becomes a "psychosocial transitional state necessitating a readjustment of assumptions" (Parkes, 1998), where one needs to "relearn the world" (Attig 2001).	Professionals and experts are generally excluded from support groups. **Goal of Grief** To celebrate diversity: therefore, depends on individual personal choice and the community with which one identifies. Mourners construct and reconstruct the story of their new lives	Expressing one's grief openly does not uniformly benefit the bereaved (Bonanno et al., 2007). The current science of bereavement has been driven primarily by Bonanno, who suggests that the ability to rebound remains the norm throughout adult life. Bonanno's Four Trajectories (arising out of his studies on resilience and its place in grief): Resilience,	frameworks (Konigsberg, 2011). Postmodern grief theorists also criticize counselors/ therapists for "disciplining grief" to achieve conformity to social norms—but indirectly through diffuse power rather than force. (Interestingly, self-help groups have sprung up that create and recreate a set of social norms.)

(continued)

Table 2.4 *(continued)*

Social Structure within Which Grief Is Situated			Cultural Response to Grief		
Modernity			**Modernism**		
Societal Characteristics	**Grief Characteristics**	**Grief Norms**	**Response to Grief**	**Grief Experts**	**Criticisms**
Postmodernity			**Postmodernism****		
	Typical Death All ages **Primary Survivors** Individuals in social and virtual relationships	Out of the struggle to resolve the conflict between holding on and letting go of the old assumptions there gradually emerges a new and more mature model of the world (Parkes, 2015).	in the absence of the lost entity, thereby assimilating the multiple meanings of loss into the overarching story of their lives. **Approach** Rejection of norms of grief. Maintaining continuing bonds with the deceased.	Recovery, Chronic dysfunction, Delayed grief or trauma.) The Dual Process Model (Stroebe and Schut, 1999) reflects mourners' oscillation between moving through grief and learning new skills to move forward with their own lives (oscillation between loss and restoration orientations).	Grief trajectories were set out (tasks according to Freud and others), but grief work lacks definition when it is out of the norm, and what is the norm, has been criticized and/or dismissed (Konigsberg, 2011; Stroebe et al., 1992). Medicalizing grief deflects away from recognizing the physical and social consequences of grief.

Doka (2002) identified five categories of disenfranchised grief (e.g., abortion, AIDS, being over-expressive, when the griever is developmentally delayed). Ambiguous loss ("frozen grief") arises when there is uncertainty regarding the nature of the loss (e.g., brain injury, kidnapping).	Mindfulness practices become common (Cacciatore and Flint, 2012).	Stroebe and Schut acknowledge that excessive rumination may be a form of avoidance and is not conducive to healing; therefore, optimal time lines between RO and LO remain uncertain. Attig (2011) emphasizes that this is a different process from "relearning the world," which requires relearning a sense of safety and	**Impact on Women** The pathology of grief was associated with the stereotype of feminine behavior (Silverman and Klass, 1996). Therefore, women have had to defend their reactions and responses to grief (or hide them). Now, they are more likely to search out support groups of other individuals who have shared similar

(continued)

Table 2.4 *(continued)*

	Social Structure within Which Grief Is Situated			Cultural Response to Grief		
	Modernity			Modernism		
	Societal Characteristics	Grief Characteristics	Grief Norms	Response to Grief	Grief Experts	Criticisms
	Postmodernity			Postmodernism**		
			Because of the focus on individualism, new norms may emerge. The bottom line: Both the experience of grief and the frameworks within which is it interpreted are in flux (Konisberg, 2011).		belonging with a new way of negotiating the world.	experiences of loss and grief, in an effort to make meaning of the grief experience, that is, to find one's current place in a changed social context, and to align (or not) with the cultural context the griever finds herself in (Neimeyer, Klass, and Dennis, 2014).

*Adapted from T. Walter (2007), "Modern Grief, Postmodern Grief," *International Review of Sociology*, 17(1), 123–134.

**B. McHale (2008), "1966 Nervous Breakdown: or, When Did Postmodernism Begin?," *Modern Language Quarterly*, 69(3), 391–413 doi: 10.1215/00267929-2008-004.

Several researchers and practitioners alike have recently steered away from stage/phase theories of grief. James and Friedman (2009), for example, support common responses to grief (to which no time frames are attached) as reduced concentration, a sense of numbness, disrupted sleep patterns, changed eating habits, and a roller coaster of emotional

Table 2.5 Examination of Task-Based Theories of Grieving

Theorist	Number of Tasks	Specific Tasks	Pattern
Lindemann (1944) Coined term *grief work*	3	1. Relinquishing attachment to the deceased 2. Adjusting to the environment without the deceased 3. Developing new relationships	• Grieving is something we do. • Actively engage the challenges presented by our longing for, and need to let go of, those we care about.
Parkes (1983)	3	1. Acknowledging and explaining our losses 2. Emotionally accepting the losses 3. Assuming a new identity	• Struggle to gain control of, or constructively expressing and directing our emotions
William Worden (2009)	4	1. Acknowledging the reality of the loss 2. Working through the emotional turmoil in our lives 3. Adjusting to the environment where the deceased is absent 4. Loosening our ties to the deceased	• Work through our crisis in self-identity and disruptions in our usual behavior patterns, and develop alternatives; seek to build new relationships; make sense of our new reality; and find meaning in life without the deceased.

energy. But Attig (2011) has taken his criticisms of stage/phase and medical analogies one step further in stating that they lack a general understanding of what grievers actually experience, that there is a lack of discussion about the challenges faced including the critical role of choice, and current practices miss that grievers grieve as whole persons. In developing an

Table 2.6 Transposing Worden's Tasks into Relearning the World Tasks

Worden's Tasks (2009)	Attig's* Comparison to His Four Principal Facets of Coping	"Relearning the World" Tasks (Attig, 2011)
Acknowledging the reality of the loss	Intellectual/spiritual: Struggle to take in and make sense of the loss.	Attig's key criticism: Worden's tasks are not circumscribable, modest in scale, or completable.
Working through the emotional turmoil in our lives	Emotional/psychological: Acknowledge feelings, express/process them.	Relearning the world: • Coping as whole persons involving all facets simultaneously
Adjusting to the environment where the deceased is absent	Behavioral: Explore and adopt the life pattern changes that the loss demands.	• Coping in ongoing work until we die—a constant renegotiation with the dead and fellow survivors
Loosening our ties to the deceased	Social: Find new way to relate to those/what we have lost; accommodate the loss in relationships with our fellow survivors (changing social relationships have biological significance and are organic, and we are not fully conscious of the process).	

Doka's (1993) spiritual task: reconstructing faith or philosophical systems challenged by loss. (Note that Attig combined intellectual and spiritual tasks.)

Neimeyer's (2001) primary task in bereavement: meaning making or reconstructing meaning.

*Note that in Table 2.6, Attig has also incorporated the work of Doka (1993) and Neimeyer (2001).

approach that resonates with his observations of the grief experience and his research, Attig reexamined the work of grief—the tasks, and in them he discerned a pattern: that of active engagement in reconstructing one's identity and relationships in absence of the one or thing we held dear. Table 4.1 summarizes his examination.

For Attig, there are four principal facets of coping with grief that involve intellectual/spiritual, emotional/psychological, behavioral, and social dimensions. Relearning one's world requires that we work on all parts simultaneously, and we work until we die. Losing someone or something dear is not a one-time event. We embody our losses, and we recalibrate our lives in ways that make sense to us within the culture and society of which we are part.

This position resonates well with our social construction approach to examining and situating women's grief. Essentially, the concept of relearning one's world requires identifying, testing, and recovering trust in what remains viable in one's world after loss. It is about choice—the most basic choice requiring a "distinctive kind of hope, and optimism rooted in faith and conviction that supports and sustains the capacity to affirm life without the one we have loved and cared about" (Attig, 2011, p. 52). In respecting the individuality of grief and promoting grieving as active coping within the dimensions of one's physical and social worlds, and existential and spiritual being, the model is consistent with a postmodern view of the world. And what is more, for women, relearning the world incorporates both feminine and masculine capacities, which the modern/postmodern woman is already living with and through.

Notes

1. Note that Rando (1988) suggested that the traditional six-month time frame was variable and that "backsliding" should be regarded as part of the normal grieving process. In other words, time lines should be individually variable.
2. McHale, http://mlq.dukejournals.org/content/69/3/391.abstract.

CHAPTER THREE

Women's Socially Constructed Grief Response

With a backdrop of the socially constructed roles of women on one hand, and the social and cultural context of the loss and grief on the other, it is useful now to merge the two for a better understanding of women's possible experiences of loss and grief.

The Traditional Woman's Response to Loss and Grief

Generally, the traditional woman deals with her grief in the most productive manner of the three sex roles (transitional and modern/postmodern being the other two). Her grief is profound and intense. Again this has to do with the traditional woman following the blueprint for what a woman is "supposed" to be, and according to traditional ideology, women are emotional (generally far more emotional than men). Historically, the display of emotion was assumed to indicate weakness; therefore it is appropriate that women (the weaker sex) are the ones who show grief.

The traditional gender role, though constrictive and limiting in most of its other manifestations, does allow for a productive manner in dealing with grief. In fact, it could be taken as a model for grieving because as humans we not only have emotions but also an inherent need to express them. To deny or repress those emotions leads to many physical and emotional problems otherwise easily prevented (Charles-Edwards, 2005). In dealing with loss and grief, the cultural premium placed on stoicism, or "taking it like a man," is particularly destructive, and a healthy acceptance of our emotional natures is called for. Emotion is not a sign of weakness or of inability to deal with the world. Grief is the natural response to loss and cannot and should not be denied.

Traditional women's identities are dependent on their relationships, so a loss of those relationships necessitates an immediate confrontation of that loss. It is difficult for a traditional woman to subvert her feelings and divert herself with work. She must deal with the loss immediately. She must confront her role and its dependence on the one or thing that she has lost. The most extreme reaction a traditional woman could have in this situation is typically severe depression or even suicide. Less frequently, she can choose to reevaluate her role, perhaps even assuming the role of a transitional woman—someone whose identity expands beyond the boundaries of the task-specific, caregiver role so tightly bound up within the traditional role.

Because women tend to live longer than men, a very common loss for a traditional woman is that of her spouse. When her husband dies, a traditional woman is likely to face being alone for the first time in her life. For a traditional woman, the most common initial reaction to the death of a spouse is usually shock, numbness, and disbelief (Silverman, 1981). Even when a traditional woman anticipates the death of her spouse (as in "anticipatory grief"), the length and pervasiveness of these reactions may be lessened, but they are seldom alleviated. Intervals of irritability and anger continue in the day or two preceding the funeral. During this time, the woman continues to function in her role as wife. Physically, she may have trouble concentrating and may not feel well. However, the funeral is often a time of breakdown. The widow may cry uncontrollably, fluctuating between agitated distress and silent despair. Following the funeral, she will probably continue to meet her social obligations, but otherwise she is withdrawn. She may have trouble accepting that her husband is really gone, a reaction known as denial. Her emotions may include guilt, depression, insomnia, anxiety, and blaming herself and others. Guilt is a common emotion for the grieving traditional woman. She may feel that she could have done something to prevent her husband's death, that she should have treated her husband differently. Or she may feel guilt for having felt relieved by his death (if the relationship was a negative one). She may be overcome with executing the acts associated with her husband's estate, or she may avoid those responsibilities altogether, relying on someone else to deal with them.

In short, a husband's loss is considered a great one to the traditional woman in terms of her position and dependence (emotional and possibly financial as well) on her spouse.[1] She must come to terms with the fact that she is no longer a wife, and so she has lost the identity with which that role provided her. Without her husband to care for, her role as caretaker is drastically reduced, and she may lose self-esteem because of this. For a woman who saw her value as a person as being bound up with being able to please and care for her husband, the death of her spouse often means she is likely to feel less worthy. She must find a new identity or other reason to live and value herself as her self, possibly for the first time in her life. This is no easy task. The grieving process, then, for the traditional woman, is often a long one. (Interestingly, when a woman is widowed, she is five times less likely to remarry than a man.)

For a traditional woman, the death of a child tends not to challenge her role as a mother to the same extent that the death of a husband challenges her role as spouse. The traditional woman does not rely on her children to create her identity to the same extent as she does her spouse. In the case of the death of a child, the grieving and recovery process will necessarily entail that the traditional woman comes to terms with herself as a person, and although the process of self-discovery may be painful and difficult, it will probably open up possibilities that are both fulfilling and liberating. The fact that lack of an identity outside the relationship (particularly with a spouse) forces the traditional woman to deal with her loss, and is productive in that sense, it is less so in both transitional and modern women's lives in the sense that it is often easier to suppress grief and avoid dealing with loss because these women's identities are not so dependent upon their relationships (particularly with spouses or significant others). Avoidance of dealing with loss is not healthy on several fronts. In this regard, an argument can be made for the traditional woman dealing with loss and her grief more productively than women in transitional and modern/postmodern roles.

The Influence of Cultural Diversity on Traditional Roles and Response to Loss and Grief

Many ethnic cultures encourage women to mourn a loss by reacting with hysteria, which is consistent with the view that women are inherently more emotional or even that emotion is a feminine trait that men do not have. Of course we think differently today, but in Western society there is still an emphasis on logic and thinking that is an important part of being human. In other cultures, woman may be encouraged to express their emotions openly, such as in Latin cultures. Caucasian Americans are less involved with dying and death than most cultures, and as a result, have a much more difficult time dealing with grief and loss.

The Transitional Woman's Response to Loss and Grief

When a transitional woman is undergoing an identity crisis and is then confronted by the loss of someone she loves, the manner in which she reacts is dictated by the role that she most identifies with. She may try to be strong like the modern woman, or she may resort to her traditional role and be more consumed with her grief.

As stated earlier, the traditional woman's reaction to grief is one of expression. The transitional woman, in some ways, still identifies herself by the people closest to her and is therefore greatly affected by another's death, such as the death of a spouse. The transitional woman is also already in the process of reevaluating her role in relation to others, so she is not quite as profoundly affected by her sudden state of widowhood, for example, as a traditional woman would be. She thinks of herself less in terms of being someone's wife.

The death of a parent of a transitional woman may accelerate the woman's progression through her identity reevaluation, especially if the parent was instrumental in impressing upon her that she must conform to certain values. A key point is that many traditional women, upon experiencing a loss, become transitional women. This is only after a period of intense grieving when the woman is forced to reassess her role now that the person that essentially defined her is gone. Similarly, transitional women are more likely to become modern women once the experience of loss leads them to even more directly confront their sex-role classification. The transitional woman who is in a rapid state of transition is more likely to be preoccupied with her role reassessment and will be distracted by loss. Her emotions, as she tries to analyze them and fit them into the context of her changing role, are confusing to her. She is more likely than the traditional woman to deny the loss. As she fluctuates between the two roles (traditional and modern/postmodern), she alternately adheres to the way each typically reacts to loss. Some days she feels good, putting up the strong front of the modern woman. She is affected, but she feels as if she must attack the problem head-on in order to come to terms with it. Other days she feels devastated. She expresses her anguish as a woman adhering to a traditional role would do.

Because there is a conflict of how she should react, the grieving period may last longer for a transitional woman than a modern/postmodern woman, for example. She may suppress grief and experience delayed reaction and response. The progress of a transitional woman through grief is less smooth than that of the traditional woman, in that she must handle her identity crisis and reconcile her loss simultaneously.

The Modern/Postmodern Woman's Response to Loss and Grief

The modern/postmodern woman tends to respond to loss and grief as an expected life occurrence. The Internet has exposed her to death and dying in many ways, levels, and cultures around the world. Generally speaking, she is more able than the traditional or transitional woman to put her grief into the context of the universal experiences of loss and death. Although she relies on family and close friends to help her deal with her loss, she is also likely to call on virtual communities for comfort and support. This broader circle becomes important to her, and over time she tends to rely on them less and less as she assimilates her loss into her life. It is not that she is any less affected by loss and grief than women in other role classifications; it is that she is generally more equipped to place it within a larger context. As caregiver, and receiver, regardless of her role at home or at work, her family, friends, and the communities to which she aligns acknowledge that she will need some time to adjust. The extent to which various cultures define her role in grief influences her expression of grief, but cultural influence is ameliorated by her modern/postmodern stance in her own interpretation of her life. Typically, the modern woman pays homage to her cultural role within the context of loss and grief, but she assimilates those expectations into her life and resumes her "regular" life fairly quickly. If she feels more help is required, she will turn to her designated support groups or professionals whose specific expertise she feels she needs.

However, age of the woman is a factor influencing the ease with which she assimilates death into her own life. Women who are middle-aged or elderly may have experienced changing roles in the course of their lifetimes. They may have been exposed to or raised in households that reflected the patterns and values inherent in any of the role classifications, and any one or more of them may have become the norm of how they were raised. So that regardless of the age of the woman at the time of her loss, she may feel obligated to pay some homage to each of the roles she has transitioned through, and perhaps to, the various groups of people that fit those roles (e.g., family members who adhere to traditional roles), as these people are still significant in her life. This makes her expression of grief more complex and in some cases more schizophrenic because of her feeling that she needs to meet multiple role expectations simultaneously. (Age and life circumstance are addressed more fully in Chapter 5: Factors Influencing Grief Response.)

A Word about Gender and Its Influence on Grief Response

Historically, in the Western world, where individuation is prized and autonomy is the goal of human development (Erikson, 1959), little value has been placed on a model of interdependence when it comes to dealing with loss and/or grief. In fact, dependence has been linked to chronic grief as a pathology (Parkes and Weiss, 1983). From a gender perspective, autonomy in grief has been ascribed to masculine (or manly) traits, and dependent behavior has been ascribed to feminine (or womanly) traits (Lassonde, 2002).

In our view, the pathology of grief that has been associated with stereotypical feminine behavior has been mis-assigned (others also support this view, e.g., Silverman and Klass [1996]). We acknowledge that research exists that indicates sex-role conditioning whereby men and women grieve differently and have different needs in grief (Rando, 1988). But even in Kübler-Ross's last book (2004), she explained that there is no typical response to loss. Grieving is individual. And more recently, Attig (2011) looks at grief from a gender-neutral human, rather than a gender-centric, perspective, a phenomenological perspective.

Some people have successfully integrated the masculine and feminine within themselves and have come to terms with and given significant value to each. These individuals generally experience fewer problems dealing with loss. To them, the emotion does not indicate weakness, but possibly even strength. The woman (or man) who has rejected the feminine tends to experience problems when someone she cares for dies. She rarely permits herself to cry on receiving news of the death and at the funeral, but after this, she may suppress her emotions when she would otherwise be progressing through this difficult time in her life. She adopts a stoic position, keeps a "stiff upper lip," and though the people around her would certainly comprehend and sympathize with her feelings, she appears to be "handling it well." This suppression of such strong emotions is not a healthy way to grieve. The unexpressed feelings will manifest themselves in more detrimental ways later. Physical symptoms, which may come from this suppression, include colitis, back pain, severe headaches, ulcers, or other stress-related diseases. In her avoidance of appearing feminine or weak, the woman who has not integrated her masculine and feminine principles experiences an unnecessarily difficult and complicated grieving process.

Gender roles in today's society seem to make little sense. Rigid role definitions separate rather than unify in the most essential sense: they separate us from ourselves, causing us to suppress characteristics that are inherent to human nature. All of us have both masculine and feminine tendencies—tendencies of equal value and equal weight. In learning to cope with loss and grief, it may, in fact, be the traditional women's process of coping that can be used as a model for grieving. This would apply to both men and women equally, and to women who have adopted what has traditionally been masculine, antifeminine, anti-emotional characteristics. Our argument is not for the obfuscation of traditional gender roles and standards, but for accepting and valuing the "feminine" capacity to deal with grief and loss. It is a more natural and healthy way of coping than is the masculine mode of denial and suppression. Both feminine and masculine traits are embedded within each human being, so assigning these traits to either women or men exclusively denies the dual capacity inherent in each individual. Both those capacities are important when it comes to grief response.

Note

1. A Kalish and Reynolds study (1976) identified that all age groups except the 40- to 50-year-olds found the death of a man and the death of a woman to be equally tragic. (The 40- to 50-year-old group fit within the traditional role classification, and women were more impacted than men.)

CHAPTER FOUR

The Complexity of Grief

A Constructivist Approach to Grief and Mourning

Much has been written about psychosocial responses to death and bereavement, from which professional specialties and nonprofessional bereavement programs have developed. The conceptual models of loss and the clinical programs flowing out of them reflect outdated theories that have restricted the important questions that need to be asked, including the methods used to interpret findings (Neimeyer, 2001). Various authors have criticized the "standard model of grief," and they point to a new direction—from the function of mourning being a conservative, restorative process to one that is transformative; mourning as a private, intrapsychic process, to one that is social and relational; mourning as having normal, standardized characteristics, to one being personal and unique; mourning's central task as detachment to one of continuity; mourning leading to full resolution, to one being open and evolving (Hagman, 2001).

The criticisms raised on previous ways to grieve and mourn, and the transitions in mourning described above, reflect a contextualist, constructivist, and interpretive shift in psychology and allied disciplines—a new wave in grief theory. New models exhibit a skepticism about some of the fundamental tenets of standard grief theory: the universality of predictable emotional trajectories (i.e., stages, phases, etc.) and the presumption that grieving requires withdrawal of psychic energy from the deceased so staunchly supported by Freud and his followers. A constructivist approach supports greater awareness of the implications of loss on the individual's sense of identity, and a broadened focus on individual experience and the patterns and processes by which loss is negotiated within the individual, within families, and within broader social contexts (Neimeyer, 2001). This approach acknowledges that grief is an emotion that is influenced by social factors, but its shape, its meaning, the length of time it is expressed, and how it is expressed vary not only from one individual to another but from one cultural and historical group to another (Lofland, 1985).

A central process in grieving that involves meaning reconstruction in response to loss has begun to replace former approaches to clinical practice (Neimeyer, 2001): that of "meaning making" (inferring that we are self-consciously active and deliberate in making new meaning out of our lives), and "meaning finding" (less self-conscious and more passive or receptive to meaning that arises spontaneously out of our grieving)—processes that reflect Attig's (2001) "relearning the world." Grief response is inherently active and unpredictable, shaped by a person's personality, through exercising freedom and choice, by relationship to the deceased, and by familial and cultural backgrounds (Hagman, 2001). Loss results in a crisis in the meanings by which our lives are given structure and substance, and in bereavement we respond as multidimensional beings (Attig, 2011).

The Individuality of Grief Response—a Woman Whose Grief Works through Her

Jenn, a registered nurse and clinic administrator, is married to Mike. She is a mother and also a grandmother to little Jeremy, who is barely two years old. Jeremy's father—Jenn's son, Steven, a firefighter—died in a sudden and tragic accident almost a year before Jenn's own car crash, which she describes below. Her story describes a journey through the confusion and complexity that loss and grief have visited upon her as she works her way through grief, and it works its way through her.

> Mike was still in the shower and the children were busy getting ready for school. It was late. I was due at the clinic at 7:00 a.m. It usually took an hour to get there, and in my rush to the freeway, I failed to see the black ice on the road just as I came over the last hill out of the woods. The rear of the car slid to the left, and I maneuvered it out of the skid, but then it slid again. Again I maneuvered successfully, all the while my car was picking up speed. I started to spin out of control in the middle of the road, like I was caught in a whirlwind. In that flash, I knew that I would not be able to correct anymore, so I just hung onto the steering wheel and braced myself.
>
> I don't know how many times the car spun in circles. The more it spun, the farther from reality I felt. It seemed as if I was looking through a long

black tunnel, and I felt as if I was going to pass out. Soon everything was moving in slow motion. Then I felt a crushing pain as the right side of my car slammed against the curb. The jolt somehow cleared my vision long enough to see that that I was heading into a roll down a steep embankment. That's when I must have passed out.

I awoke to a tomb of silence. Everything was blurry. I wondered if this was death. But then I began to hear falling glass and I was relieved to feel the cold morning mist sifting in through the broken windows. I just sat there, afraid to move, my mind stalled. I remember not really knowing what to do next. Should I stay in the car or get out, stay still or move, scream or be quiet? I closed my eyes, hoping that when I opened them again, I'd find myself back home, slicing oranges for breakfast. But when I opened them, all I saw was twisted metal and broken glass.

Nothing made much sense to me. I was in a car. I thought it was my car, but when I reached to the right, I felt the bark of a tree. I was still in the driver's seat, but my door was above my head. I reached for the door handle and tried to push it open, but felt a horrible pain in my chest. It was a twisting, grinding pain that seemed to echo throughout my whole body. Breathing became difficult. I wanted to be free of all this, but at the same time I didn't want to move, so I sat there, closed my eyes, and pulled my coat close around me.

I could feel myself growing sleepy, and that's when I started to panic. I tried to get out again. I couldn't see my glasses or my purse, and I had on only one shoe. The keys weren't in the ignition anymore either. I could hear cars behind me, but they were high up, and no one was even stopping.

The windshield was shattered, but it was still intact. My only way out was through the broken window of the passenger side door. I put all my effort into climbing out, cutting my arms and legs with each move. When I got outside the car, nothing looked familiar. I heard a car come close, and I tried to scream, but I couldn't take in enough air to even yell. My car was hidden, and so was I. I knew that somehow I had to climb up the embankment or I would likely freeze to death. I started to crawl up the embankment.

Mike came to mind. He had asked me where his burgundy sweater was, throwing his parka on the bed, saying that it was only 19 degrees outside. I remembered that we didn't say goodbye. Then Steven's face came to me.

"Well, isn't this another fine mess you've gotten yourself into?" He laughed. "I blew it this time, Steven," I said. It was so strange. I felt his warmth all around me, but I knew he wasn't there. I closed my eyes and smiled. I think I passed out again. "Get up! *Get up!*" I could hear him yelling at me, but I couldn't see him—even with my eyes closed.

Steven had been a fighter. He'd loved life. He'd seen the tragic results of "dangerous" living every day at work. The night he died, he had been on call, and others working with him said it had been a very busy night. Steven was just tired and fell asleep. He wasn't wearing a seatbelt. He was tired and he just forgot.

Steven's voice kept getting louder and louder. *"Get up!"* "Oh God," I thought, "I must be going crazy." Steven had been dead for over a year, but he kept yelling.

It took several tries. I'd make it halfway up the hill, and then I'd slide back down. The pain was excruciating. I'd close my eyes, and again the long, dark tunnel would appear. But Steven was at the end of it now, laughing. It reminded me of when he would swim out to the waves and dare me to swim after him.

I don't know how long I tried, but finally I could feel the concrete curb. There was still so much pain, and Steven was gone. That long cold aloneness of his never being there was back again. How I missed talking with him, hugging him hello and good-bye. I should have died that day—could have, but didn't. I likely would have if it hadn't been for Steven—or I guess the memory of him.

When I think about him, I wished that I had died. It would have been easier to avoid all the pain I felt with him gone. I felt angry, numb, helpless as I tried to deny that he was actually gone, and it had been a year. I would vomit every time I ate. If I didn't vomit, I'd make myself. I felt better when I did. There were other things too.

I was in a world and didn't feel a part of it. I walked through familiar places and saw no one. One night I awoke from a dream with hives all over my body. I couldn't stand the itching, so I drove myself to the emergency room. It was three in the morning.

I didn't know what I was going to tell the doctor. I sat in the parking lot, wondering what I would say—that my son had died and I was actually going crazy and now I had hives? I just wanted relief and some sleep. So, being a nurse (which I did not mention), I presented the doctor on call with my real symptoms (generalized hives) and a fake history of having unknowingly eaten fish in a salad that evening (I have an allergy to fish). My blood pressure was elevated and my pulse rapid, and I looked like a normal case of allergic reaction. Except that I didn't feel normal.

No one asked me if there was another reason I was crying. No one questioned the fact that I said I was married but had driven myself to the hospital. No one wondered why I was 400 miles away from the home address I gave them on the admission form. No one really cared, or cared to know.

My allergy was not from fish, but from the pent-up feelings of grief I was experiencing—denial, anger, sadness, and guilt. Like being out of control on the icy road, those feelings were part of the whirlwind I was spinning in and couldn't free myself from.

> After my car accident, I resigned my nursing position. How could I help anyone when I couldn't even help myself? Even simple decisions seemed confusing and difficult.
>
> I talked about my turmoil with a friend, who immediately blamed the chaos in my life on my falling away from the church. Actually, I'd never felt closer to God than when I decided to get away from the chaos and drove to the Grand Canyon alone for a weekend. I stayed out all day wandering along the edge of the South Rim. I watched the sunrise and the birth of color against the sculptured canyon walls at dawn, the dancing colors as the day passed, and the somber peaceful colors of sunset.
>
> I wanted to believe that change could be good in my life too. Climbing up the embankment from the wreckage was exhausting. Just as exhausting as searching for who I am now. Surviving the accident was a lonely journey encouraged by the beautiful memories of Steven. Surviving this grief is another lonely journey. Like memories of Steven, the help of friends has been inspiring—at least some of them. An old friend, 3,000 miles away, listened and talked me through a time of wanting to give up on life, and a new friend taught me to accept that nothing is forever, that it's okay to cry, and especially to concentrate on living. I run down the path and still trip over pebbles, and bike down the road and fall off, but it is a lot easier to get up and keep going, and someday I know that I'll swim out to the waves where Steven is.

What Jenn experienced as a time of chaos and confusion with even simple things did not really surprise her. She was a modern woman easily fulfilling her job as nursing administrator. She was also already familiar with the bereavement process. She understood, as Eliot had described long ago in the 1930s, that grief could cause a sense of abandonment, shock, denial, guilt, and anger, and most of all, an intense longing for the deceased. She had experienced depression too, but she had not realized the extent to which her depression had been prolonged and that perhaps she had allowed the busyness of her life to mask and maybe even stifle it. Jenn was aware of some of the physical reactions to grief (dyspnea, tight sensations in the throat, physical exhaustion, sleeping lethargy, feelings of emptiness, decreased appetite, gastrointestinal disturbances, crying, auditory and visual hallucinations, and insomnia), and some of these had been part of her grief too—but in mild form. It wasn't until the nightmares and the hives that Jenn was shaken by what her body was telling her—that she had not yet dealt with the mental anguish of her son Steven's death. And like the skidding tires and the seemingly endless spins of the car on the icy road and then careening down the embankment, her life was out of control. Strangeness in her own body, out of sync with her world, emotional flatness—these were the signals to Jenn that it was time to surrender to her loss.

Jenn turned to nature—to a weekend of solace alone in the Grand Canyon. To family and friends, it may have seemed dis-regarding. To work colleagues, it may have seemed neglectful. But to Jenn, it marked the first real step to begin reconstructing her life without her son in it.

Some time ago, Deutsch (1937) remarked that every unresolved grief is given expression in some form or other—that the process of mourning *must be carried through to its own completion*.

Should church have been the place for resolution of Jenn's grief? Was Jenn's car crash the impetus for her to know that connecting with Steven was real for her, but it just happens in a different way now? Will that memory sustain her? Clearly, Jenn's path is her own. No one can really tell her what will work best for her. Friends and family can support her, but her journey is one of making meaning from and out of her life now.

Meaning Reconstruction

Perhaps as Bowlby (1961, 1998) suggested, both overt and hidden reactions to grief do occur in overlapping stages—sometimes as disbelief and numbness at the news of death and its denial; of disorganization of one's own personality as the loss is accepted; and eventually, as reorganization of one's own personality as it reestablishes connection with the deceased—in Jenn's case, with Steven and the memory of him.

Through Jenn's symbolic association between the reactions to the death of her son and then the experience of her own automobile crash, the intensity of the grief she felt and the precious value of her lost relationship became disclosed to her. As discussed earlier, although grief has been categorically described in stages or phases, behavioral responses of the survivor of loss are not so clearly defined or differentiated (Hagman, 2001). They are complex and often intertwined, more closely reflecting oscillation between loss- and restoration-oriented coping and life reconstruction (what Stroebe and Schut's portray in their Dual Process Model, 1999). And certainly, it reflects what Neimeyer and Attig refer to as "re-learning one's world."

Backsliding is a normal experience. Just when the bereaved seem to be progressing well into the reorganization stage, a particular incident, day, or time of year that holds specific association with the deceased may plunge the survivor back—like Jenn sliding backward down the embankment. Typically these incidents occur with increasingly less frequency, and with less intensity. The most important thing to remember is that when these backslides do occur, this is not indicative of the individual's failure to cope. Jenn, like other survivors of loss, should not be held to the pressure of "getting on with it" or "letting go." These kinds of pressures cause an unhealthy suppression of grief. Falling back into depression is a normal occurrence and does not mean that Jenn or other survivors are "losing it" or that they should feel guilty about their feelings for not recovering quickly enough. The path through grief, or grief's path through us, is complex, inherently active, and yet unpredictable (Attig, 2011). It is an individual process that is influenced by many factors—as the next chapter explores.

CHAPTER FIVE

Factors Influencing Grief Response

Factors Further Individuating[1] the Grieving Process

Grief is shaped by many social factors,[2] and as discussed in previous chapters, today women (and we suggest men as well) often experience both inner turmoil and social dissonance due to their search for self-identity through their choice of role in a constantly changing society. Some women live within a traditional role orientation; others, within a transitional or modern/postmodern framework. Women may not identify with any one role exclusively. As well, outsiders may interpret a woman's role very differently from the one she identifies with. What is important is the woman's self-perception, for it is this perception that will most affect her grieving process.

Traditional, transitional, and modern women are each potentially vulnerable to the effects of bereavement because of society's respective standards, norms, and pressures embedded within each role orientation. Such feelings as guilt, self-blame, and anger are strong for anyone who has experienced a loss. A woman who struggles with role orientation is at risk of stagnating in her guilt and self-blame, but she can also choose to find an inner stability clarifying her own identity and fit in her world that is changed through loss.

Some of the key factors that have a significant influence on a woman's grief include the value of her lost relationship, her age, personality, ethnicity, educational level, and financial status. The sum of these determinants, along with her choice of social role (traditional, transitional, modern/

postmodern), call forth a very individualized and complex "grief response"[3] (Attig, 2011). And although each woman experiences her grief individually, societies and cultures establish mourning practices that provide stabilizing expectations of behaviors during times that women often experience as confusing and chaotic (Noel and Blair, 2008). When the loss of a close relationship occurs during a transitional woman's reevaluation of her role, for example, the emotions of grief and the entire grieving process are intensified. What is more, these factors typically do not occur in isolation, but rather in some combination to shape a woman's grief response, and unacknowledged, or misunderstood, they may put women at risk of developing problems dealing with their grief. An individual's maturity; tolerance for frustration and inner conflict; capacity for adaptation, substitution, and sublimation; as well as intelligence, education, and life experience, all affect her capacity to resolve grief (Doka and Martin, 2010).

Value of the Lost Relationship

In any individual's life, not all relationships have the same value or intensity. The greater the value of the lost relationship for the woman, that is, the degree of its closeness and uniqueness to her, the greater will be its influence on her response to grief (Lofland, 1985). "The more the deceased is interwoven into the tapestry of our lives, the greater our vulnerability to having to reweave the fabric" (Attig, 2011, p. 77).

According to many, the death of a spouse is considered to be the most stressful loss (Holmes and Rahe, 1967; Norris and Murrell, 1990). Others feel the death of a child has a greater impact on the bereaved parent due to the significance of children representing the parent's hopes and dreams for the future (Deits, 2009; Klass, 2005; Rando, 1993). To the elderly, the death of a brother or sister is significant because that lost sibling may have been the only person left from the bereaved person's past (Shah and Meeks, 2012). Memories, no longer shared by siblings, serve to further isolate the elderly, who often in American society already tend to live a lonely, segregated existence. Although the elderly are generally more accustomed to the idea of death than younger people, the value of the lost sibling relationship tends to be very high.

For the bereaved woman, if the relationship was deemed a positive one, whether with a spouse, child, or sibling, successful completion of the grieving process is less difficult. Similarly, if the relationship involved conflict, the survivor is no longer able to resolve the conflict with the lost person. She may anguish over unfinished business (Doka, 1989) and become even more vulnerable. The accompanying grief is then more difficult to work through, and this may result in the woman experiencing a "complicated grief."

A number of factors determine grief and whether it is uncomplicated or complicated. In an uncomplicated grief process, loss is typically accepted, assimilated, accommodated, and transformed. In complicated grief, the bereaved experience significant functional impairment longer than six months, and they suffer psychiatric comorbidities such as depression, anxiety disorder, and/or PTSD. However, to make that determination, a number of factors must be considered (Love, 2007). Predisposing factors may include previous loss, conflict with the deceased person, dependency of ambivalence in the relationship, and beliefs about death. Protective factors may include personal resilience, adequate social support, opportunities to redefine and create relationships. Precipitating factors may include traumatic loss following accident, other significant attachments, and whether the death is associated with stigma or shame. And finally, perpetuating factors may include inadequate social support, conflict with the deceased person, dependency, or ambivalence in the relationship. All of these factors have to be assessed and considered with respect to the depth of bereavement the woman is experiencing.

Social Role

A woman's social role also affects her response to grief. A young adult woman, for example, with a traditional upbringing, could initiate an intense grief reaction to feelings of insecurity through the loss of a parent (possibly a dependent relationship). On the other hand, the loss could initiate a sense of freedom and new possibility for the woman. To an older woman in a traditional marriage, loss of her husband could mean the loss of her perceived purpose in life because she had functioned primarily as her husband's caretaker. For older women who have adopted a transitional or modern role, again the loss of a husband could produce an intensified grief reaction if the woman feels that she has somehow let the deceased down by deviating from a traditional role, or she could feel a strong sense of liberation if her husband had been restrictive in accepting and supporting a more modern role for his wife.

Social Class

Grief is dealt with privately, but also publicly. The social class with which the woman identifies has a definite impact on her experience of grief.

Generally speaking, the working class publicly displays a greater commitment to the deceased through their overt expressions of grief. The middle class in the United States recognizes grief as an accepted consequence of a significant loss, but the bereaved individual is expected to "snap out of it" and get on with life rather quickly. For the upper class, stoicism in public is insisted upon, for grief is considered a private affair. The public image of strength and being in control in times of trouble must be maintained. The private life, including its sorrow, must be protected and withheld. But rules of proper behavior do no more than complicate the woman's experience of loss, and what is considered proper deportment actually sets up barriers to successful grief resolution.

Age and Life Circumstances

It is generally believed that the young who experience loss of a significant other have intense grief to resolve (Christ, Siegel, and Christ, 2002; Rask, Kaunonen, and Paunon-Illomonen, 2002; Worden, 2009). This includes young adults (Balk, Walker, and Baker, 2010). Societal attitudes give the impression that death is not possible in youth, and its occurrence is likely to be shocking to a young person who has little exposure to death (Lench and Chang, 2007). The reckless lifestyles that many younger people live (drinking and driving, speeding in cars or motorcycles without wearing seat belts or helmets) reflect an attitude and perhaps belief of infallibility and immortality. When death is visited on a young person, there is a sobering and frightening effect on youth (Arnett, 2007). Death by suicide (and therefore choice) makes it especially difficult for youth to grieve, particularly when the suicide victim is another young person. In American society, where death is a subject that is generally avoided or covered up, young women are likely to be hit very hard by the death of someone they know.[4]

There is little research conducted on the impact on young women who experience the loss of a spouse. However, to a young widow in a traditional relationship, the loss will likely be greater than if she were in a transitional or a modern relationship. She may be feeling abandoned by her husband, left to raise young children alone (if she has children), having to become the sole income provider and financial manager, and possibly having to learn new skills for employment as well. And when she is told, "Don't worry, you'll find someone else," she is torn between feeling that her friends and family believe her husband is easily replaced, and/or that she cannot function or manage on her own.

There is some research to indicate that loss of a partner for a young woman results in peer discomfort because they too are unfamiliar with loss. However, young women can also experience a kind of "rebirth" after losing a spouse (Walter, 2003). When the young woman continues bonds with the deceased and actively incorporates the death into her new life, she is likely to suffer a less complicated grief (Neimeyer, Baldwin, and Gillies, 2006). Technology too has an influence on a woman's grief response. The Internet allows her to connect with others with similar experiences, and moving forward through online dating sites, for example, can help her connect to a possible new mate. At the same time, these experiences can conflict a young widow in feeling that she is somehow betraying her deceased spouse (Walter, 2003).

Loss to a woman in middle age has different impacts. A decreased social life becomes even more important to a widow who has already lost her primary companion. Often, when a middle-aged woman becomes a widow (or is divorced), her married friends eventually drop her from their guest list because she is no longer part of a couple. Friends might become uncomfortable, assuming she's "on the prowl," looking for a new partner. One recently divorced woman explained:

> One of the nicest things that happened to me eight months after my divorce was being invited out to dinner by a couple who were old friends of my ex-husband and me. I felt awkward and crushed when the waiter looked at the three of us and inquired if we wanted a table for four saying, "Is there another gentleman coming?" Keith turned and winked at Jennie, and I immediately requested a table for six, giving the waiter fictitious names of three additional women, adding, "I'm expecting my other dates soon." The look on the waiter's face was priceless. The ice of uneasiness was broken; we were given a table for six, I relaxed, and the three of us enjoyed the evening. A lot of the hurt is knowing how other people view you. You can see them fitting you into a mold when actually you're just trying to figure out who you really are. No one seems to understand that.

For someone who has fit comfortably into a social structure only to be displaced because of the loss of a significant other (through death, divorce, or loss of other kind of relationship), being marginalized is painful. On the other hand, the loss experience can also be an opportunity for personal growth. Society, though, generally fails to recognize this and instead stigmatizes displaced individuals.

Women at midlife also experience other types of loss and grief, resulting, for example, from the death of one parent while having to shoulder emotional, caregiving, and possibly financial responsibility for a surviving parent. This may require the woman to juggle multiple role orientations simultaneously—that expected by the surviving parent as well as the one she chooses as an independent individual. At the same time, the woman may also be in a parent role if her own children (regardless of their age or life circumstance) still live in the family home. The fact is that many women in midlife experience a whole range of losses from which grief can arise: loss of a spouse, a partner, siblings, parents, relatives, jobs, and health. (Some of these are covered in subsequent chapters.)

For the elderly, coping with loss may be less difficult because they have more exposure to, and are more accustomed to, the idea of death itself. Research indicates that older women report less fear and anxiety about dying than do men, but that losing an adult child can be as devastating as losing a spouse (Hooyman and Kiyak, 2007). For an elderly woman who lived her life primarily in a traditional role, redefining herself after the death of her spouse is typically very difficult. Having other supportive relationships and continuing active involvement in the companionship of leisure activities with friends help her to develop new positive self-concepts (Montpetit and Bergeman, 2010). More than with any other age group, death is accepted as a fact among the elderly since more friends and acquaintances are dying of old age. Death is regarded as "normal" and if the bereaved's own life has been rewarding, it is easier to accept than when life has been fraught with hostility and conflict.

Education Level

Usually, the higher a woman's educational background, the better able she is to take control of her life and handle responsibility for life experiences. This is very important in determining the outcome of her grief. A college education, for example, typically means exposure to various ideologies, and this encourages the individual to actively participate in forming personal values rather than merely accepting or conforming to traditional ones. An education also typically encourages a more mature and broader approach to problem solving. These skills are relevant and important with respect to loss and grief in that with them comes the need for personal examination, redirection, and adaptation to life without a significant other (a spouse, a partner, a child, a parent, and so on). A higher education level eases some of the burden of redefining one's life in the face of loss, especially, for example, for the widow who becomes the primary income provider. Employment opportunities are greater with a college education, and when education is coupled with some past experience, maintaining a position or reentering the labor force is less difficult.

By comparison, a low level of education means a more difficult path toward personal and economic independence. Research indicates that many aged widows experience a decline in their standard of living upon widowhood, a pattern that is pronounced among those with limited education (Weaver, 2010). Replacing external pressures of tradition with individual freedom might not be customary, as the tendency is for women with less education to lead more traditional lives. Recovering from loss in this instance would be a slow process that involves guidance, counseling, and further education.

Financial Status

Grief is a difficult experience in itself, but when compounded by financial problems, it can be disorienting and overwhelming. People who experience financial decline following their partner's death are at greater risk of poor psychological health—women more so than men, and for longer periods of time (Cordon and Hirst, 2013).

For the young traditional widow, loss of a husband means the immediate burden of becoming the major breadwinner. (This is exacerbated if there are major outstanding medical bills.) If the traditional woman has a profession (or had one prior to being married), getting back into the workforce may be challenging as she attempts to deal with her loss on an emotional level. Concentration is a problem during bereavement, and this may also create problems at work as the following widow's experience indicates:

> As soon as I sold my home in the country, I took a trip to the town I planned to move to. With my résumé and past experience, I was able to secure a position the second day I looked. Everything was happening so fast, and I felt I was a robot who was saying all the right things. I heard words coming in and bouncing off, but I had trouble remembering what was said. During my new job orientation, I was shown several forms and what to do with them, but I couldn't remember any of it. I found myself having to look things up in the procedure manual—something I had never had difficulty with before. I found myself listening to conversations, but not participating in them. When I finally tuned in, I realized that I had been thinking about what had happened to me in my life and wondered what I was doing in this strange place anyway.

Disorientation after loss is common, as is a reduced ability to reason and concentrate on duties that once seemed trivial. Without the grounding force that the lost relationship provided, it may seem very difficult, if not impossible, to recenter and focus oneself on new tasks. If the young widow in the story above, for example, had been at home caring for children, the added costs, frustration, and fears of leaving the children with friends, relatives, or at a day care center would add further stress to the chaos she already feels. The necessity of making decisions at a time of also attempting to resolve grief can hinder the grief process and significantly disrupt life. For a woman in this situation, both support from friends and family, and possibly counseling as well, is probably a necessity to help ease the enormity of her burden and to help her put things into perspective. As well, the immediate necessity to solve economic problems and find employment puts her at high risk for developing problems in grief resolution. If older children are at home, she also might feel she is a failure because she is financially unable to assist them in their educational pursuits as previously planned. This is complicated by the fact that she has difficulty providing her children with the stable emotional support they need during their experience with the loss of a father.

For the middle-aged widow, financial problems are also a significant factor in assessing the outcome of her bereavement. One study indicated that widowed individuals in 2011, especially women, reported fewer social and financial difficulties than their counterparts in 1979. However, the effect of widowhood on depressive symptoms and psychological difficulties did not differ significantly across these points in time. The authors concluded that social changes in the late 20th century may be protective for older adults' physical, social, and financial well-being in the face of spousal loss, yet these changes do not alleviate widow(er)s' psychological distress (Perrig-Chiello et al., 2016).

In the United States, data indicate that almost half of older women (46%) age 75+ live alone. Over 48 percent of the poor elderly are widows, even though widowed women account for only 26 percent of all persons age 65 and older. Compared to the slightly more than 4 percent of couples age 65 and older who are poor, about 20 percent of widowed women are poor. This poverty rate is considerably lower than the 50 percent of widows who were poor in 1970. However, on average, married women in the United States experience a decline in income when their husbands die. Although widowers are somewhat more likely to be poor than are married couples, data that follow couples over time do not show a decline in average economic well-being for men when wives die. The median income of older persons in 2013 was $29,327 for males and $16,301 for females. Older men were much more likely to be married than older women—72 percent of men, 46 percent of women. In 2014, 35 percent of older women were widows.[5]

In Canada, the story is not much different. Statistics Canada reported that in 2001, Canada had just over 1.2 million widowed men and women aged 65 and over, a 6.4 percent increase from 1996, according to census data. Senior widows outnumbered senior widowers four to one. In fact, widows accounted for 45 percent of all women aged 65 and over. Because of widowhood, more senior women were entering low-income status over the years. Five years after the death of their spouse, the proportion of widows entering low-income status exceeded the proportion of their still married counterparts by two to one.

Financial security does not guarantee successful grief resolution, but the threat of financial insecurity can be further disorienting and may make it seem that there is just too much for the widow to handle. In short, death of a spouse often still means the loss of the main source of financial support for a woman and a drastic lowering of her standard of living. (Unfortunately, divorce can have a similar result.)

Resilience: The Capacity to Cope with and Recover from Loss

Although an array of social and personal variables influences an individual's coping ability, there is little agreement on which factors have the most influence. However, the most predictive factors have been found to be positive self-esteem and personal competencies of the bereaved in managing the tasks of daily living (Doka and Martin, 2010). These two characteristics are similar to what Bonanno (2004) calls "resilience." In his studies of widows, Bonanno found that although personality does play a small role, resilience (the ability to maintain relatively stable, healthy levels of psychological and physical functioning following the death of a spouse) is not a personality trait, but rather healthy adjustment to loss. Bonanno found that laughing and smiling are more helpful in adjusting to loss, along with the repression of negative emotions (Bonanno, Ray, and Gross, 2007; Keltner and Bonanno, 1997). This is quite contrary to the emphasis grief culture has placed on tears or anger as healthy expressions of grief. According to Bonanno, resilience reflects the ability to maintain equilibrium and healthy levels of stable psychological and physical functioning as well as capacity for generative experiences and positive emotions, even in the face of trauma.

Other research supports those results. For example, widows who remained connected, rather than isolated, felt that their grief was manageable and under control; and those who embraced and learned from new experiences, rather than avoiding or feeling threatened by them, were better able to bounce back from widowhood (Rossi, Bisconti, and Bergman, 2007). Having appropriate social support and minimizing other sources of stress, such as financial stress, were also helpful.

Resilience, as an important factor in recovery from loss and grief, is gaining increased prominence throughout the literature. Bonanno and his colleagues have found that mourners with more robust self-narratives that assimilate traumatic loss seem to respond with resilience and resourcefulness, maintaining continuing bonds with the deceased when the loss makes sense spiritually, existentially, or in practical terms (Bonanno, 2004). One of the practical meaning-making strategies of maintaining continuing bonds and assimilating loss is through narrative (also referred to as "therapeutic journaling"). (This is also supported by other grief researchers [Attig, 2011; Deits, 2009; Lichtenthal and Cruess, 2010; Nagel and Clark, 2012; Neimeyer, 2014; Noel and Blair, 2008; Pannebaker, 1997) as well as other researchers throughout the social sciences.)

Thomas Attig (2011) expresses his view on resilience this way:

> [O]ur resilience resides in what is not broken. . . . our daily lives are shattered, our life stories disrupted, our connections to larger wholes threatened or undermined, and our ego's illusions undone. Yet, much in the tattered web of our life remains intact. . . . [n]either the soul nor spirit is broken. The home-seeking and meaning-seeking drives that animate our lives, though shaken, can and do address our brokenness and overcome our sorrow. Resilient souls find sustenance in familiar surroundings; draw from roots in family, community, history, and tradition; care and love deeply, and find grounding in the great scheme of things. Resilient spirits find hope, faith, and courage to rise above suffering; stretch into the new and unknown; change and grow; seek understanding; and open to joy again. And the love that still pulses in our soul and spirit can cherish precious memories and lasting legacies, revive connections with fellow survivors, and open to new relationships. As our unbroken and resilient soul and spirit do these things we relearn how to be our selves again in life in separation from our loved one. (p. xlix)

Although "grief work" may be helpful to those bereaved individuals experiencing significant distress (Neimeyer, 2000; Stroebe and Stroebe, 1991), there is a lack of evidence to substantiate its positive effects over time (Wortman and Silver, 1989). In some cases, grief work has actually been shown to have harmful effects (Bonanno and Kaltman, 2001), leading seminal grief researchers to support building resilience as key to overcoming grief.

Ethnicity and Culture: Their Influence on Grief and Its Expression

Cultural norms and traditions significantly influence bereavement. They become "shaping agents" of grief that reinforce both women's (and men's) roles in the grieving process (Doka and Martin, 2010). Culture has also been said to "colonize" a person's public identity and private self-concept (Neimeyer et al., 2006). In short, societies "police" bereavement practices through the culture(s) they support and sustain.

Cultures have rules for expression of grief and for managing continuing bonds with the deceased (Walter, 1999). Grieving too much (prolonged or chronic grief), or at the wrong time (delayed grief), or not at all (absent grief), all are examples of contemporary psychotherapeutic culture where aberrant grief is considered pathological (Neimeyer et al., 2014). Knowing how a particular ethnic group views death, then, is important in understanding how a woman is expected to express her grief, and how members of her ethnic community will judge the appropriateness of her response.

Sometimes, the influence of the cultural group to which the woman belongs has an enormous and lifelong impact on her, as the following vignette illustrates.

> My grandfather died in 1950 in an accident at sea. My grandmother, an independent woman from the Madeira Islands, owned a fresh fish market and restaurant in New England. When my grandfather died, her in-laws no longer felt it proper for her to be a business woman, and they strongly suggested that she not shame her dead husband by working in public. My grandmother then sold her business and supported herself by selling her Madeira embroidery creations that she made and sold from her home. From the time of my grandfather's death, my grandmother dressed completely in black until she died 33 years later at the age of 96.

Although the woman described above was considered fairly modern for the 1950s, the pressures that traditional family members placed on her after her husband's death plagued her with the guilt of possibly shaming her deceased husband. To reconcile her personal loss and grief, she succumbed to family pressure and lived out her days in a fashion "acceptable" to her ethnicity. She gave up the business she enjoyed and withdrew from the outside world. For a woman who in some ways had experienced movement from a traditional to transitional role in her early life, cultural moirés dictated her reversion to the very traditional lifestyle she had begun to transition out of.

Cultural traditions that dictate, or at least direct, the role of women in their expressions of grief are deeply embedded historically. In the Bible, for example, when Mary Magdalene mourns the death of Jesus and bends to look inside the empty tomb, and is asked by the stoic disciples, "Woman, why are you weeping?" Mary replies, "Because they have taken away My Lord and I don't know where they have laid him." (John 20: 10–13). By tradition, it would have been disgraceful for the disciples to display emotion or grief. Mary, on the other hand, as a woman, fulfilled the traditional requirements of her role by crying. Traditional gender roles see women as more openly expressive of their grief and more invested in familial relationship than men, based on their reaction to grief and because women generally may pay more attention to their own and others' emotional states than men (Doka and Martin, 2010).[6] The Women's Movement itself was a significant factor in allowing for a more feminine expression of grief in the public sphere (Doka and Martin, 2010).

In some cultures such as the Far East, India, the Middle East and in many smaller societies, death affects the immediate family but also the community of which the family is part. Grief is openly expressed by everyone through crying, weeping, sobbing, and wailing. In many North American societies, particularly Britain, America, and the Scandinavian countries, death is largely private and dignified, and limited to the immediate family. Although open expression is not discouraged, neither is it encouraged. Funeral services proceed with restraint and quiet dignity (Parkes, 2015).

Some ethnically diverse examples that illustrate women's roles in grief and mourning include the following:

- In the Thanga tribe of South Africa, women's wailing begins after the ritual burial and prayer. The women get on their feet and shout loudly, throwing themselves on the ground. The wife of the deceased cries more loudly than anyone else. (Junod, 1962).
- Among the Awande tribe of Sudan, the correct social behavior of women in mourning is explicit. Women who go to mourn must wear a simple girdle of bingha grass; they must tear their hair and sprinkle ashes over their head and body. In the hut, the women stand near the corpse to wail and sing while others stand near the door. The men glance inside where the body is and then squat down under the granaries in the shade of some tree to talk about what is happening.
- In the Refugaa tribe indigenous to the Philippines, a female relative first arriving at the death chair will always wail, usually with her blanket over her head. This wailing will probably be joined in by the other female relatives that are present.
- In Latin American societies, only the women lament the dead. For a period of seven nights following a death, female friends and relatives gather in a darkened, flower-adorned room lit by candles. The deceased is eulogized, and the women wail, weep, and pray. Men do not attend these ceremonies.
- To the Jivaro tribe in the Andes of South America, there is no such thing as natural death. The reaction to death is always violent because the survivors feel someone or something has caused this death to occur. But again it is the

function of the women to express the violence. The kinsmen of the deceased shake their fists, curse, and swear vengeance on their unknown enemy. By custom, wailing is the duty of the nearest women relatives of the deceased. Although some wailing has a formal or ceremonial character, much of it is personal and sincere. The Jivaro wife, for instance, calls her dead husband by pet names, praises his virtues, and speaks of the joys they shared and of her loneliness in his loss. The wailing widow moves about the body throughout the night, addressing it in piteous language. However, in the midst of all this, the widow will suddenly burst out in violent, supposedly murder-like behavior (Habenstein and Lamers, 1963).

- In Egypt among poor families in Cairo, relatives scream, wail, and lament for several weeks, venting their suffering and pain. They believe that unhappiness must find a way out of the body to avoid it weighing down the soul and causing mental illness. An Egyptian mother who remains withdrawn, mute, and inactive seven years after the death of her child is considered to behave normally by the standards of her culture (Parkes et al., 2015). In contrast, in Bali the bereaved cry a little upon a death, but they see laughing as a sensible, protective measure to keep one's psyche strong (Wikan, 1988). A Balinese mother who remains calm and cheerful after the death of her child is considered normal, as emotional upset is believed to make one vulnerable to illness and "malevolent sorcery" (Parkes et al., 2015).
- In the Hindu faith, wives of seriously ill patients pray, fast, and call upon the help of astrologers. At death the widow wipes out her wedding mark, and close female relatives wear white saris for a year after death. Shedding tears is encouraged, and professional mourners may be hired to evoke such emotion (Parkes et al., 2015).

There are many other examples from around the world that illustrate women's traditional mourning practices. Although some practices may seem very foreign to American culture, others may be more relevant given the influx of immigrants and refugees into America. Women who have been exposed to, if not raised according to, diverse cultural beliefs and traditions, experience loss and grief in ways unlike our own. The degree to which women assimilate their diverse ethnic practices into American culture influences not only how a woman responds to her grief but also the extent to which her movement through grief is considered appropriate both by the new ethnic group into which she is trying to assimilate, as well as by the group from which she originates. Not only women but also families, communities, and cultures construct meaning by integrating the experience of grief into their larger cultural and religious narratives. In multicultural societies, the question arises as to which culture controls meaning. Neimeyer, Klass, and Dennis (2014) contend that when power arrangements (political, religious) change, continuing bonds with ancestors also change to reflect those power arrangements. In short, "[P]ublic voicing and performance of grief and its associated rituals are functionally scripted . . . to support broader social systems and those who wield power within them" (p. 496).

Crying as Expression of Grief

The loss of a close relationship calls forth some form of emotionality in almost all bereaved individuals, whether female or male. The manifestation of that emotionality is typically crying. Indeed, an enduring visual associated with grief over time and across cultures, and through various art and linguistic forms, is that of a woman weeping.

According to Paul Rosenblatt (Rosenblatt, Walsh, and Jackson, 1976) in his book *Grief and Mourning in Cross-Cultural Perspective*, expression of emotion is exhibited in the form of crying, anger, and fear.

Rosenblatt conducted studies measuring the frequency of crying in both females and males after experiencing a significant loss. Of the 28 societies he studied, women were found to cry more frequently than men (Rosenblatt et al., 1976). Why has this role of ritual griever been assigned to women? According to Rosenblatt, there are several explanations, all of which stem from the traditional role expectation of women.

Due to traditional socialization practices, women may experience losses more strongly than men if they have been trained to perceive themselves only in relation to others, that is, as caregiver/caretaker. Loss of this identity would be more upsetting to someone whose self-esteem is bound up in her relation to others rather than being focused solely on herself as an independent personality. The focus on relationships may cause women to form more extensive emotional attachments if they have been taught that their personal value lies in functioning as a wife or mother.

Rosenblatt also theorized that differences in frequency of crying among females and males stems from the socialization of women to express aggression in a nonaggressive or self-directed manner. Ritual grieving, such as that performed by women at funerals, may have been one of the few acceptable outlets available to women who were indoctrinated to be "seen and not heard." Indeed, in classical Athens, religious events, along with funerals, furnished women with the only opportunity to participate in the public life of the community. Trained to subvert aggression in every way, the wailing tradition, which seems to be a part of so many societies grieving practices, may have functioned as a nonaggressive way of channeling grief and its accompanying anger and frustration.

As well, Rosenblatt concluded that women may express emotional distress because they feel societal pressure to do so. Traditionally, women have been seen as being of lower status in society, and their role has been to serve as males' emotion-expressing or respect-expressing surrogates. In short, women may not experience a death more strongly; they may only be used as the persons who symbolize it publicly (sometimes in burdensome or self-injuring ways) (Rosenblatt et al., 1976).

A woman weeping, then, is one of the most prominent of the traditional gender roles of women. According to traditional lore, women are considered the more emotional sex (Walter, 2003), but Doka and Martin (2010), in examining the assumptive roots, highlighted three predominant movements with respect to expression of grief: the feminization of grief, which reflected a counselor bias toward emotional disclosure; distinctive male patterns that emphasized biological differences between genders; and emphasis on grief as a continuum from intuitive to instrumental. The terms *intuitive* and *instrumental* carry less baggage than *masculine* or *feminine styles of grieving*, derived from Jungian psychology, which regards both masculine and feminine traits on one continuum and existing within each individual. Intuitive grievers naturally gravitate toward exploration and expression of turbulent emotions following loss, whereas instrumental grievers respond in an intellectual or action-oriented manner. Doka suggested that women are predominantly "right-brain," or intuitive, whereas men are predominantly "left-brain," or analytical (Doka and Martin, 2010). So, despite the pathology of grief expression being associated with stereotypical feminine behavior (Klass, Silverman, and Nickman, 1996), Doka contends that people with the widest range of response to grief (intuitive to instrumental) and who integrate all aspects of self seem to have the greatest capacity to respond to grief. Doka also reminds that the cross-cultural designation of women as emotional outlets for the male, or for the group as a whole, carries with it ideological implications related to the universal subordination of women and the devaluation of the feminine. A healthy expression of grief is an individual process that occurs independent of ritualization and within each individual's personal experience, which is not only influenced by socialization practices but by basic inborn temperament or preferences for emotion regulation.

In some countries, the influence of global communication has affected historical grieving patterns. In her chapter entitled "Grief for Export," Konigsberg (2011) points out that even Australian ways of grieving are not outcomes of local experience, but rather "socially constructed ways of understanding inherited from a variety of dominant foreign influences"

(p. 182). Japan and Hong Kong reflect similar patterns of the influence of the Western world on their Asian grieving practices. Still, grief expert Rosenblatt concluded that no feeling, meaning, or understanding of grief is universal across cultures or even within a single culture (Konigsberg, 2011).

Expressions of Anger and Fear

The experience of losing a loved one is chaotic enough, and when combined with the accompanying consequences of the loss, can produce feelings of anger or betrayal by deceased. Feelings like "I have to start all over now. Why did you leave me now when we seemed to be putting our lives together?" or "It's not fair. Why do I have to raise our child alone?" These emotions are not unusual for the bereaved (Bowlby, 1998). However, when anger is directed inward, as it frequently is during the grieving process, the potential for suicidal thoughts and behavioral problems greatly increases (Worden, 2009). Prolonged anger, especially the self-deprecating kind, must be recognized as a risk factor and treated as such.

Fear is expressed through anxiety. There is a restless feeling of panic that engulfs the bereaved, but it is not something that is always identifiable or tangible, further increasing the confusion the bereaved experience. One cannot run from it like fleeing a stranger in the dark or turn it off like a horror movie on television.

What follows is one woman's expression of her experience of anxiety.

> Is it normal to be so restless? I can't explain it, but I just want to keep running. Am I trying to run away? I just moved again for the third time. I thought it was the small apartment, so I moved to a larger one. I love it because there's room to jump rope and dance and exercise. I made a special effort to decorate it with things that say, "This is me!" But there are still times when I feel like running away again. It's not the place, is it? A friend told me that I can't run away because it goes with you. Just what is "it"? How can you fight off something you can't understand?
>
> I don't know what comes over me sometimes. I have to leave the house. Sometimes I run until I can't run anymore. Once I jumped in the car and kept driving down the freeway with no destination in mind. It was late at night, and I remember finally coming to a town, and I didn't realize I'd driven all the way to Nogales and was blinded by the bright white lights at the port of entry. I'd never been there before, and as I drove around, the activity and intermingling of cultures consumed my thoughts. I noticed I began to feel exhausted and sleepy. The fear disappeared, although as I think about it now, being alone there at night was certainly not very safe. My body

> was relaxed, and I was exhausted, and I had to drink coffee to stay awake for the long drive back home.
>
> Later my friend described to me the fear he experienced after the death of his wife. "No one ever told me that grief was feeling afraid, but the sensation is a fluttering in the stomach. I don't like being afraid."

Fear, manifested through anxiety, is a common experience of grief. It is often bewildering to the one who experiences it, and it is difficult to pinpoint its source. Fortunately, over time, it subsides.

Risks of Nonexpression and Gender Assumptions

One of the most devastating consequences of relegating the expression of grief to women is that emotions are a fundamentally human characteristic that knows no gender bias or boundaries. Although some studies have shown an increased expression of grief by women, indeed in many cultures, and as already discussed, denial of emotion can have harsh and devastating results. Vulnerability to loss transcends the social construction of grief, which packages emotion as unmasculine or weak.

In the vignette below, a woman describes the grief experience of her husband following the death of their child.

> My husband was a victim. Here was a man, a father, who watched his child being buried and, according to convention, was asked by society to "keep a stiff upper lip." In the months that followed the funeral, my husband discovered that the demands on him were very unfair. He was the one who went to the funeral home to make burial arrangements. At no time was I asked to participate in any of the macabre arrangements the living make for the dead. The atmosphere around us was one of comfort for me, but for my husband, it was a matter of facing things head on. As time went by, instead of coming out of his grieving, he sank deeper and deeper into his sorrow. Finally, he reached a point where we both knew he needed psychiatric help. He does not remember getting much help or guidance, but, and maybe this is what it was all about, he spent many sessions crying. Just crying. (Schiff, 1977)

The need to express grief through crying is present in both sexes but is generally ascribed mostly to women. Seen as a sign of an inherently weaker nature, it is obvious why men would prefer not to display emotion. It contradicts the image society wishes to bestow on men. But if expressing emotion is no longer so consistently derided and devalued, both men and women could escape the burden of the traditional role when it comes to grief reaction and response. If the feminine becomes more universally accepted, then the interchange of male/female roles should produce a corresponding change in the ability of individuals to express emotion, which would be healthier and more conducive to the successful completion of the grieving process in both women and men.

As it stands now, with vestiges of the feminine still experiencing devaluation, only women who plan no career past marriage and accept the traditional role seem to feel comfortable with emotional expression. Among female acquaintances who are career oriented and who plan to be financially independent following college, very few overtly express their emotions. Many have adopted a more masculine approach to work and life.

Acceptance of the "feminine" characteristic of expressiveness would be much healthier for all individuals who have experienced loss. As Konigsberg (2011) emphasized, "The attempt to 'gender' grief—just as marshaling it into stages—does it a disservice. . . . Whether someone is a man or a woman has little predictive power about how he or she will adjust to bereavement" (p. 180).

One Cultural Approach to Grief

Cultural traditions have a significant influence on one's grief. Knowing how a particular culture views death is important in understanding a woman's experience in mourning. For some cultures, death is accepted as a natural part of the process of life, but for many, death is hidden and denied. When a society denies death, pressures are placed on the bereaved to conform to societal denial of death. The bereaved are expected to get on with their lives as quickly as possible and not let the loss affect them—an expectation that is virtually impossible to fulfill.

Although much has been done in recent years to "naturalize" death in American culture, the majority of people continue to deny it. They see death as a failure, and they shield themselves from the sight of it. In some cases, practices persist where the dying are prematurely buried in isolation in rooms at the end of sterile hospital wards, away from family, friends, and the familiar surroundings of home. Because these individuals are tainted with death, they must forfeit their right to continue to live among the living.

Burial rituals also indicate denial of death. Mortuary practices in body preparations or viewing ceremonies are based on unreality, with the goal of trying to make the deceased appear to be "just resting" or looking as lifelike as possible. The family is led away from the viewing room before the coffin is closed and before cemetery workers lower the coffin into the grave and shovel dirt onto the casket. These events constantly give the message that death is to be avoided and denied.

Unlike the Anglo culture, the Jewish recognize death as a natural part of the life process. Throughout the Jewish funeral ritual, time limits help to structure mourning. There is a sense of community associated with these rituals that provides opportunities for the bereaved to progress through grief with social support. In *The Psychological Wisdom of the Law* (1974), Audrey Gordon documented the rituals of Judaism that work to assist the survivor of loss, and these aspects are instructive to avoid many of the negative impacts of grief.

- The bedside vigil of the dying person assists the family in reducing denial of death later experienced by many bereaved individuals. They are present at the time of death and thus cannot deny that death has occurred.
- The bereaved must actively participate in burial plans. This also lessens the numbness phase of grief—the phase of disbelief.
- Judaism supports simplistic burials, which relieve the family of financial burdens incurred by elaborate funeral plans. Elaborate funerals are also seen as expressions of guilt and are discouraged as the belief exists that the bereaved must work through these feelings rather than hide them in expensive funerals.
- The rending or tearing of clothes is a Jewish ritual that provides psychological relief. It is an expression of grief that encourages open grieving and signifies the wounds left by the loss of the deceased.
- After the burial, the "meal of recuperation" begins with the community's emphasis on the bereaved. Bagels are often served because roundness is a symbol of personal, inner grief. The Shiva is a week of intense grief where community members and family share their memories with the bereaved.
- A year is set aside for mourning. Aside from the first month of intense grief and gradual readjustment, the year involves memories and healing for the bereaved. The most significant finding in Jewish mourning practices is the importance of community and its accompanying social support for, and encouragement and acceptance of, expressions of grief in mourning the loss of a loved one. Mourning and grief is not only a personal experience, something that is "wrong with" the survivor of loss, but it is a community affair as well.

Although we do not suggest universal adoption of the Jewish view of mourning or as a prescription of how to handle grief, the Jewish model (acknowledging multiple customs within the Jewish faith) (Parkes et al., 2015) could well be used as a starting point for bereavement counseling and intervention. The open expression of grief and individual progression through the grief process promotes healthy grief resolution with less opportunity for stressful or negative impact on the bereaved individual, regardless of their role orientation.

Notes

1. Individuation is derived from Jungian psychology. In Hollis's terms (2005), individuation refers to recovering our own personal story among provisional stories wrapped up in familial limitations and constraints of tribal claims on us.

2. Doka and Martin (2010) identify a number of factors that affect the grieving styles of individuals, including culture, gender, socialization experiences, birth order, and temperament, among others. Rando (1988) categories factors affecting grief as psychological, social, and physical.

3. Attig (2011) distinguishes grief reaction as a specific reaction to grief emotion, whereas grief response refers to the full range of experiences of emotional, psychological, physical, behavioral, social, cognitive, and spiritual impacts of bereavement. Mourning refers to both grief reaction and response. Grieving response is unpredictable and shaped by an individual's character and their choices.

4. Losses experienced by youth of varying ages are comprehensively covered in McCoyd and Walter (2016).

5. "Administration on aging (AoA)," Administration for Community Living, http://www.aoa.acl.gov/aging_statistics/profile/2014/2.aspx. Note that the site reflects principal sources of data for the Profile are the U.S. Census Bureau, the National Center for Health Statistics, and the Bureau of Labor Statistics. The Profile incorporates the latest data available, but not all items are updated on an annual basis. http://www.aoa.acl.gov/aging_statistics/profile/2014/docs/2014-profile.pdf.

6. Note that Mark Mercer (2012) suggests that women do not understand male grief and that men grieve as "hard" as women; they just typically don't show it as openly as women do ("What Women Should Know About Male Grief," http://thegrieftoolbox.com/article/what-women-should-know-about-male-grief).

CHAPTER SIX

Death of a Spouse or Partner: A Widow's Grief

Introduction

Losing a spouse is considered the most stressful of all life events (Holmes and Rahe, 1967). In fact, research has shown that people can (and do) die of broken hearts at twice the rate of nonbereaved people matched for age and other demographics (Carey et al., 2014). Widowhood is no small matter.

This chapter presents women's experiences of spousal death: first, as loss arising from an anticipated death due to terminal illness; second, as a sudden, unplanned death as the result of a workplace accident; and third, as a result of suicide. The chapter examines women's experiences of loss and their ability to progress through grief within the context of their relationships to their husbands,[1] and the roles arising from the nature of those relationships.

Spousal Relationship and Its Influence on a Woman's Role

In marriage, wife and husband are partners. In a good marriage, this is a loving relationship. The relationship can have defined boundaries (loosely or rigidly), which also define the woman's role and her relationship to her spouse. In a traditional sense (as described in Chapter 1) the wife's role is primarily that of caregiver, while the husband's role is primarily that of protector and provider. Historically, this configuration resulted in women being perceived as dependent since the material aspects of the marriage were given higher value than the emotional or personal. It is not uncommon that older women in today's society have lived traditional marriages, but this can describe a contemporary marriage relationship as well, although certainly less common.

In a transitional or modern/postmodern role configuration, boundaries in a marriage relationship are generally more flexible with spouses sharing roles and responsibilities. Today's marriage relationships more typically fall into this categorization where it is common to see a strong element of interdependency between husband and wife, with this dependency leaning more toward one partner or the other, depending on the individuals involved and their individual needs at the time. In these contemporary relationships, equality replaces dependency in the financial realm, and domestic responsibilities are shared. There is a partnership, but individuality thrives and nurtures the relationship. A loving relationship grows with each partner's experiences being shared by the couple. Within the context of such a relationship, a husband is not only his wife's partner but her lover and best friend, and she his. When death of the husband ends the relationship, which statistically occurs far more frequently than the death of the wife, the wife has lost a very important aspect of her life.

Widows' Bereavement

Most women react to death of a spouse in a manner similar to that described by Dr. Erich Lindemann in 1942. A woman's grief reaction typically includes a period of numbness and disbelief accompanied by a tendency to deny reality. This may last a few hours to several weeks. There is usually a display of strong emotions, such as crying, along with various other physical symptoms related to mental distress. A state of panic may arise as survivors find they are unable to stop thinking about their loss. Overwhelming feelings of guilt and preoccupation with the deceased may surface, including hostile reactions of having been abandoned by the deceased spouse/partner. Anger and jealousy toward those who are left alive may occur, as may hostility toward the medical establishment, which may be blamed for the death. Customary daily routines are disrupted, and incapacitating feelings of sadness or loneliness may persist for several months.

In their study of over 100 widowed persons, Clayton, Halikes, and Maurice (1971) noted that during the first month of bereavement, the most common symptoms included crying, depressed feelings, difficulty sleeping and concentrating, poor memory, lack of appetite or weight loss, and heavy reliance on sleeping pills or tranquilizers. More recent research (Walter, 2003) indicates that the bereaved woman may experience anger, loneliness, and isolation. Her grief is intensified because of losing the partner she mourns, the relationship she lost, and her identity embedded in that partnership. Essentially, her world shifts from "we" to "I."

Age and Its Influence on a Woman's Bereavement

Widowed in Young Adulthood

When a woman loses her spouse when she is young, the loss is out of sync with her stage of life. Her peers may experience discomfort with her loss because they have little or no experience of the death of a spouse. They do not know what to say or what to do to help the widow (Shaffer, 1993). However, because of the age of the widow, starting over (e.g., changing a career) reflects a forward-looking response to moving on from death (Young and Caplan, 2010).[2] When young widows are intentional about engaging in new activities to define who they are, research indicates that they generally experience less stress and fewer symptoms of complicated grief (Neimeyer, Baldwin, and Gillies, 2006).

Widowed in Midlife

At midlife, the most common death women experience, next to the death of their parent(s), is that of a spouse. Like the woman who is widowed at a young age, people often do not know what to say or do, isolating the woman in her grief (regardless of whether she has adopted a traditional, transitional, or modern/postmodern role). Unfortunately, those women who do become widows in midlife, and never remarry, experience the greatest depressive symptoms (Sasson and Umberson, 2009) that can endure into old age (Hughes and Waite, 2009). This includes greater incidence of chronic disease and lack of mobility. For those women who are partnered, but not married, research indicates that they receive less emotional support from friends and community (Doka, 2002), prolonging the grieving and healing process.

Widowed in Older Age

The majority of widows and widowers are 65 years old and older. The loss of a partner/spouse in later adulthood can result in increased mortality, disease, depression, and sleep disruption (van den Berg, Lindeboom, and Portrait, 2011). At the same time that spousal relationships become even more significant for the elderly, widowhood emphasizes decreased social networks, reduced number of family and friends available to offer support, and reduced numbers of social circles in which the widow can participate (Moss, Moss, and Hansson, 2001)—all this occurring at a time that the elderly woman herself may be experiencing chronic health problems, disability, or reduced mobility and physical stamina (Hansson and Stroebe, 2007). Preoccupation with the image of the deceased partner, lost interaction with him, and the quality of the feelings aroused by his image usually diminishes over time as the widow accepts the fact of her widowhood and begins reorganizing her life.

Factors Complicating a Widow's Grieving Process

Changed Financial Status

As discussed earlier in this book, the change in standard of living created by loss of a spouse often complicates a widow's grieving process. This was particularly true in the last century. Fortunately, changing sex roles in society are helping somewhat, for now most women are not completely dependent on their husbands for financial support and many, if not most, have careers of their own.

Reduced Engagement in Social Roles/Relations

In addition to financial adjustment, changes in social roles due to the death of a spouse can also negatively affect the widow. Although this is dated information, some of the precepts set up in Lopata's 1973 study of the social involvement of American widows are still applicable today. The study reported the degree of change in the type and level of engagement in social roles the widow performed. Three degrees were reported: medium to high levels of interaction, similar to those in the widow's life before the death of her husband and dependent upon the availability of social groups that do not require the husband's presence (including kin, longtime friends, neighbors, work associates and voluntary associations); interaction in new types of social roles; and relative isolation. A study by Williams and Loeb (1956) indicated that at that time many American widows had minimal levels of interaction. Many widows were found to be only minimally involved in social relations even previous to their husband's death. The death of their husbands caused a further drop in social activity. Lopata reported that about one-half of the widows she studied felt a strain in couple-based social activities, saying that they often felt like a "fifth wheel." Lopata went on to argue that American widows are largely restricted in both the availability of social roles and in their ability to actually become involved in new social role patterns. Lack of education, training, and skills limited the widow's choice of occupational or voluntary experiences.

Insecurity, inexperience, and poor motivation often prevented her from even thinking about new activities, let alone risking trying something new.

So, although American society boasts that many social roles are now open to the new widow, in reality, the choices are restricted to the woman's level of financial security, education, health, and motivation. This is particularly true for the older widow. As well, current awareness and tolerance of the single person has eased the fifth-wheel awkwardness somewhat, as living either singly or in relationships other than marriages is occurring more frequently, which may also reflect changing sex roles.

Impact of a Death-Denying Society

In a society in which death is considered unnatural, almost taboo, and something to be avoided or covered up, other people are often not helpful to the bereaved. According to Parkes (1972), every widow discovers that people who were previously friendly and approachable become embarrassed and strained in her presence. Expressions of sympathy often ring hollow, and it is as if the widow has become "tainted with death."

The bereaved themselves have described their experiences in a similar manner. They find that people do not want to talk about the husband's death, nor do they understand the widow's pain—not even close family members, and sometimes not professionals either.

When confronted with a woman who has suffered a major loss, the behavior of others can make progression through the grieving process much more difficult for the widow. A society which requires survivors to "keep a stiff upper lip" and "get on with it" isolates the widow, not so much as a result of her own withdrawal, but as a result of the behaviors of others and their inability to deal with death. Further, when a death-denying society prevents the adequate expression of mourning, a widow is likely to feel intense preoccupation with her own physical health, sometimes even conjuring up images of her own terminal illness and death. A widow is likely to become preoccupied with fears of being physically or emotionally alone when having to face this illness. Unless a widow is encouraged to express her feelings and talk out her fears, the fears may be repressed without being resolved, thus enhancing a widow's risks of mental and physical breakdown. Talking about her loss helps a widow to accept it.

Women's Experiences of Spousal Grief

Three case studies follow. The first is a woman's experience of her husband's terminal illness (an anticipated grief). The second deals with a widow who experiences her husband's accidental death (a sudden grief). The third is also about surviving the sudden death of a spouse—this time through her husband's suicide. In each case, note the influence of the age and role of the woman, and any complicating factors delaying her grieving process.

A Woman's Experience of a Husband's Terminal Illness

Nancy is a 44-year-old woman who was 37 when her husband died of cancer. He was 45 at the time of his death. Nancy is a professional health care provider and now has her own business. She is financially stable and a single parent who lives with three of her five children. She is comfortable in new relationships, both professional and personal, and seems to have resolved her grief without complication. Nancy has lived both a traditional first marriage, and in her second transitioned into a modern/postmodern role where she is/was an equal partner with her husband John.

> A man's dying is more the survivors' affair than his own. My husband's tumor was a cylindroma—a rare form prevalent in the Philippines. He had been a fighter pilot there. That was the only connection we could find. The tumor was initially discovered in his left lung in 1972. At that time, he had surgery. His left lung was removed, and he was started on radiation therapy with no growth noted after years. That's when I met him. He and I dated for a while, and we lived together. We discussed whether or not we should marry, considering the fact that the tumor could reoccur. We had each endured long difficult marriages that became unbearable before we met. We were both divorced, loved and enjoyed each other very much. We decided no tumor was going to frighten us away from sharing our lives together as man and wife, no matter how much time we would have together. We had been married 19 months when John died.
>
> About six months into our marriage, John started having difficulty swallowing. We were in a restaurant, and he almost choked. Like always, John made light of the incident, but the difficulty swallowing began to happen more often. John saw his doctor in Tucson. A fiber-optic bronchoscopy was done; no tumor was found, and the X-ray of his right lung was fine. We were relieved, but the difficulty in swallowing continued, and further X-rays showed a narrowing of his esophagus. A CAT scan was performed, and a tumor was discovered surrounding the esophagus. I thought, "Simple enough, they'll just remove it by surgery like the last time." But no. The news was that, due to its position, the cylindroma was now inoperable. I was angry. John and I had finally found happiness with each other. I was angry with God too.
>
> Several procedures were done throughout the course of his illness to alleviate pain and discomfort in eating. But the effect only lasted a couple

weeks at a time. John was getting tired. The tumor was growing and causing more constriction of his esophagus. We joked about our new liquid gourmet meals, but even they became difficult to swallow. Amazingly, John had maintained his weight.

Our next trip to the University of Arizona Medical Center brought strong recommendations of chemotherapy because of the rapidly growing tumor. John was getting more uncomfortable, so he reluctantly agreed to chemotherapy. From September to December 1978, he did well, but the side effects of chemotherapy caused him to lose 60 pounds and tire easily. He was miserable. At Christmastime John said, "Enough of this." He had been told this time it was terminal, and he refused to continue chemotherapy. I felt helpless. Everyone felt helpless.

I begged him to try something, and late in January we went to a clinic in Mexico. John was on Laetrile for six weeks. Again I almost lost him due to choking. I decided to keep an oxygen machine in the house, which I used two times.

Sometime before Christmas and Mexico, John started talking about death. I tried to change the subject, but he kept encouraging me to talk about it. Do you believe that guy? Here he was dying, and he was preparing me for his death. John taught me how to be an independent person. To my first husband, I was a possession, and I felt like a baby factory. (He wanted a big family, and we had four children in the first five years of our marriage and then another one after that.)

John encouraged me to do what I wanted to do with the rest of my life. It was a new freedom that I enjoyed, and now he was teaching me to be free and how to live independently without him. I remember one weekend we went to the coast. We had a copy of Elisabeth Kübler-Ross's book *Death and Dying*. We read it together, and we spent time walking along the beach, talking and crying together. John was having some problems with his oldest son (from his first marriage), and one day he said, "I can understand why people commit suicide—not because of illness, but because of rejection by your children."

He continually encouraged me to make decisions on my own about the children, financial matters, returning to work (which I did part time), even calling a tow truck when the car stalled (he sat on the curb watching and laughing as I raised the hood of the car, pretending to know what all those parts were supposed to do). He showed me that these little problems were nothing to be upset about.

About three weeks before Easter, John agreed to another procedure to ease his difficulty in swallowing and the accompanying pain. It did provide relief. He was home for six weeks. I was already back to work as an operating room nurse, and I received a phone call from my mother, who stayed with us and helped with the children. She said John had been out jogging as he usually did (he kept active because he said he didn't fear death as much as he feared being an invalid before dying), and he'd started to vomit blood and was in the emergency room where I worked. My coworkers at the hospital were my support system too. They were aware of John's terminal illness and adjusted my schedule or provided backup help for me whenever I needed to be away.

I found John in the emergency wing, and he said, "Hi, babe, I don't feel so good." He looked so pale and tired, and still he smiled. I said, "John, damn you, don't you go and die on me now." He laughed and then we both laughed. The doctors were pumping blood into him and had stabilized him enough to move him to intensive care. There was talk of surgery, X-rays, etc., but John wanted none of it. His surgeon took me aside and told me that John did not want to be revived if his heart stopped. I said that John and I had agreed to this already but when the surgeon told the ICU nurses, they objected and questioned his decision. This was my first outburst of anger. I said, "How dare you nurses hit on the dying and his decision. Why mutilate him?"

The surgeon reviewed John's blood count report with me. John continued to bleed, but they couldn't tell from where. The doctor said he didn't think John would live through this crisis. I knew he wouldn't and John knew he wouldn't. The nurses let me stay with John constantly (which is unusual in ICU). John dozed off and we talked a little when he woke. He said, "I think this is it." I left his side long enough to call his oldest son. I explained what was happening, and John's son said he'd pick up the other children and come right away. John had tried to prepare his son for his death too.

John cried when he saw his children. They all talked with him. I sat there holding his hand, and somehow we both seemed to feel a peacefulness as his children all said goodbye.

Shortly before he died, John thanked me for the time he spent with his children, and I kissed him goodbye.

Nancy's stopped her story at this point. She recalled choosing a song for her husband's funeral because of a line that talked about those who die young but have lived, and about those who are alive but choose not to live. John (Nancy's husband) had told her when they started to talk about death and life, "Nancy, you have to each be your own planet. You can't be a planet and a satellite." Nancy said, "John helped me to be that before he died. That's how I handled my grief."

Anticipatory Grief

Preparing for the loss of a loved one can lessen the potential for extreme grief reaction. The duration and nature of the illness, particularly with respect to changes in the spouse brought about by his illness, also appear to affect the widow's grief reaction and her later adjustment to his death.

When a husband has a terminal illness, the grief process of the wife begins when the news of the illness is received. That news affords a couple the opportunity to acknowledge and try to enjoy what remains of their relationship. With the support of each other and the understanding and caring of family, friends, and health care professionals and volunteers, the widow is better able to complete the part of her life that she has lived with her husband.

When deciding how this last phase should be lived out, it is important to note that in a hospital, which is an institution that emphasizes curative care, a person with a terminal illness can be shunned as an embarrassing failure on the part of the medical community. One nurse who recently was assigned to the surgical ward in a community hospital noted how little time was even spent discussing a cancer patient at the shift report: "When it came to me to discuss Mr. J. (a man with terminal lung cancer), all that was reported was that *'He's still here.'* It was like being here meant nothing, and to see his family standing around in a daze was uncomfortable for the staff, who were caught up in their busy work of monitors, tubes, drains, catheters, and superficial chatter. In contrast, the palliative care setting with its hospice concept accepts where this couple is in their lives and encourages the dying man and his wife to express their feelings about death and their grief. Staff associated with this setting support the widow and other family members through the death and the grief process. Cicely Saunders of the St. Christopher's Hospice in England sums up the hospice concept of the palliative care setting this way: "You matter because you are you. You matter to the last moment of your life, and we will do all we can not only to help you die peacefully but to help you live until you die" (Buckingham, 1983).

This coming together in the final phase of a couple's relationship is accomplished by providing a comfortable, familiar environment in their own home or a palliative care setting. This, together with symptom and pain control for the dying, a relaxed atmosphere, and a caring multidisciplinary team and bereavement counseling program, provide the wife with a sensitive transition from being a wife to becoming a widow and then an independent individual.

The Experience of Sudden Death

Sarah's Story

Sarah is a 32-year-old woman who experienced the sudden death of her husband. She was 26 years old at the time of his death. He died in a workplace accident. Sarah was a college student at the time of the accident. Following the death of her husband, she completed her teacher's training and is now moderately financially secure. She values religion in her life but has a more modern approach to living with religion than the traditional, strict believer.

Evan was on call at work that evening. He came home for dinner at 6:00 p.m. but said he had one more call in Newburgh to make and then he'd be home—except that he never did make it back home.

At 11:00 p.m. that night a "representative" (who I later learned was actually the coroner) came to our home and said there had been an accident at work and that he would like me to call someone to come over. My parents lived two blocks away. I called them and they said they were on the way. The representative would not say what had happened, just that there had been an accident.

It seemed like it took my parents hours to arrive. I was very anxious to go to the hospital. I assumed that Evan was badly hurt and that he was in the hospital. The representative said nothing. As we waited for my parents, I started thinking and talking incessantly.

I tried hard to remember everything Evan had told me before he left the house at 7:00 p.m. He had one more stop to make in Newburgh to work on the big machine. The "representative" just sat there as I rattled on and on. "You know Evan always said he didn't like to work on that damn machine; it was too dangerous. There is no safety switch at the bottom where they have to check its operation. He said that if anything ever happened to him there, he would be a dead man."

There was a long silence.

It was like I had slapped myself in the face with what I had been avoiding all along. "Oh, my God! He's dead isn't he?" I asked. The representative said, "I'm sorry, Mrs. Roberts. I'm sorry."

Those words kept ringing in my ears as I felt my blood drain from my head and down through all my body. I started running around the house. But every time I came to the living room, the representative was still there. Then I began to fill my head with what I would tell my parents, how I would tell his parents, how I would tell his brother and sisters, and how I would tell our son. My parents arrived and we sat together and cried. My son was still asleep in his bedroom.

I remember a feeling of emptiness, terrible thoughts of the agony Evan must have endured, trying to imagine what he'd felt. For some reason I felt the need to know every last detail of his last moments, and when I asked the coroner, he said I shouldn't think about that. It's strange; it frightened me, but I needed to know.

My thoughts shifted to birth—of labor and delivery, and how Evan and I shared that together and how after the discomfort of labor, there was beauty—peace after the struggle. I found some peace in believing that Evan found peace after his struggle, but I wish I could have been there to support him.

The coroner had opened his briefcase, and he removed a manila envelope from it. Inside was the concrete proof of his big announcement. The wedding ring I'd given Evan, his watch, his wallet, some change, and his keys. That was all—things that I saw every day and hardly noticed, but now I was clinging to them.

I heard the coroner tell my Dad that he needed someone to identify the body. I said, "I don't want to see him." More thoughts of Evan's torn, bruised body lying in the morgue. I repeated, "No! I don't want to see him."

My Dad called our families, and I sat in the kitchen with my mother, remembering that I'd eaten an orange about 8:00 p.m. That was close to when he'd died. How could I have not sensed something was wrong? I'd been eating food while Evan was dying! (I find food repulsive now.) I won't be able to smell him anymore. I smell his ring and his watch. They are still dirty from him working on the machine. I put them on. It comforts me. I wore them for a month, every day, smelling them in private and crying.

I remember he changed his shirt this evening. I went to the hamper and smelled his shirt. It smelled like Evan! I got a Ziploc plastic bag from the kitchen and put his dirty shirt in it and put it in a bedroom drawer. I kept it for a year. I'd go to it, smell it, and cry.

I had been trying to find a teaching position before Evan's death and was offered one two weeks after he was buried. It was good for me, although I was still numb about his death. Working helped me make decisions and got my mind off how things used to be. I decided it was better for my son and I to live our lives enriched by the time we spent with Evan rather than clinging to things which only made the hurt worse. One by one, I put the ring and watch in a chest to give to my son when he was older. And finally, one day when I was ready, I put the shirt in the garbage.

Jocelyn's Story

Jocelyn was 34 years old when her husband took his life. She was left with three small children, ages 2, 4, and 7. The following is her account of life with her husband before his suicide and how the stigma of suicide affected her grief after his death. Jocelyn remains very active in the Catholic Church. She had held a position in the health field prior to marrying her husband, but left her career shortly after marrying to devote herself full-time to the role of wife and mother.

It was not uncommon that I would not know if Tom would make it home for dinner. I would make dinner for the family, waiting, and then usually deciding that Tom must have stopped for more cigarettes and beer. Life was too difficult for him to cope with, and he had become an alcoholic.

I loved Tom, and our three children loved him too, but the situation was becoming unbearable. One night as I prepared dinner, I remember hearing sirens and finding myself hoping that Tom had been killed in an accident. I discussed my conflicting feelings of loving and disliking Tom with our pastor, as I began seeing similar conflicted reactions to Tom from our children. I knew that I had to make a decision about our lives.

Our pastor helped me by suggesting that I look at our family life and individual lives and ask myself questions such as, 'Who is benefitting from this situation? Was anyone? How could I change our lives? Would a change benefit anyone in our family? Would it benefit everyone?'

I wrestled with these questions and some of my own for some time, and one day after Tom and I had had yet another argument, I told him that I felt we needed to be separated until he could figure out how to deal with his life without alcohol, because our being together under these circumstances was killing our relationship and hurting our children. Tom moved out.

The months that followed brought his games of manipulation and denial of his drinking problem. He refused to seek help through counseling because he did not believe that he had a problem. Financially, life was difficult for me. I could not work because Patty, our youngest child, was in and out of the hospital for surgery to correct a congenital orthopedic problem, and she required a great deal of follow-up home care. When our pastor suggested that I apply for food stamps, I was devastated. However, seeing no other alternative, I did attempt to apply, but we did not qualify because Tom and I were still married. Following that, Catholic Social Service was very helpful to me, and to our children.

Eight months passed in the same futile manner until Tom finally agreed to counseling. I attended some of the sessions with him. He seemed to be handling life better. He took a more active interest in the children, and our relationship improved. Christmastime came, and I planned a traditional family brunch. All of our relatives were happy, and Tom and I spoke of getting back together. We were on good terms.

Three weeks later, Tom sat in his apartment alone, pointed a gun into his mouth, and pulled the trigger.

I remember the day vividly and always will. The phone rang and a man identified himself as a police detective. He asked me many questions. Was I Jocelyn F.? Was I Jocelyn Mary F.? Was I Mrs. Thomas F.? I asked him what was going on and if something had happened to Tom. He would not answer me but said he would come to the house shortly.

The next half hour was a chilling and frightening time. I did not know if Tom was drunk, in jail, injured, or dead. The uncertainty of what had happened was coiling up inside of me, and when the doorbell finally rang, I ran and opened it and yelled, "Is Tom dead?"

I didn't realize it, but that question immediately made me a prime suspect in a possible homicide because Tom was dead, and no one had yet informed me. None of my questions were answered, and the next hour brought even more painful questions about our relationship. After I was ruled out as a suspect, I was told of Tom's death and the circumstances surrounding it.

What was I feeling? It's strange, but I wasn't hysterical. I felt a huge abyss—a big black hole deep inside of me. I couldn't articulate anything. I wasn't afraid of material concerns. I just felt a black emptiness, a sadness that is indescribable.

My feelings shifted from sadness to anger as I recalled how the children begged Tom to spend time with them during our separation, but his excuse was that he couldn't bear to leave them each time he had to go. Why had he been so selfish again in choosing death?

I was crying. Then I heard our children in their bedroom, innocently playing and laughing. My concern immediately turned to how I would communicate this tragedy to them without causing any further trauma in their young lives. I knew that they could not cope with the fact that there was an element of choice which led to their father's death. They would see this as abandonment. And I knew they could not cope with all the details that were too grotesque for children to live with.

In explaining their father's death to the children, I felt that gentle truth was important. I wanted to be able to build on that truth as they grew older, so I went to their bedroom door and announced that I had something really sad to tell them. Tom and I had always saved that introduction for serious matters, so they knew something was very wrong. I sat on the bed with our children and told them that their Daddy had had an accident with his hunting gun and that he had died. We cried. We hugged. And we prayed. I felt like I had a ton of bricks on top of me.

I was glad I had decided to tell the children of Tom's death right away, because we had our own quiet time together before the demands of the funeral arrangements took over.

The detective stayed with me and the children until Tom's brother, Jim, arrived. Jim was very supportive of me and understanding of my previous decisions about the separation. He would visit often, and he saw how Tom and I had been living. Frequently, Uncle Jim would stop by, see our refrigerator near empty, and take us all home to have dinner with his family. To ease my pain, he would joke about how his wife, Susan, always cooked twice as much spaghetti than what was needed for his own family. But other people were cruel.

The night before the funeral, I received what I thought was another one of many phone calls of condolence from Tom's coworkers. The caller coldly told me, "I don't like what's happened, Jocelyn." He said that I did not know him, but that he knew me, and that he would be at the services the next day. I was frightened and hung up. To this day, I shudder when I hear an unfamiliar voice on the phone.

That call was the first of a series of incidents involving comments, repeated rumors, and strange looks toward me by friends, relatives, and even strangers.

The funeral was short, simple, yet comforting. Our pastor had known Tom and me for years, and his talk brought some peace by helping us recall the husband, father, brother, and son we loved. It diminished the dramatic, awful last moments preceding his death.

The women from our parish prepared a lovely dinner, but I couldn't eat, and it was at this time that I began to feel the coldness and rage of Tom's sisters who had flown from back East. This was so horrible for me because even though they lived far away, I'd always felt I had a close relationship with them, sharing much through phone calls and letters. But the day of the funeral, they were cold as if they were saying, "What has she done to our brother?" I felt like I was being judged. At one point that afternoon, as I looked around the room, everyone seemed to be looking down at me. It reminded me of a television commercial where a young bride invites her mother-in-law over for lunch for the first time, and when the mother-in-law enters the room you see a woman with sharp, ugly features. She scans the room, unable to find anything amiss, but comments on the lingering food odors anyway. That's how I felt Tom's sisters were looking at me. I felt inadequate, and to me, they looked ugly and distorted.

The following week Jim moved Tom's chair back to the house from the apartment Tom had been renting. It was the chair I had bought for him for Father's Day two years earlier. Mary Ann, our eldest child, wanted to put the chair in the family room. The children liked having Daddy's chair there. It was special to them, and they took turns sitting in it. It was as if that was as close to Tom as they could get, and the chair gave them comfort. But I couldn't look at the chair without thinking of Tom's life in the apartment and his suicide. I'd look at the chair and start defending my actions regarding the decision to separate all over again. Had my suggestion of counseling been too strong? Had I been unfair? Had I caused Tom to commit suicide? When I looked at Tom's chair, I saw 10 months of loneliness that had led to despair.

It took me five years to work through the guilt and what I saw as my part in Tom's death. Because of Tom's increasing amount of alcohol consumption, financial insecurity had been a big problem before his death. After his death, the children and I had financial security. We had his veteran's benefits, social security, and retirement benefits. It took a long time for me to admit that I was relieved by this, even though it meant that Tom was gone. I had enough money now to pay bills and buy food and clothing, and even enough to drive the children to California for a week the following year. It felt good to enjoy life with them for a change. But along with financial security came the burden of decisions. This was frightening at first because there was no one to share this responsibility with—especially when it came to signing a consent form for one of Patty's serious operations. If it was unsuccessful, it would mean the amputation of her left leg. I felt so alone.

The most difficult part of having your love commit suicide is getting over the guilt you put on yourself. Working through it was hard, but when a friend invited me to attend a workshop on self-esteem, we went through some exercises on self-forgiving. Figuratively, I placed Tom in a chair and was able to see him in an entirely different perspective. I forgave him for dying, then sat myself in the chair and was able to forgive myself for any contribution I felt I had made in Tom's death. Being an "impartial observer" to our relationship, and to Tom's suicide, helped me accept Tom's decision about death and my decision about life.

I attended several more workshops and widow groups that helped me cut the ties of guilt and to finally let go. I remember my first dream about Tom after his death. I went to him and we hugged, and it was a truly good feeling. I woke up feeling like we had finally kissed goodbye.

Sometime during the five-year period following Tom's death, two people asked me why I never wore dresses. That really startled me. Pantsuits were in style at the time, that's all. I had never thought of myself as masculine—maybe neutral, but not masculine. It took me six years to feel comfortable in developing relationships with other men, and I have noticed that dresses have replaced many of the pantsuits in my closet. Today I am happy in my life with my present husband and our children, and I find peace in knowing that I am who I am today because Tom was a part of my life yesterday.

Making Sense of Sudden Death

J. William Worden (1982) outlined significant features of sudden death that make grief more difficult for the survivor, and some of these both Sarah and Jocelyn had experienced: for example, a sense of unreality about the loss, a need to fully understand the circumstances surrounding the death, exacerbation of guilt feelings ("if only . . ."), a need to blame someone (even God), a sense of helplessness that can turn to anger and rage, agitation and extreme depression ("flight or fight" response), and regret over unfinished business for things not said or done with the deceased.

Sudden death of a husband robs the widow of the opportunity to say goodbye. Unlike Nancy, who had some time to prepare for her husband's death and even to discuss what life would be like after Tom's death, Sarah and Jocelyn did not have this opportunity. Sarah used articles (her husband's shirt, his wedding ring) to help her maintain some kind of contact with her husband while she came to terms with her loss. In some ways, Tom's chair also provided that linkage to the deceased for Jocelyn, and especially for her children. Sarah's and Jocelyn's behaviors were not abnormal or destructive, but rather emotionally constructive in overcoming feelings of devastation, disconnection, and emptiness.

In the case of terminal illness of a husband, such as in Nancy's, anticipatory grief is possible and can provide for earlier acceptance of death when it occurs. The influence of an appropriate care setting and compassionate health care providers are particularly important. Such care can encourage the expression of anticipatory grief by the widow, which assists her in progressing through the grief process. In the instance of sudden death as in heart attack, accident, or even suicide, coping mechanisms play an especially important part in the initial impact of widow's grief. It is important to look at the special case of suicide.

The Special Case of Suicide

Prevalence. In 2014, suicide was the 10th leading cause of death in the United States (homicide ranked 17th), and the second leading cause of death among 15- to 24-year-olds. Every day approximately 105 Americans die by suicide, that is, one death approximately every 12 minutes. (The rate reported in Canada in 2014 was slightly lower at 11.3 per 100,000 population compared to 13.4 per 100,000 people in the United States, the highest recorded rate in 28 years.) Across the world, there is one death by suicide every 40 seconds (World Health Organization [WHO], 2014).[3]

Completed suicides are more likely to be men over age 45 who are depressed or alcoholic. The ratio of attempted to completed suicides is likely 10:1.[4] Suicide among males is four times higher than for females, with male deaths representing 79 percent of all U.S. suicides. Females attempt suicide three times as often as males. Male deaths occur most frequently by firearms; female deaths, by poisoning. Suicide rates for females are highest for those aged 45–54; and for males, aged 75 and older. Twenty percent of the population and 40 percent of suicide victims are over age 60. After age 75, the rate is three times higher than average, and among white men over 80, six times higher than average. Rates among the elderly are highest for those who are divorced or widowed.

The untold story is that these rates may, in reality, be much higher. Many suicides go unreported because they are listed as accidental deaths, violence, or poisonings. And, although the media dramatizes suicide, particularly among the rich and famous, for a family, suicide is a dreaded word. In our society, suicide is a taboo subject—one that stigmatizes the victim, but also the survivor.

Before the 1900s, Durkheim's *Le Suicide*, published in 1897, pioneered efforts to understand suicide. He tied the incidence of self-destruction to the environment in which people lived. Briefly, Durkheim's theory included three types of suicide: egoistic (the individual had few ties to family, religion, social controls, or community); anomie (the individual failed to adjust to social change); and altruistic (the individual loses his own personal identity and wishes to sacrifice his life for another cause). About a century later, the Suicide Prevention Center of Los Angeles devised three psychological classifications for suicidal death: an unintentional death (one in which the individual had no real or active role in the decision of his death); the intentional (one in which the victim actually deliberated and caused his own death); and sub-intentional (the victim unconsciously caused his own self-destruction). These classifications point to the complexity of suicide, and the multitudes of factors that influence the choice to take one's life.

Some common precipitating factors that appear to coincide with suicide include: depression (30% to 70% of suicide victims suffer from major depression or bipolar (manic-depressive) disorder);[5] a long and painful illness (many people take their lives, leaving behind memories of themselves as they were—hearty and vigorous), economic distress, or the death of someone close.

Women who are survivors of suicide (typically of their spouses) may have teens under their care, so it is important to recognize the signs and address teens' feelings about it, as the period following the death of a loved one is an especially trying time for teens (Manor, Vincent, and Tyano, 2004). Among teens, suicide ideation peaks between ages 14 and 17. Males with decreasing suicide ideation are more likely to attempt suicide, whereas female teens with increasing suicide ideation are more likely to attempt suicide (Rueter et al., 2008).

However, suicide may also surface in situations of divorce.

When a person dies, at least there can be some sort of explanation, for example, "He had cancer." With divorce, the practical explanations and questions are harder to understand, especially when children are involved. The feelings of guilt and failure affect both the parents and the children. Studies have revealed that many people who kill themselves are either products of a broken home or have recently gone through a divorce. These specific stressful situations—illness, economic distress, death, and divorce—can often overwhelm a person's defenses. Despair and helplessness often cause a person to panic and resort to suicide. Older adults who are less resilient and overcome by their losses may also decide to end their lives. Men over age 75, for example, have one of the highest suicide rates (Dombrovski et al., 2008; Sisask, Kolves, and Varnik, 2009). Various meaning-making interventions seem to help older adults and depressed veterans (for example) avoid suicide. (Veterans are reported to be at higher risk of suicide than nonveterans in the United States (Braden et al., 2015).)

In many cultures, suicide is seen as forbidden (e.g., Muslim) and spiritually extremely harmful to the deceased. Some cultures and religions regard suicide as shameful or sinful, which prevents families from grieving openly and receiving social support (Catholics, Orthodox Christians, Protestants, and Jews) (Parkes, Laungaini, and Young, 2015). Perceptions and views on suicide may be less radical under sociopolitical or economic pressures, weakness, or madness, or as an honorable act serving a higher cause (witness the increase in suicide bombers in Europe and the Middle East).

Loneliness, disbelief, heartache, torment. With self-inflicted death, add to these guilt, shame, and self-blame. "Why?" "What could I have done to prevent it?" These are often the most common questions survivors ask.

In our death-denying society, we are ill prepared to handle the loss of a loved one, especially when there is no illness preparing us to accept the ultimate outcome. When a person kills him- or herself, life is over. But for the family, the real tragedy is just beginning. Unfortunately, the stigma associated with suicide is attached not only to the individual who committed suicide but also to the family and friends connected to that person. For the widow, suicide may intensify feelings of abandonment, alienation, guilt, shame, anger, depression, and meaninglessness. "The suicidal person places his psychological skeleton in the survivor's closet" (Grollman, 1971).

Unnatural, sudden death puts the bereaved at a higher risk of complications in their grief process (de Groot, de Keijser, and Neeleman, 2006). Survivors themselves can become victims of physical, emotional, or behavioral disorders. Acute bereavement brings about symptoms of distress such as preoccupation with the image of the deceased, vivid memories of the circumstances of the death (many people repress this thought because it is so painful), hostile reactions, loss of acceptable social behavior, and a tendency to push away from friends and relatives. All this emotional turmoil decreases the surviving family's ability to cope with consequences of the death. Practical problems of finances and settling the estate can be very difficult for the survivor. Even attending church, which is traditionally a comfort to the bereaved, may feel alien or awkward (Cain, 1972). Family members may even turn against one another, and in their attempts to explain the event, they may blame one another. For the family, the suicidal person may have been difficult to live with over a period of years. The husband may have been mentally ill or may have been an alcoholic or abusive (or both) to his family. The feelings of finally being rid of the abuse can doubly intensify feelings of guilt of the survivor(s) (Wolman, 1976). The widow may also blame her husband for leaving her to cope on her own. Most widows have children, and the effects on them must be handled delicately so they do not grow up hating the father who "deserted" them. Many women are faced with the problems of having to move to a smaller, less expensive home in a new neighborhood because of financial problems. This alone can cause and increase the feelings of disorientation and change. As well, many widows constantly seek answers for the cause, which may have sparked the suicide in the first place. There is always the lurking thought: "What did I do wrong?" But sometimes the spouse may deprecate her husband by saying that he was weak, cruel, or no good, however consciously or unconsciously, as a way to minimize her sense of loss. This rather wicked smorgasbord of psychological and emotional turmoil causes considerable angst in the life of a widow that may prolong the grief process.

Coming to Terms with Suicide

The funeral offers an important opportunity to comfort mourners: it is the rite of separation. Elisabeth Kübler-Ross stresses in her book *Questions and Answers on Death and Dying* (1974) that when a family is faced with a sudden death, it is important that they not be prevented from viewing the body, even though it may be mutilated. It is important for the family to be able to identify with the deceased in order to face the reality of the death. The presence of the body can transform the process of denial into one of accepting reality. During the funeral, the clergyman/woman should avoid any reference to "sin" or "crime." The man who took his own life was still a man, with strengths as well as weaknesses. The positive and negative aspects of his life should be mentioned so that people can recall the happy times with him and the many ways in which life was enriched by his presence. The funeral must bring about the feeling that the total years of this person should be remembered, not just the isolated moment of his death (Kübler-Ross, 1974).

One of the key areas in helping the woman grieve is helping her face the fact that she is now a widow. Cain, in his *Survivors of Suicide* (1972), characterizes grief as a process with three stages. He refers to these stages as impact, recoil, and recovery. During the impact period, the widow seems to be dazed, almost unaware of what has happened. She is in a zombie-like state, goes through the motions of the funeral, and deals with the immediate needs of her family. It is during recoil that her awareness of what has happened reawakens, and she begins to understand that she is a widow. This is a time of great pining, of trying to recapture the lost husband, weeping, and sleeplessness; of being very angry with him and herself; and general disarray. This is a very important time for intervention in order to avoid a situation where the widow feels stuck in the past. Recovery marks the acceptance of widowhood and a willingness to look for new relationships.

Suicide, as a special kind of death, must be taken into account. Friends should be neither judgmental nor prejudiced of the actions of the deceased or of the survivors. Conversation should be natural, and interest in the survivor should be sincere. One should not try too hard to assist the widow, as over-solicitation may induce further guilt reactions. The most important method of encouraging grief is by listening. It is of no help to say, "Don't talk about it." The bereaved widow is going through an intense emotional crisis, and she needs to talk about it. Especially in a case of suicide, the bereaved needs to pour her heart out. What Sigmund Freud called "dissolution" is the sharing with the survivor of both pleasant and unpleasant memories of the deceased. When each pain is felt, the widow slowly begins to dissolve herself of the emotional ties to her dead husband. A gradual working over of such old thoughts and feelings is necessary to ensure completion of the mourning process and the acceptance of the reality of her husband' s suicide.

Survivors of suicide carry the stigma for life. Years afterward, a woman is still remembered as "the one whose husband shot himself." Suicide is never completely forgiven or forgotten by society. But someone has died and must be buried, so no matter how difficult the situation, the grieving must be faced (Wolman, 1976). For some widows, their grief feels disenfranchised (Doka, 2002), that it is not acknowledged or condoned, much less supported. After all, there must have been a reason, and unless there was a note clearly stating the reasons, who knows? The stigma of blame, including self-blame, makes the widow vulnerable to disenfranchised grieving, and others may not acknowledge the grief as legitimate, or they may stigmatize it.

The question of suicide means breaking taboos. The law labels it "criminal," and religion calls it a sin. But whatever the label society places on suicide, it is still a way of death that many people choose. The survivors who bear the burden of guilt and the stigma of having had a loved one who has willfully taken his or her life are the "living victims" whom friends and health professionals must support.

Healthy Adjustment to Loss of a Spouse

Living through loss and grief is difficult for anyone. If a woman's whole life has been centered on her husband (as in a traditional role), without an independent existence of her own, adjustment can be especially difficult (Lopata, 1973). Parkes, in his 1964 study of widows, found a sharp rise in the number of widows' psychiatric complaints in the first six months following the death of their spouse, but a return to normal after that. Another study conducted in the late 1960s and early 1970s in the United States (Silverman, 1986) indicated that widowhood was difficult because a woman's identity is so tied to a relationship with her spouse, including the roles associated with it (again, the traditional role of women). However, women outside the study (the nontraditional women) were doing just fine. The "husband sanctification" (a term coined by Lopata in the early 1970s) served to elevate the widow's own self-worth and at the same time allowed her to regard her deceased husband in a benevolent way. Both Silverman and Lopata admitted that viewing widowhood as a prolonged state from which recovery was nearly impossible was likely more a reflection of "social convention than psychological reality" (Konigsberg, 2011, p. 59).[6]

Other research (Boerner, Workman, and Bonanno, 2005) has confirmed that although loss is forever, acute grief is not. When a widow suffers prolonged grief disorder, it is likely due to her being dependent on the deceased for a sense of role in life or identity (again, a traditional role). Unfortunately, when the traditional widow does attempt to restart her life or transition to a different role, she may be seen as unfaithful in keeping the memory of her deceased husband if she dates too early, cohabitates, or remarries too soon. The widow is somehow seen as suspect in the trueness of the love she had for her husband, or as cold, unfeeling, or even in denial of the death itself (Konigsberg, 2011). Konigsberg cites research to indicate that, as an American population, although we have become more aware of the diversity of romantic relationships and relaxed in our attitudes about interracial dating, cohabitation, divorce, homosexuality, and gay marriage, "[W]e have actually grown *more* conservative about remarriage after spousal loss" (p. 39).

Contrary to these negative views, Boerner, Wortman, and Bonanno (2005) found no significant differences in distress between widows who recovered from their grief quickly (e.g., within six months) and those who took much longer (2–4 years). Over time, symptoms of distress just declined. The authors concluded that resilient grievers appear better equipped to accept death as a fact of life, and tend to have a more positive worldview, whereas chronic grievers seem less confident about their ability to cope and are more dependent on their relationship to the deceased. A study of Canadian widows and widowers reflected similar results, indicating that the securely attached were less angry, less socially isolated, and less prone to guilt, despair, and depression following spousal loss than were insecurely attached persons (Waskowic and Chartier, 2003).

Both Silverman and Lopata acknowledged that some widows enjoy their new independence and financial security (collecting Social Security benefits) following spousal loss. Others (e.g., De Giulio, 1989) point out that widowhood is temporary and can be an opportunity for self-expression and self-discovery. And finally, Konigsberg (2011) reminds us of the paradox that the prevailing "grief culture" supports widowhood as being a punitive event in a woman's life. After all, pain is good and it is the only way out of grief. But, many widows, she contends, find the subtle message of grief culture very sad and discouraging—and refuse to abide by it.

So, for a widow—and acknowledging that adjustment can be complicated by emotional challenges, financial insecurity,[7] social isolation, and lack of meaningful life purpose—the development of new roles, relationships, and activities are critical to help her transition out of grief and into a new life. Adjustment of this kind involves finding meaning in her own life (Coleman and Neimeyer, 2010)—a kind of individual reconstruction of a more meaningful and purposeful identity (Klass, Silverman, and Nickman, 1996). In particular, an older widow's self-concept may undergo a kind of structural reorganization following spousal loss (Montpetit and Bergeman, 2010), and this may include revisiting positive memories, having conversations with the deceased, sensing the deceased's presence, or sustaining activities once enjoyed together—something Carr (2010) referred to as restoration-oriented coping, which is also reflective of the Dual Process Model (Stroebe and Schut, 1999). For the widow, activities may involve replacing some familiar activities with new ones such as painting, reading, writing, or playing an instrument. These may divert or wean the widow (especially the traditional widow) from craving the relationship previously provided by her spouse.

Nancy's, Sarah's, and Jocelyn's journeys through grief involved first becoming a widow, then an individual woman. In coming to terms with being a widow, all three showed a healthy "feminine" capacity for grief, and a "masculine" sense of themselves as independent and valuable individuals who are important in and of themselves and not just in relation to their families or primary relationships. Individuating their grief, according to their own life circumstances and proclivities for enriching their own interests and lives, helped them to recreate a life shaped by, but not defined by, their deceased spouses.

As society begins to recognize and address the special needs of the widow who has been socialized according to traditional doctrines and traditional sex-role boundaries, greater understanding of and support for the widow's grief experience is required to encourage women to develop identities that are not completely limited to the role of familial caretaker and caregiver. The modern widow is more likely to have a better education, more occupational skills, and a wider repertoire of individual and social functions,[8] which allow her to make the transition into and out of widowhood with less difficulty than the traditional widow. Social support and healthy social networks (Jackson, 2013), and the degree to which the grieving spouse finds those supports helpful, is critical to healthy recovery and positive aging (Hill, 2005).

Notes

1. Note that this chapter generally refers to male/female spousal relationships, with full acknowledgment of variations of spousal relationships involving LGBT (lesbian, gay, bisexual and transgender) individuals. Note also that *relationship*, as used in this text, refers to several configurations of relationships, including those that have been sanctified through a religious or civil ceremony and those recognized as common-law.
2. However, even though the economic well-being of widows has shifted from widespread hardship to being reported just above the poverty line (Weaver, 2010), it remains pronounced among those with limited education.
3. World Health Organization (2014) "Preventing suicide: A global imperative," (http://www.who.int/mental_health/suicide-prevention/world_report_2014/en/).
4. Mental Health America (n.d.) (http://www.mentalhealthamerica.net/suicide).
5. Ibid.
6. Incidentally, in the instance where a woman is not legally married to her partner with whom she cohabitates, she generally experiences less support both at the time of the death and following the loss (Walter, 2003). In these cases, the woman experiences additional stresses either from lack of support or from the lack of predictability of the support that does come her way (Bent and Magilvy, 2006; Walter, 2003).
7. Interestingly, although financial status is perceived to decline for widows, a 2004 study from the Institute for Research on Poverty in the United States found that women widowed less than three years and more than seven years did not report being less satisfied with their finances. (Note that earlier findings in this book indicate evidence contrary to this finding.)
8. For widows, generally, technology (e.g., online dating sites) affords a sense of safety in her anonymity and her privacy, as well as insulation from judgment of others, some control over her relationships, and her ability to search possible new relationships with individuals who have had similar life experiences (i.e., loss of a spouse) (Gilbert and Horsley, 2011).

CHAPTER SEVEN

Death of a Marriage: Divorce Grief

Introduction

Divorce is no longer taboo or socially unacceptable. In fact, it seems almost a way of life. Statistically, in the United States one out of every two marriages ends in divorce, with one-half of divorces occurring within the first seven years of marriage (Cherlin, 1981). Today, midlife adults comprise the group most likely to be divorced (Amato, 2010) because many baby boomers have experienced divorces in their early 20s and 30s, and now in their 50s and 60s they continue to have high divorce rates.[1] Incidentally, baby boomer women are the group most likely to have been raised in traditional households and assumed traditional roles in all or a good part of their marriage(s) (most likely past marriages, but perhaps also present marriages).

Emotional Impacts of Divorce

Divorce is a complex social phenomenon that can have traumatic effects on a woman. Psychological changes can include depression, anxiety, bouts of crying, self-doubt, and a lack of self-confidence. Physical changes can include weight loss, lack of appetite and sleep, and an apathetic outlook on life. Social changes occur when, for example, the divorcee becomes excluded from social gatherings once enjoyed with her husband (or partner). These physical, psychological, and social impacts of divorce make the initial experience of divorced life difficult (Bohannon,

1970), and although divorce is devastating for everyone involved, it often has the most detrimental impact on women.

Divorce represents a major loss (Deits, 2009), which influences relationships, roles, routines, and self-concept (Lloyd, Sailor, and Carney, 2014). Loss through divorce can be compared to the death of a loved one because the same grief process occurs. In some cases, divorce can be even more painful than death in that in death the loss is final and there is no hope of bringing the person back. In divorce, however, there may be some hope (however false) that one is able to recover the relationship and unite with the partner.

Emotional impacts of divorce, then, are many and can include anger, destabilization in wondering whether you did the right thing, worry about what family and friends will say and whether sides will be taken, and how one will fare as a single woman (Lloyd et al., 2014). If the woman initiated the divorce, she is likely to experience lower levels of anxiety, loneliness, and depression than if her husband initiates divorce action (Sakraida, 2005), but in either case divorced individuals tend to have lowered immune systems (Sakraida, 2005), making them susceptible to illness and disease.

Women who divorce in midlife typically not only experience the loss of a partner and a sense of family but also changes in their living situation and an uncertain sense of self (Baum, 2003). Due to traditional gender-role socialization patterns, women often experience financial instability and a lower standard of living following divorce (compounded by the irregularity of child support payments because women are also more likely to gain custody of the children). In addition, women who were socialized to believe that it was their duty in life to get married and have a family before all else often lack the skills necessary to be competitive in the labor market. These women also worry about what impact the divorce will have on the children. This decision is especially difficult for midlife women "at the confluence of menopause and empty nest" (McCoyd and Walter, 2016), as they may have decided to wait to divorce until the children were out of school and perhaps out of the family home. Little wonder then that divorce causes considerable upheaval in a woman's life—the pain of which leads to mourning (Maata, 2011). Paul Bohannen (1970) writes that "emotional divorce results in the loss of a loved one just as fully as does the death of a spouse." The "natural" reaction to this loss is grief, as human beings mourn the loss of every meaningful relationship. And although outdated and criticized earlier in this text, Kübler-Ross's five-stage model can be applied to the loss experienced in divorce (Herman, 1974).

Denial, the first stage, sees the newly divorced person not fully comprehending the emotional investments he or she made and then lost in a marriage shared over a period of 5, 10, even 20 or more years. Even though the marriage may have been difficult, there was at one time a meaningful relationship for those involved. Denial functions as a temporary defense against the shock of separation or divorce and the losses associated with it. Denial in the grief process is necessary to help collect oneself and to mobilize other defenses. The time it takes to pass through this stage of grief is determined by the history of the marriage and the degree of positive memories held therein.

The next stage in the grief process is anger. Most often anger or hostility is projected at the ex-spouse, who is blamed for the failure of the marriage, the unhappiness, the confusion, the hurt, the fears, and the loneliness. At times anger is expressed inwardly, which usually leads to depression. For a traditionally socialized woman who has not worked and is not independently wealthy, there is often little or no money readily available immediately following divorce. Besides financial problems, the decision to go to work, move, or assume full responsibility for the care of the children places additional stress on the divorced woman. Lacking money and direction, and sometimes alienated by parents and friends, the traditional woman may find it especially difficult to put her life back together.

The third stage of the grieving process involves bargaining. A divorced woman may second-guess her decision. Could she have done more? If she changes, will her ex-husband return to the marriage? If she continues to feel good about herself, will she be able to make it on her own? As the bargaining continues, the woman becomes less apprehensive about new ways of life and new responsibilities and begins to form more productive relationships.

In the fourth stage of grief, depression, the divorced woman senses a great loss. She now realizes that the full emotional investment she made in the failed marriage, and whatever that marriage meant at one time, is now gone. Her role in relation to the marriage is gone, and with it the old structure, clearing the path for new, more enabling structures to support her future.

The final stage is one of acceptance. The divorced woman has probably been living alone and is more aware of who she is, what she wants, and what she can do. It is now possible for the divorced woman to tell others that she is divorced, without going into details or feeling great remorse. At this point, the woman is able to look back at the marriage realistically, seeing both its good points and its negative ones.

The time it takes to move through these stages is indeterminate. Also, depression does not always occur. Sometimes euphoria is a primary reaction to divorce. For many couples who divorce by mutual consent, divorce provides welcomed and sustained emotional relief. Euphoria arises from the realization that the attachment figure is no longer needed and that one can do very well alone. This is another way to manage the loss; the woman rearranges her emotions so that the loss is much less significant. She no longer needs the spouse, and this realization makes available new opportunities for self-realization (Weiss, 1975).

An Alternate View

However, comparing divorce to death is not a view held by all researchers. Susan Gettleman and Janet Markowitz (1974), authors of *Courage to Divorce*, do not compare divorce with death. They do not feel that mourning rituals are necessary in divorce, although there is, even in welcomed divorce, a sense of loss. They recognize that a person who is abandoned or divorced against her will is likely to feel a profound sense of regret and anger, but that in many cases divorce is, for the woman, a welcomed solution.

In Gettleman's view, mourning rituals only enhance feelings of despair and loneliness, and symbolize love and respect for the deceased person. In the case of divorce, why should people mourn the "loss" of someone they prefer to be rid of or have outgrown? How can one think of the spouse as dead when he is around to demand visiting privileges to the children? Mourning is needed to establish the fact that a loved one is gone and is never coming back. Divorce means that two people no longer share their lives, not that they will never see each other again. Gettleman and Markowitz suggest that divorce is not proof of the moral decay of American society, but rather part of the "passing of patriarchies and feminism in America, and of the revolt of women." Divorce can be loss, but it can also be a transitional point from which to start a life that is more self-realized and conscious than the passive acceptance of dated institutional norms that governed assumptions about sex roles, marriage, and families. As early as the 1970s, Gettleman contended that we were living in a world in which patriarchies and the sex-role ethic that says men work and women clean and care for children, and the countless implications of inequality that accompany such a situation, were "passing." Authors such as Betty Friedan (*The Feminine Mystique*, 1963/1997) and a host of other feminists would wholeheartedly agree.

Psychological and Physical Impacts of Divorce

Along with the emotional aspects of divorce, a person will often develop psychological and physical symptoms. In Cabot and Wanderer's book *Letting Go* (1987), the authors discuss obsessive, compulsive, depressive, phobic, hysterical, anxious, and psychosomatic symptoms, which a person going through a divorce may develop. Under obsessive symptoms, the lack of ability to concentrate places one's whole concern on the ex-spouse, wondering whether there is another woman or man involved, guilt over wrong-doings in the marriage, lack of ability to make decisions, and other issues. Compulsive symptoms may include questioning mutual friends about the ex–husband or wife; constantly talking about the lost relationship; suddenly turning very spiritual; drinking, eating, or smoking excessively or relying on drugs; or making preparations for when the spouse will return. Depressive symptoms may include intense fatigue, crying, neglect of duties, feelings of failure and rejection, and basic loss of interest in most activities. Phobic symptoms may include feelings of being closed in, panicking at the thought of meeting new people, needing to be with someone constantly, leaving lights on and doors open, and a generalized fear of many ordinary events. Some hysterical symptoms are irritability; minor concerns causing panic; forgetfulness; carelessness and frequent accidents; and emotional outbursts. Anxiety symptoms may become manifest through difficulty sleeping, eating, and breathing; gritting of teeth; excessive perspiration; and excessive nervousness. All of these problems that may accompany divorce or loss of a meaningful relationship can lead to many actual physical problems that have underlying psychosomatic causes.

Kerry's Experience of Divorce

The following case study shows the danger of others' expectations and the traditional expectation that the woman in a marriage is supposed to live to support and fulfill the man's dreams and not have any dreams of her own. This points toward a probable cause for the frequent incidence of contemporary divorce: the idea people have that others live to fulfill their dreams. The case study looks at this problem from a personal point of view, which is more realistic than theoretical in its analysis. This is Kerry's story.

> I found the statistics on the rising divorce rate interesting, but the figures never really meant much to me. Interesting, yes, but not my problem.
>
> Today, they say approximately every one out of two marriages ends in divorce, and after 21 years our marriage became one of those statistics. This one-out-of-two ratio does have meaning to me now. It's my reality.
>
> With marriage came a celebration—the birth and bonding of a growing relationship filled with love. With divorce comes grief. Mourning tends to avoid or forget the bad times.
>
> The weather was turning when we reached the decision to divorce. The air was crisp already, and as I sat in the kitchen, gazing out the window, I noticed that the aspens were beginning to change color, and soon the mountain peaks would be splashed with the vibrant colors of fall. I chuckled as I heard the hum of chainsaws in the forest. The woodcutters had arrived again to cut firewood before snow blanketed the forest floor and capped

the mountain peaks. And I remembered the wise old Navajo medicine man who also did interpreting where I worked as an emergency room nurse on the Navajo Reservation. He said he always knew when fall was coming. I asked how he could tell (I was sure he had some mystical explanation). And he would say, "Because many white men leave the forest with their U-Haul trailers filled with wood." This always made me laugh.

There was a chill in the air, though, which brought back the reality of the emptiness around me, and I wondered how I could laugh at a time like this. For a moment, it was as if I had been frozen in my chair. I couldn't look at or do anything without being reminded of an incident or time in my husband's and my life. Everything I looked at in our home brought back memories.

It was cold in the house, and I found myself mechanically walking to the bedroom for a sweater. Without thinking, I automatically picked up my favorite one. It was cold like the air around it. Mike had bought it for me when we were in England. It was in the window of the little store next door to the fishing shop where he first discovered fly fishing. I remembered the afternoon he'd given me it. He had gone into town with Ian (one of the British tutors) on the student van that morning to get the fly rod he had admired for some time. While he was there, he stopped by the wool shop and bought me the sweater.

It rained often while we were in England, and I was always chilled during our walks up the long drive of the college to the pub at the end of the road. The sweater felt good back then. Wearing it always brought back pleasant memories, but as I stood in the bedroom doorway now, starting to put on the sweater, the flood of happy memories—and now their loss—really hit me. I took it off the sweater in a hurry and put it in the box I had set out to collect things that I no longer wanted. I suppose I felt that if I discarded the sweater, I could also cast off those old memories. Good memories were too painful now.

So I found an old sweatshirt, put it on instead, and went back to the kitchen for a cup of tea. It seemed to help if each time I thought of a bad memory I tried to think of a pleasant one. Maybe it helped me understand why we had slowly grown apart over the years.

As I sipped some tea, my thoughts shifted back to the college in England. Mike had been a visiting professor at the British campus of the Midwestern University where he taught. One afternoon I was touring Lincoln Cathedral with the American Visiting Professor in Nursing, and she told me of her success arranging a day at St. Christopher's Hospice and invited me to join her and her six other students. Being a nurse, I was thrilled at this prospect. I had read a little about the hospice concept of care and its beginning at St Christopher's, but to actually spend a day there was a great opportunity for me to see what was being done for the terminally ill and their families.

That evening I anxiously told my husband of the planned trip, and he reminded me of a tea that had been arranged on the same day by the bursar's wife for all visiting faculty wives, and I was expected to attend.

I didn't go with the nursing group to St. Christopher's.

That was the first time I remember feeling like a possession instead of a partner. Faculty wife teas? Strange how everyone looks so prim and proper and bored to tears, no matter which side of the ocean you are on.

I smiled as I looked at the box of Earl Grey tea sitting in front of me now. At least I had finally developed a taste for good tea, though 10 years had done nothing to improve my interest in faculty wife gatherings.

I thought of the last faculty wife tea I had attended. This one was truly a saccharin society of polyester politeness whose members' main goal was to get one's secret recipe published (next to the dean's wife's recipe) in the Faculty of G Club Cookbook. Picture nine months of teatime deciding which chocolate cake recipe of the 35 chocolate cake recipes submitted would be published. Who cares which one was the best? Each was best to someone. Was this to be my purpose in life?

Not long after I decided not to attend the faculty wives tea, I began to make my own choices. I just stopped going to teas and started attending emergency care conferences to obtain my emergency room nurse certification. Maybe that's what I'd done wrong. Someone asked me, when they found out we were getting divorced, "What happened? We thought you two were the perfect couple!"

What happened? How dare they ask that question? That question assumes there's a short, simple reason to the end a 20-year relationship. What do they want me to say? "Mike didn't take out the garbage," or "I didn't cook chili the way he liked."

When a relationship dies, it is a slow process and usually a complicated one. The decay in our relationship was both. Sometimes I wish there was an easy answer. Perhaps we could have recognized it sooner and saved ourselves a lot of grief. We both said things that hurt. One of the most sobering things he said to me was *"How are you not interested in my dream?"* When I first heard his words, I was devastated and I couldn't do anything but walk away. I was tired of arguing, and the only release that seemed to help was to jump in the car and drive away. I had no idea where I was going, but I just had to leave. I kept on driving until I saw a road sign saying Cottage Grove Lake. It was an exhausting drive, and I was glad I was tired, because I fell asleep as soon as I got to the hotel room. I guess I saw driving away as an escape.

I awoke at 5:00 a.m. and looked out on the lake. It was still and peaceful, and I kept replaying his comment. Didn't he understand that I was denying myself dreams of my own, and I just could not do that anymore?

Medical problems and other life events were all given as reasons for our problems at one time or another, but as I look back, these were only crises that brought out the real problems between us.

Afterthoughts

Everyone hugs you when your husband dies. Very few hug you when you get a divorce. I never realized how much that meant until my father came from San Francisco to help me close up the house. When I picked him up at the airport, he didn't say anything. It was so nice not to feel like I had to defend myself. People were busy rushing here and there, and Dad just stood there in the middle of the airport and hugged me for a long time. It felt so comforting.

The day I returned home from a relative's funeral was the day my husband chose to discuss our divorce. At the airport. It wasn't the only bad memory I had. I remember a day he came home angry from work because a female colleague was fighting his idea for making some changes. I asked him how he was going to convince her that it was really a good idea and he said, *"I'm going to intimidate the hell out of her!"* He said she was crying in someone's office a few days later, and now she had moved on. That happened to me too. The intimidation always came when we were alone. No one else saw it, and no one will ever know.

After I moved away, waking up in the middle of the night to new surroundings, I was confused and frightened. For a few months after the divorce, I kept having dreams of how things used to be. One dream is especially vivid to me. We were cross-country skiing past the pine trees by our home. I fell (as usual) and my husband collided with me. We tried in vain to get our skis untangled (our athletic teenagers called us Laurel and Hardy), and we lay there in the snow, exhausted and laughing. I awoke from the dream laughing. I didn't know where I was. Then I realized that it was a dream, and I started crying.

I guess that dream was my way of trying to hold onto the good times. Maybe it was also my way of denying that the good times were now gone.

Sometime later I had another dream. I had moved away and started back to work. The dream was so strange. My ex-husband, Mike, was lying in a bed dying. His every feature was clear. I was looking through a window in a door, and no matter how hard I tried, I couldn't open the door. He was just lying there. He was alive, but I couldn't reach him.

I don't dream much anymore except when we have to communicate about our children or business matters. Then there seems to be a period of about a week or two when I seem to experience the entire process of the loss, the grief, and the letting go again. The last significant dream occurred just a few weeks ago, and it was a nightmare.

Something had happened to one of our children, and I called to let Mike know. I didn't feel like I was speaking to a person. It felt as though I was leaving a message on an answering machine. For the first time, talking with him made me feel cold and empty. That night I had another nightmare. I was looking down at Mike's face and arms, and I was screaming because his face was decaying—just rotting away before my eyes.

> The next day I called Roger, an old friend back East. I told him about the dream I'd had the night before. First he went on to explain his own divorce grief and how he had handled it. "Treat grief like the weather, Kerry," he said. "When the weather is extreme and harsh, you must do things to protect yourself, like putting on a jacket or rain hat. But when the weather eases, enjoy the comfortable feeling. You'll notice that these comfortable times will slowly be more frequent and last longer, like the unpredictability of spring weather as it passes into summer."
>
> Roger and I talked about grief and the passing of time. Then he asked me to think about the three dreams that I had discussed with him. He said the last dream was a good sign, and I snapped at him and said he had a sick sense of humor. He didn't laugh. He just said no, that I had acknowledged the bad times and was finally letting go of the good times.
>
> It has been a year and a half since my divorce, and I find difficulty trusting all relationships now. That really bothers me because in the past I found it extremely easy to trust. I asked myself why trust is so difficult now. To have faith in someone leaves you vulnerable to pain. But to never trust leaves you empty. I want to have faith again, but it takes time. Building or rebuilding relationships with friends and family are necessary for all of us in life, but right now, for me, relationships are like roses. You want to get close enough to enjoy their beauty, but you are afraid of the thorns.

Kerry's experience shows some of the problems associated with a woman's traditional role and her husband's expectation regarding his wife being there to fulfill his dreams. This points to the unrealistic portrait of romantic love that the mass media has perpetuated. Simply put, it is unreasonable to expect anyone to fulfill one's dreams—except one's self. We must take care of ourselves first, become whole in ourselves first.

The expectation of a traditional role for Kerry, which she seemed to fulfill for a time in the marriage, failed when she transitioned into a more modern role of making her own decisions and choices to fulfill her own needs for education and career. At midlife, this transition for women as their children leave or have left home is not uncommon.

Divorce[2] can mark a transition to renewal and a process of reassessing goals and priorities, from which growth occurs. One doesn't really ever "get over" divorce. The former spouse remains part of one's personal history (Deits, 2009). Releasing your attachment to the former spouse does not mean that you forget or deny the importance he or she has had (and may continue to have) in your life. Deits suggests that it is not unusual to need a year or more to begin recovering a healthy self-image. And it takes a strong sense of purpose and direction to get through divorce in a healthy manner.

"To 'go through' grief is to 'grow through' grief" (Deits, 2009, p. 92). Deits reminds us that reaching for a new life means giving yourself permission to reorient your interests and activities in new directions—congruent with Attig's (2011) concept of reweaving the tapestry of one's life as an essential part of relearning one's world after loss.

Research indicates that the divorce rate in the United States is highest in the world at 54.8 percent (Nugman, 2002).[3] Forty-three percent of marriages end up in separation or divorce within 15 years, 33 percent within 10 years of marriage, and 20 percent within five years of marriage. Bramlett et al (2001) indicate that the duration of marriage is influenced by age at the time of marriage. The older the woman is at the time of her first marriage, the longer the marriage is likely to last.[4] However, an article in the *New York Times* (December 2014), presenting research conducted by economists Betsey Stevenson and Justin Wolfers, tells a somewhat different story.[5] Trends indicate that the high divorce rates of the late 1970s and 1980 are falling for couples wed in the 2000s. Some factors attributed to that trend include women marrying later and entering the workforce later.

Notes

1. "Gray" divorce, labeled in the United States in 2004, is initiated by females in 66 percent of cases. Older adults account for the overall increase in divorces in the United Kingdom. Reasons offered for the increase include infidelity of older husbands due to the availability of anti-impotence drugs, human longevity, cultural values of the baby boomers, and women's increasing financial independence (Brown, 2015).

2. Statistics Canada indicates that divorce rates in Canada continue to decline (a decrease by 8 percent from 2006 to 2011, dropping steadily each year). Report author Mary Bess Kelly pointed to several factors: "The proportion of married couples has been steadily decreasing over the past 20 years while common-law unions are becoming more numerous," as are lone-parent families, which have proliferated since the mid-1960s (Kelly, 2012).

3. G. Nugman (2002), "World Divorce Rate," Nugman, Gulnar of the Heritage Foundation, 2002, http://www.divorcereform.org/gul.html.

4. M. Bramlett and W. Mosher (2001), First Marriage Dissolution, Divorce, and Remarriage: United States. Advance Data 323, Centers for Disease Control and Prevention, May 31, https://www.cdc.gov/nchs/data/ad/ad323.pdf.

5. Claire Cain Miller (2014), "The Divorce Surge Is Over, but the Myth Lives On," Upshot, *New York Times* data blog, December 2, http://www.nytimes.com/2014/12/02/upshot/the-divorce-surge-is-over-but-the-myth-lives-on.html?smid=fb-nytimes&smtyp=cur&bicmp=AD&bicmlukp=WT.mc_id&bicmst=1409232722000&bicmet=1419773522000&_r=4&abt=0002&abg=0.

CHAPTER EIGHT

Death of a Child: A Mother's Loss and Grief

A mother's grief is unlike any other. It is more difficult. It is more lasting. It arises from the bond between mother and child at the genesis of the child's conception. The bond is indelible, and it endures no matter when the child leaves the mother's life, and regardless of the reason or cause of that departure or what the nature of the relationship between mother and child was.

When a woman is a mother, the potential for grief follows her throughout her life. The potential of the gift of the child to the mother's life is what sustains her. She does not live in the shadow of love or the fear of loss. She lives in the potentiating force that new life bestows on her. Her child is, in many ways, her future. When a parent dies, the past is gone. When a child dies, the future is.

When a child's death arrives, it is painful. It racks the very bones of a mother's existence. She should have gone first. She *would* have gone first—no matter the age of the child. No matter what was said, or whispered between child and mother; no matter how well intentioned the actions or advice, it is all too late. Death steals the window that mother and child were meant to share.

A mother's grief becomes the door to the rest of her life. She can shut it or open it and walk through, but loss of a child marks a significant transition that changes a mother's life forever.

Leah lost her son David to cancer. He was 12 years old. This is her story.

> "What was it Mom?" David whispered, still groggy from the anesthetic and surgery. "It was a tumor, David." Too sleepy for more questions, David closed his eyes and slept.

It was Thanksgiving Day. David was admitted to hospital in the late afternoon to give us time for a family dinner. David's Grandma and Poppa (my parents) brought a stuffed chicken to our home, but none of us felt much like eating. After a short nap, David was ready to go to the hospital. "I don't think we should be late, Mom," he said.

David refused the wheelchair at the hospital door and answered all the admission questions himself. He was, after all, 12 years old. His dad, Tom (my ex-husband), and David's twin, Douglas, arrived later that evening from their home in northern Arizona. We were divorced and Douglas lived with his father; and David, with me. While Douglas visited his grandparents, Tom and I walked David to the operating room. David held my hand, loosening it just as the OR doors opened. Then we waited. . . .

I spent most of the next two hours in the chapel and then went back to the crowded waiting room. The pediatric surgeons arrived shortly after and motioned me to the hallway.

Cancer. A large tumor on the liver that had metastasized to David's chest and lungs. The story was repeated again a few minutes later for David's father. The surgeons said they would send more samples to the lab to learn more about the specific type of cancer. I didn't want David to be told, but the surgeons said, "No, he must be told the truth. He's a bright boy, and we'll be doing many unpleasant things to him. He'll need to know why."

For the first time in a long time, Tom and I held each other and cried. "This can't be real," I heard myself saying over and over again.

David was then taken back to his room, tubes running from his arms and nose into his stomach. When I went home to change to come back to the hospital for the night, David had asked his father, "Was it cancer?" Tom nodded yes.

For the next few days, David just stared at us with large sad eyes. Friends rallied round. Some answered the phone for me at home, sparing me from having to go through the story again and again. Some brought food and thermoses of hot tea to David's room for Tom and me while we stayed at the hospital. I was dizzy and I tried to pray, but only tears would come.

The evening after his surgery, David motioned me to his bedside and asked me to pray with him. He asked God to heal his liver—"even if it means more surgery," he said. I prayed too—not to heal David's liver, but to take away his pain. All the while I kept thinking, *"I don't want to be here. I don't want this to be happening."*

The next few days were filled with more tests and more surgeons explaining what tests had been done and what the results were. Each piece of news was worse than the last. In the end, it was a type of cancer resistant to both radiation and chemotherapy. David asked the oncologist why he couldn't just take out the tumor. The doctor replied that the tumor was connected to tissues David still needed. That seemed to satisfy him. When the doctor left, David asked, "Do you think doctors are sorry to tell a boy he has cancer?"

David's incision ran across his abdomen and up into his chest. When I tried to help him sit or stand, he would get angry and tell me I was doing it wrong. The social worker met with us and explained that it was safe for him to vent his anger on me. That helped me take it less personally.

Across from David's bed was a boy who had bruised his liver during a bicycle accident. Another was covered with scratches, casts, and bandages from a mountain bike fall. David whispered to me, "Wish that's all I had."

As David's incision began to heal, his spirits lifted. But instead of going directly home with me, he decided that he would like to have a "little vacation" at Grandma and Poppa's house. So, out of Grandma's supply of clay in her art studio, David sculpted a tiny devil-like figure with a big grin. He did not comment on it. Back in our little house, he drew cards for all of us too, but no longer airplanes or animals that he used to like to draw. One day he drew a fantasy space 'scape in soft pastels, small bubble-like planets with a golden podlike shape in an upper corner. Inside it was an inner pod surrounded by green plantlike spikes. At the center was a tiny embryo with a lovely sprouting seed in it. Again, he had no comment on it.

One lovely lady told David that cancer was just a name and that he should do what he could to get well. She encouraged David to think about his illness as confused cells that weren't getting messages from his brain. David liked that, and he called her a "messenger."

Over the next few months, we worked with a therapist on healing imagery, autogenics (deep relaxation), and meditation. These helped David a lot, and he had less pain. He also cried for his Uncle Richard, who had died a year earlier. At the time of Richard's passing, David did not show grief, but after one of his autogenic sessions, he cried and cried. He explained to his father and brother on the phone that night that he was learning about his feelings, about suppression, and about disease. A couple more sessions and David announced, "I forgive everybody for everything!" I believe these sessions (in addition to the meds he was on) helped David to handle his pain.

A few weeks later David's oncologist held a meeting at the hospital for anyone who wanted to come and learn more about David's cancer. (David said he didn't want to go.) What surprised me were all the friends who attended—nearly 25 in all. Some had taken time off work to learn more about what sort of chemotherapy David could have, that it would shrink the tumor a bit, but with nausea, hair loss, and so on. It would have very little chance of success. Poppa asked why the cancer had not been discovered sooner. The doctor explained that it was a very rare form of cancer, and that even major cancer centers saw no more than one case like this per year. Everyone there began to understand the gravity of David's illness. We left the hospital that night with lighter hearts, our burden shared.

Our weekly clinic visits to the hospital continued, with ultrasound every other week. In December, David wrote a letter to his brother:

I wish you were here, Doug. I miss you, but I'm not bored. It seems like every day I have plenty of things to do like seeing the acupuncturist, the three-times-a-day relaxation tape, seeing Dr. Hutter or Cample. I'm really busy sometimes. For favorite pastimes, I listen to Mark Twain story tapes from the library, or Mom reads to me from fiction books. I can't wait till Christmas. Aunt Gwen and Uncle Jim mailed some Christmas presents for me and you, and Mom won't let me open them till Christmas. Love David.

And to his father:

I miss you and want to see you. Today I had another ultrasound. I can't wait to see you. Also I can't wait for Christmas. Yesterday I got a hair cut and I look exactly like Douglas. I'm having a very nice time. Yesterday I had an acupuncture treatment and felt real good, full of energy and this good feeling has lasted all day. It's just one more reason I feel I should try this before chemotherapy. I'm eating well and feeling good. Love David. Merry Christmas.

And to Tom's girlfriend:

I miss you and I enjoy your warm feelings. I'm glad you're coming and can't wait to see you. I feel real good and more energy than normal today and yesterday. It rained today. I like this weather a lot. It's more like Christmas. Yesterday was hot. I'm living in a real cute house with a cute little Christmas tree that's only three feet tall. Love David. Merry Christmas.

David was eager to give everyone presents, and he pushed himself to go shopping. We chose the quieter stores, but he still tired easily. He spent more on gift wrap and bows and matching paper than on the gifts themselves and took considerable care wrapping each one. His cards and letters were decorated lavishly, and he sent them to everyone he knew, including the doctors.

As David's illness progressed, his printing became tinier and tinier.

Both sides of the family came to our house for Christmas dinner. It was the first time in a long while that everyone had gotten together. Doug was good-natured about all the gifts David got, and he helped David unwrap them. They chuckled over most of them, but David soon grew too tired to finish opening them all. Everyone tried to be cheery, but Tom cried silently in the corner of the room, and I was too upset to eat. David felt the stress too.

We were up more at night now because of the pain, and it was harder for David to relax. The pain meds were increased. Doug developed a sore throat over Christmas and proclaimed that he wished he were either on fast forward or rewind.

David changed too. He became less interested in boyish things, which was hard for Douglas. He began to feel cut off from David. He even had a dream, he said, in which David refused to talk to him.

The New Year began with David weak, tired, and depressed. But he insisted on looking his best to see the pediatric oncologist. He would change out of pajamas and slippers and into street clothes. He worried about his appearance. "I'm so skinny now," he said, "Will people think I look different?"

Since early childhood, David had wanted to be "normal." He explained the difference between his social self and his real self. He said, "God helps people to be their real selves. My real self's coming out with this illness. I used to have one for the crowd."

He worried about finances too. "I don't want to be the boy who took all the bacon," he declared one day. My disability payments were low, and Tom's insurance didn't cover illness. But other agencies covered surgery, hospitalization, and visits to the oncologist. One day a hide-a-bed showed up at our house. David and I relaxed after that, believing that our needs would be met, and they were.

Relatives sent us a little money, and when it came, David would quietly decide what presents he could buy with it to give to his Poppa, his friends, his nurses, and so on. He would share ice cream with any child who came to see him. David gave his small savings to Douglas to go fishing in Michigan ''cause I don't need anything', he said. We never said it, but in a way, David was making out his will.

In January David moved to the living room, sleeping full time on the hide-a-bed. Friends helped me rearrange furniture: the vacuum was retired because it was too noisy and bothered David's stomach, and even Sounder, the singing canary, was moved away from David's bed. A stopper was put on the screen door to deaden the sound. Soft running suits replaced David's jeans, to make him more comfortable.

David began to want more and more of my time. He was distressed when I spent too long at the clothesline, and soon I let friends help me with the laundry. One day, David said very simply to me, "I'm not afraid of dying and I won't mind it, but you'd mind it." It was as if he was living for me. And he was right. It would be hard to let go. I did mind it. One day when the hospice nurse asked David if he thought about death, he told her that he did and that "Mommy will be sad." The nurse told him that "Mom will be sad, but she can take it." I assured him that I could.

David's acceptance of his death helped me accept it too. And as much as Grandma and Poppa were disturbed by David's and my discussion of death, they also began to accept it.

David's and my conversations turned frequently to death. Sometimes I described my belief that there was really no such thing as death, that the spirit or soul, the part that was of God, survived. David's face would glow, and he would say, "You understand." The peace that surrounded us was so great, it was as if we could feel God protecting us. Even the visiting nurse would comment on it. I would say to David as he lay in his bed, "We are so fortunate, David," and he would nod his head in agreement.

David created many poems during those days. He hesitated sharing them, though, for fear people would think he was showing off. After reciting this one to me, he said his guardian angel's name was "Leaves, with both meanings."

The leaf falls from the tree's arm,
Doing loops and rolls in the autumn air,
And as it tumbles to the ground it sends a
Small breeze gently over the green grass.
Not moving it,
Not disturbing it,
But quenching it,
Cooling it.

Late one January night, David complained of difficultly breathing. I took him to the emergency room, and X-rays indicated that the tumor was pushing against his lungs, making less space for him to breathe. He stayed in hospital for about three days. One afternoon one of my friends wheeled him to the pediatric ward. David had developed a deep concern for sick children. Outside the ward, David met a man whose daughter was named "Karma." The man knew about David's cancer, and he said to David, "So you're one of the lucky ones who doesn't have to wait until he's old to be good enough to leave. You're good enough now." That comforted David. He called him a "messenger" too—another person that understood.

David returned home, this time to a hospital bed and oxygen that had been loaned to us, but he refused any more acupuncture. He tried to do everything he enjoyed doing—going to a birthday party, and a lunch out with Grandma and Poppa. A friend remarked, "He did whatever he could until he couldn't anymore. Then he'd give it up without looking back."

By February David was bedbound except for walks to the bathroom. He could sit up to eat from a tray, but switched from pajamas to large tee shirts to accommodate his distended abdomen. Even with all the paraphernalia, oxygen tanks, and small TV, the living room was comfortable. David picked out pictures of animals and decals for the walls and told me where to hang the crystals. He was surrounded by flowers and Valentine cards, and soft music played on the tape player. From his bed, David could see hummingbirds at the feeder on the tree outside the window. Quiet, no longer able to read or write, David said he wasn't bored because he had a lot to think about. With growing acceptance, David's depression was gone. No tears, no self-pity, just occasional irritability because the disease was so "frustrating." He apologized for his "grumpiness" and prayed to God for help. Grumpiness was understandable with diarrhea, vomiting, constant pain, weakness, painful urination, legs that felt like a "thousand ants biting," headaches, backaches, and nosebleeds. Yet with all this, no complaints. His message to us was "I am happy, and I will be happy!" He wanted everyone he loved "to understand the way I want them to" before he died. He wanted to teach others, especially Tom and Douglas. He felt that they might not be ready for another year. One night, after a shot of Demerol, he said to me, "I'm comfortable. Don't fill your mind with thoughts and trouble yourself."

One evening, on the way to the bathroom, David recalled how he used to be, how he used to run and be active. "But I'm not complaining," he said. "I wouldn't change anything. I've learned so much. I'm not sorry I got cancer." Another night Douglas and David talked about death. David was very practical and matter-of-fact. Douglas felt better and told David that he was glad he wasn't afraid and that "the body was to express the soul." About 1:30 that morning, David woke me, saying that he'd had a wonderful dream and knew that everything would be all right.

Most nights David and I were up between midnight and 1:30 or 2:00 a.m. David would have a snack, and I would read to him. Those were cozy times for us.

Wasting and pale, with more coughing and diminished appetite, David talked less and less. I treasured his whispered words, the closeness, and his rare kiss or hug, or "Mommy, I love you so much!" We'd play fantasy games at night too, like fishing with Douglas. One night, in distress, he told me he heard a bell and a cricket. I couldn't hear them, but I told him that that didn't make things less normal or less real. He relaxed a bit after that.

Calm amidst greater physical stress (numbness on his left side, an enlarging lump near his collarbone), David tried to comfort me. "Don't try to read my mind and upset yourself. I can feel your love." And when I'd get up to leave the room, he'd squeeze my hand and say, "It's all right; you can cry in here."

His face was less and less a child's as it became thinner. Pale, with finer hair and skeletal arms and legs, David was still beautiful. Eating was still a pleasure for him and a comfort to us. His diet had gone from natural foods, after surgery, to a mother's horror—ice cream, cake, cookies, and candies. David's liver could best assimilate sugar, and he needed calories. He seemed to relax best with small children who didn't ask him questions. Tom and Douglas drove down often from their small town. David and Douglas spent some nice moments together, watching Muppets on television. I left the room once as Doug held David's hand, and overheard him say, "We'll be close, no matter what happens." Douglas told me later about one of the nights he spent at our house when he got up and held David's hand and said quietly, "I love you." David said, with closed eyes, "I love you too."

David had a convulsion one night, and his feet swelled horribly. Toward the end of that week, David spat out a tooth while chewing a jelly bean. "I don't care," he said. "The tooth fairy can have it." He was amazing, unexcited by all these bodily changes, calm, unafraid, with no self-pity. He seemed detached from his body.

I could no longer lift David. I felt useless and helpless. Leaving David in Tom's care, I visited my friend and wept. I felt at the limit of physical and emotional strength and found myself with no time for anything but David. I felt inadequate. "What does David want you do to?" my friend asked.

"To sit and hold his hand," I said. "That's all."

My strength was limited. But God's was not. I bowed my head and left myself and David in God's care—where we had been all along.

David became interested in my life story about that time. I told him about being a little girl and a teen. He said he thought he would have liked me as a girl. He was especially sympathetic about my asthma and said he wished he'd been alive then, when I was young, to help. Who was the adult and who was the child? David was no longer a child. To me he was a wise old friend.

David had to be turned every 20 minutes to get comfortable. His chest was very red, but his body temperature was actually falling. Sunday night I prayed that David's ordeal would be over soon and whispered to him, "You don't need to stay in your body and suffer anymore." Breathing became more difficult. David wanted quiet and motioned to me to have the visitors leave.

Soon after that, David slipped into a coma. I wanted to hold him, but I was afraid I would hurt him. The doctor assured me that I would not. After all the months of worry about David's death, worry about if I'd know, or if I'd be there, here it was, in God's hands, unfolding perfectly. It grew very still in the room and outside. The wind died down; the oxygen was turned off; even the canary was quiet. Tears flowed silently. The social worker and young doctor from the hospital and two dear friends made a circle of love around us as I held David. I lost track of anything happening in the room outside of David. I lost track of time and my resolution to pray.

Perhaps it's not accurate to say that I felt God's presence. It was more that we were within His presence, His consciousness, His great golden heart. The room was so peaceful; David's death was so perfect. All our desires were fulfilled. David and I had talked about him dying in my arms, which months before he had said "would be wonderful."

I was so grateful to God for being there. We all felt such calm and joy. No more pain for David. He was free now, a joyous spirit.

Understanding a Mother's Grief

The biggest source of strength for David's mother over the 30 years since his death has been spirituality. In the same way that David's suffering had meaning, spirituality helped Leah find purpose in his suffering and, indeed, in her own suffering. In the same manner that David said he had learned a lot through his journey—about his truest, deepest self, Leah too said she had learned a great deal about death and also about herself through David's illness. Leah's fear of death was lessened, and looking back, she is grateful for being able to accompany David to a pain-free peace. Doug, David's identical twin, threw his suffering into cycling and running. He's run and cycled in races he could easily compete in, but instead he has run beside a faltering friend, encouraging him and helping just to see him finish. He stops the car to carry snakes across the road so they won't be run over. In countless acts of kindness to friends, family, coworkers, neighbors, and clients, he shows his own qualities of gentleness and generosity as well as David's influence. Leah can still feel herself in her living room and recall David's passing as a "joyful dancing ball of light." Thirty years later, Leah's simple words reveal the significance of David's passing to her own being. "This life flowed through me," she said. "It has been painful, but it has also been joyful."

David died of cancer, but he could have been any child, any age, and there could have been any number of reasons for his death. Whether loss of a child is due to miscarriage, stillbirth, illness or disease, sudden or violent, or uncertain as in the case of a missing child,[1] each parent's grief is unique. There is no set path or predictable grief pattern (Nagel and Clark, 2012). Grief is an individual event (Barnhill and Jorgenson, 2011). And for women, in particular, that path is created first out of the nature of the relationship she had with her child and, second, out of the sociocultural context of her life.

Emotional Response

When a child dies, parents' immortality is stolen. A parent's assumptive world, along with his or her future, is shaken (Rando, 1993; Sanders, 1992). One of people's deepest fears is awakened—death before fulfillment (Buckingham, 1990). It is not surprising then that death calls forth a wellspring of emotions: anger, anxiety, confusion, uncontrollable tears (or not at all), denial, despair and disappointment, guilt, helplessness, numbness, loneliness, energy loss, forgetfulness, changes in libido (Nagel and Clark, 2012). Grieving makes it hard to concentrate, focus, and organize thoughts; it impairs the ability to think (Doka, 2016). Death of a child can cause one to experience an oppressive sense of failure and a loss of power and ability (Sanders, 1992). Disillusionment, emptiness, and insecurity may follow—all stemming from a diminished sense of self (Rando, 1988).

Parents wonder what they did wrong to lose their child (Neeld, 2003). They suffer guilt over what they said, or might have said, or wished they had said. Doka (2016) identified six different types of guilt that influence both one's physical and psychological health: causation guilt (how I caused my child's death), role guilt (how I could have been a better mother), moral guilt (why I am being punished or why my child is being punished for my sins and shortcomings), survivor guilt (why I am alive and my child is not) and grief guilt (shame on me for coping so poorly).

In short, emotions arising from the loss of a child are intensified and exaggerated (Sanders, 1992), and the impact of those emotions can be complicated and long lasting (Rando, 1986, 1988). Some research indicates that mothers tend to experience a more intense level of grief or distress than fathers and that they need to talk about their grief more than do men, who more often intellectualize their grief and control their expression of it—often through problem-solving approaches. These findings apply to loss of a child regardless of the age of the child, that is, whether the child was young, an adult child or a grandchild (Doka and Martin, 2010).

In the special case of the terminal illness of a child, from the moment parents are told of the diagnosis, they begin to experience intense emotions—being stunned, shocked, or disbelieving. Sometimes it is therapeutic for parents to seek multiple opinions, but ultimately, parents feel helpless because they have no control over the illness. As the disease or illness progresses, parents must invest in the wellness of the child at the same time that they prepare for their inevitable loss. Parents will likely exhibit sadness (rather than depression, which is marked by loss of self-esteem) and guilt about not being a better protector. At the same time, the dying child may want to distance somewhat from the parent to avoid causing the parent even more pain (Buckingham, 1990). Buckingham reminds that we fear death, not only for ourselves but in particular for our children. We cannot control death; we cannot precisely determine the exact moment of death or what it means to be dead. To envision this for a child, and to be responsible or feel responsible to explain this to a child, is daunting, and perhaps insurmountable. Dying children also fear death and the dying process, and they are eager and relieved to have someone to talk with about it and to answer their questions.

In short, bereavement is a shattering of natural law because no child should have to predecease his or her parent. Parents often blame themselves (or someone else) as a way to avenge the child's death, but even self-blame allows parents to feel some control over the death or impending death of their child.

Impact on the Family

Sometimes bereaved parents strike out at one another (Rando, 1988). After all, spouses/partners are typically accessible to one another, and because grief attacks one's feelings of security, strength, assertiveness, independence, and health—all necessary for keeping any relationship positive and growing, it is not surprising that relationships often bear the brunt of painful loss.

Bereaved parents, particularly the mother, also lose a sense of family as she once knew it. Women grieve for the lost child as well as for the family system that has changed or even disintegrated. As well, the composition of families (dual parent, single parent, blended) can add complexity to both the expression and resolution of women's grief. There may be no spouse (or ex-spouse) with whom to discuss the loss of the child, or with whom memories of the deceased child can be shared.

Sometimes siblings of the deceased child contain or consciously (or unconsciously) limit their own mourning in an effort to focus on their parents' mourning (referred to as "prohibited mourning") (Barnhill and Jorgenson, 2011). The mother may also feel compelled to nurture the surviving children while simultaneously having to deal with her own grief.

Grandparents too may experience a kind of double grief in losing a grandchild and feeling sorrow for their own son or daughter who has just lost a child. Grandparents, because they have typically also experienced other losses in their lifetimes, may experience cumulative grief with the added loss of a grandchild. Again, the bereaved mother feels compelled not only to acknowledge and accommodate her parents' grief, but perhaps also the grief of in-laws and partners' parents—all that alongside her own tortured heart.

These multiple roles of mother, spouse/partner, sibling, daughter—perhaps even grandmother herself—call on extraordinary coping and nurturing capacities in women.

Longer-Term Health Impacts of Loss of a Child

It is important to understand and distinguish grief emotions from trauma response, which can become a chronic condition leading to complicated and unresolved grief inhibiting the natural healing process (Nagel and Clark, 2012). Unlike depression with its persistent sense of hopelessness, grief has an ebb and flow, with periods of intense sadness and longing as well as relief. But sometimes shock and the news of the death of a child are too sudden and too much for a mother to bear. She reels and recesses into a black, deep, stunned silence. Grief overtakes her life, and sadness turns to depression. After sudden death, the bereaved have been found to be at higher risk of complications of their grieving process (de Groot, de Keijser, and Neeleman, 2006). Similarly, some research indicates that nearly 20 years after the death of a child, parents reported more depressive symptoms, poorer well-being, and more health problems, including greater likelihood of having experienced a depressive episode and marital disruption, than parents who had not experienced the loss of a child (Rogers et al., 2008). However, research is inconclusive with respect to increased divorce rates attributable to child death. Some research indicates that divorce rates are higher after the loss of a child (e.g., Deits, 2009), whereas other research indicates that divorce rates are not higher (Doka, 2016; Fox, 2008; Schwab, 1998). Although it is acknowledged that a child's death adds inevitable stress on marriage, it may be due to lack of understanding of different ways of grieving between women and men (e.g., instrumental vs. intuitive grieving styles).

The Effect of Hidden or Disenfranchised Grief

At various times in their lives, women may also experience hidden grief associated with termination of a pregnancy (electively or through miscarriage) due to the stigma associated with abortion in American culture (McCoyd and Walter, 2016). New mothers who lose babies can experience disenfranchised grief, which can lead to unresolved feelings and isolation (Doka, 2002). Both hidden and disenfranchised grief may promote guilt feelings and thus inhibit women's healing and their ability to find new meaning after the loss of a child.

Support for Mothers' Healing

Mothers suffer physical, mental, and psychological impacts of a child's death, and it may take longer than expected to recover—perhaps even a lifetime.[2] Crying is helpful. Tears of sadness have a chemical makeup that is different from tears of joy. Sadness tears release substances that have a calming effect, and thus tears are a sign of healing (Deits, 2009).

It may be difficult for a woman to resume regular duties such as shopping, taking surviving children to sports activities, or other activities she once enjoyed. Death causes a complete reordering of priorities in life and the routines of parents. Birthdays and anniversaries, for example, may be difficult and require advance planning. Memorializing the child is common, particularly when the death involved military, medical, or justice system involvement (Blank, 2013).

These things aside, though, Doka (2016) suggests that one of the most difficult tasks in grief is reconstructing one's beliefs in the face of loss. Having a sense of purpose or renewed sense of being and reason for existing are critical to women's reclaiming their own lives and finding new direction in the face of loss of their child.

It is critical that women feel that they are supported by their community in dealing with their grief experience (McCoyd and Walter, 2016). Even joining online support groups for mothers is a way of creating an "online afterlife" (McCoyd and Walter, 2016). Supporting women reduces the risk of depression, which can have a devastating effect on surviving siblings' capacity for attachment (Gerdes et al., 2007), and their generative ability to provide strong nurturing to their own children. Survivors of child loss do find benefit by reframing painful events as opportunities for growth (Barnhill and Jorgenson, 2011). As Deits (2009) suggested, "You aren't falling apart; you are coming together" (p. 36).

Conclusion

Women mourn the hopes and dreams of the child they lost. They mourn not only what the child was, but what the child might have been. The entire family system is affected by the loss: siblings, grandparents, step-parents, and relatives as well as friends and neighbors down the street or miles away.

What grief does well is to cause us to reassess our fundamental view of the world, our assumptions about what is, how the world works, and our place in it. Grief forces women—indeed, *allows* us—to create a different world for ourselves, with a new sense of purpose, incorporating the loss of our child into it. In the wake of having no choice as to the death of our child, we are called on to rediscover choice in our life and to act on those choices.

Grief, as a transitional experience in a woman's life, opens us to look at the reality of our lives in new ways, engendering growth (Doka, 2016). "Only when the lost person has been internalized and becomes part of the bereaved, a part that can be integrated with the bereaved's own personality and enrich it, is the mourning process complete" (Buckingham, 1990, p. 101).

Notes

1. Current stats on death of a child due to various causes (United States).
2. Sanders (1992) suggested that renewal from spousal loss may take 3–5 years, but loss of a child may take 10–20, or even a lifetime.

CHAPTER NINE

Retirement Loss and Grief

Trends in Life Expectancy and Retirement

Between 1950 and 2010, the global population nearly tripled, and the U.S. population doubled. Population growth from 2010 to 2050 is expected to be much slower and to tilt to the older age groups. As well, there have been significant changes in life expectancy. Between 1930 and 1960, life expectancy increased by more than 12 years, particularly so for men at the higher end of the economic ladder. However, this trend is even more pronounced for women. Women in the top earnings bracket who reach age 50 can now expect, on average, to live another 41.9 years (the income gap surged from 4 more years for people in higher-income groups to more than 13 years).[1,2,3]

Between May 2000 and May 2016, the Pew Research Center in the United States reported that the percent of people over age 65 who held jobs in the United States increased from 12.8 percent to 18.8 percent (and that's just those people who had jobs, not those also seeking jobs). Over this 16-year period, employment rose among 65- to 69-year-old s (close to one-third work), but also among those ages 70–74 (about one-fifth work). A 3 percent increase in employment was also reported (from 5.4% to 8.4%) for the 75-plus age group. The reasons for this increased employment of seniors? Some are economic: fewer employees have fixed pensions, and the age of eligibility for Social Security in the United States has increased. Some reasons are social and health related: lengthened life spans, improved health (at least among high-income seniors), and people with higher education levels generally working longer and having more interesting and less physically demanding jobs. However, the major reason that seniors work longer is because they can. They are physically able to, and they want to.[4]

With greater numbers of women working longer, combined with the "longevity revolution" (Taylor and Mintzer, 2011; Sadler, 2000), women can expect to spend perhaps 20 or 30 years in retirement. The transition to retirement, and the various transitions *in* retirement make this phase in a woman's life very significant (Borrero and Kruger, 2015; Hovanec and Shilton, 2016; Ragg, 2013). In addition, as women typically experience a different work reality than do men, it is not surprising that a woman's experience of transition into retirement, and of retirement, is also unique to women (Borrero and Kruger, 2015; Hovanec and Shilton, 2016; Price 2003; Schlossberg, 2004; Skucha and Bernard, 2000). Further, because women are generally expected to outlive men at an increasing rate, and therefore experience loss and grief at an ever more increasing rate, the retirement experience creates yet another layer of loss for women (Span, 2015)—a loss that occasions grief.

Elizabeth's Experience of Retirement: A Culminating Grief

Elizabeth had two marriages, both long term. She regards herself as having lived primarily a traditional role in her first marriage, even though she worked full time and maintained the family home, with some support from her husband for childcare. She participated in the family business and had a large circle of family, friends, and relatives with whom she maintained and often organized regular social contact. Soon after the dissolution of that marriage, Elizabeth pursued graduate and postgraduate studies, where she met her second husband. In her second marriage, Elizabeth described her role as less traditional, with greater emphasis on a modern/postmodern role. She felt quite comfortable transitioning between traditional and modern classifications, but realized that the different social moirés between her professional and personal life presented a constant balancing act, not dissimilar from what she had experienced during her first marriage. Still, she felt she coped well with the ambiguity of being wife, mother, business partner, and independent woman entrepreneur. That second marriage ended amicably after almost 25 years. Elizabeth is now in the third year of living a single, retired life. This is her retirement experience.

> I've thought a lot about my retirement experience, mostly because I had resisted retirement for such a long time. In fact, I used to call retirement the "R word." My ex-husband wanted to retire about five years before I did, which put me under quite a lot of pressure. Simply put, I wasn't ready to give up everything that I had worked so hard to earn. We had started our business together, and we had done quite well. And then, just retire and

turn away from our business and our livelihood like we hadn't even been there? That made no sense to me whatsoever.

There were things I wanted to do besides work—things I had neglected over the past quarter century or so, but I always thought those things could wait. We didn't live what you'd call a very balanced lifestyle, that's for sure, but we did enjoy our time off. We took trips; we served as good role models for our staff; and our company had a good reputation. So, if we retired—what then? My ex-husband and I were the lifeblood of the company. It was gratifying in some ways, but it also felt like a huge responsibility, especially when it came time to close the doors.

Our business was our baby. We didn't share children, so, morning and night, conversation in our home and on the way to work generally focused on "the business." Little wonder, we ran out of energy for the marriage. But that was kind of how I saw retirement—a running out of energy, a giving up. At least, that was my sense of it. That was how I had seen my grandparents retire from their businesses (my grandmother's life hadn't changed much, other than she seemed to slow down quite a bit). But my grandfather had been a vibrant man, and when I think of him in retirement, I see him sitting in his favorite chair at the window overlooking the street—just sitting mainly, watching the cars go by. And in the summer he would spend a lot of time with his apple tree and his raspberries in his garden. By this time, many of his friends had passed away, so his world began to shrink, and I guess that's the vision of retirement that surely I did not want for myself.

After I closed down our business and became formally "retired," I enjoyed the break—for a while. And then I began to feel useless. I really missed the interaction with people—staff and clients. We had been fortunate in our business that many of our clients were very bright people; interesting to talk to and spend time discussing issues with; and, most importantly, their jobs and the decisions we made impacted other people's lives. Giving advice to those clients meant something. It was important work, and I missed it. I missed feeling like what I was doing mattered. It wasn't that I needed the accolades. I just needed to know that I was spending my time on something important, not only to me but to others as well. When I retired, all that stopped.

When I think about it now, losing all that was one of the saddest times of my life. When my father died several years earlier, it was my first encounter with the death of someone very significant in my life. It was strange how my body was remembering those same feelings now in retirement—the emptiness, the constant absence, the vacancy—always an empty place at family gatherings. The futility of a life lived far too short.

Retirement had this same feeling for me. It felt like death. And it hurt—emotionally, physically, and spiritually. It was as if I could feel the energy draining from me with every passing day. It was a cold and silent loss. No more winning proposals, closing the deals, morning meetings with staff; no discussion of concepts, approaches, frameworks, or findings; no interpretation. Nothing. No phone calls, meetings, presentations. All of the things I had built and come to enjoy, and had become pretty good at, had come to a screeching halt. Retirement doesn't really sound like a death, but it certainly felt that way to me.

And that was just the start.

Even though all the work had stopped—the scheduling, planning, assigning workloads, analysis, report writing—I still couldn't get my mind off it. People would say things like "Congratulations! I'll bet you're glad to have that phase done. No more long hours, working weekends, hassles from clients. You deserve the time off!" And part of that was true. But how do you tell them that you miss it all—*really* miss it all? That was the hard part. I tried to keep a smile on my face, fake that I was really struggling. I was missing my work like crazy. Most of all, I was missing what I had been passionate about. I was missing something to *be* passionate about.

I felt like I had abandoned my business, like it was a thing that needed nurturing and that I had simply turned my back and walked away from. It felt like I had given up on it, and now in some ways, that *it* had actually given up on me too. I found myself being hurt, angry, ashamed, guilty, and resentful, and yet I had no one else to blame but me. I had made the decision for things to turn out the way they did. But I had not expected to *feel* the way that I did!

For people who don't own their own businesses, it's different. They can just walk away; say, "Good riddance"; and it's done, and they're glad to go. I have friends who have done that and they seem very happy with their decision. They closed the employee door and left—most without regret. But I found myself asking time and again, 'What on earth was I thinking!' It seemed that I had somehow betrayed a big part of myself—given away the very things that gave me credibility. It was as if I had to clear out any memory of that life and start over. When I had my briefcase in hand, I felt like someone with a purpose. Somehow, somewhere, I needed to find a new me. I needed to redefine who I was and reclaim the energy, the spunk, the tenacity, the perseverance that led me to start a business in the first place. Clearly, my work had defined a big part of me. My children were grown now and on their own. And my family had gone through other deaths, other recoveries over the years. But I must say this retirement thing, day after trying day, felt like an increasingly isolating experience. So, now what?

Those first two years of coming down, and coming out in some ways (not the gender kind, but the "who am I anyway?" kind) were important ones for me. I realize now that so much of it was like stepping through a door. On one side was what had been familiar. On the other was what I hadn't yet discovered. It wasn't that I was so afraid: I had skills. I had resources. And I had time. But I hadn't planned for it. I was too busy. And so it became hard work. It was really hard stepping through that door—not the not knowing what was out there, but the not knowing what I wanted to do with the rest of my life. I had asked those tough questions in my late teens and early 20s, and likely again in my early 30s. I didn't remember the decision being so difficult, and maybe so important. At this age, in my early 60s, when I could see the horizon of my life a little more clearly, the decision about what to do with those remaining years haunted me almost all the time. I didn't think I had much more time to "screw up" so to speak. I'd never really done that in my life, but now it seemed a real possibility. I had the role of mother, and now even new grandmother at my doorstep. I lent some care to an aging parent, to friends who were going through difficult times in their lives, but the decision about what to do now in my life fell completely on my own shoulders.

When I'd started out, knowing I wanted to build a business, I had been driven—very driven. I wanted to know everything I could about my field and also about being successful. And now I felt like I had to start all over again in virtually every aspect of my life. Sure, I had a bucket list of things I wanted to accomplish, places I wanted to see, things I wanted to learn, and learn to do really well. I took up sailing. I learned to paint a little. I learned that in the act of doing the learning, time flew by. I didn't have to dwell in what I had lost. I didn't have to wallow anymore in my own depression and self-doubt, and even shame. I felt ashamed of myself. I was an educated, skilled woman. I had helped other people for 30 years, and now I felt stuck in neutral. I'd finish doing something exciting, helm the boat, and then I'd go back home to an empty house. I looked for every reason not to be there. Traveled. Spent time in the sun. And yet, I wasn't anywhere near settled. I made some new friends. It didn't help that I was divorced—again—I had some familiarity with that, and my ex-husband and I were still friends, so I knew that it wasn't divorce grief that was getting me down. It was the culminating grief of all of it, and retirement made room for it, made the time for me to sit in it, wash that kind of grief all over me, like a mud between me and a real life—or at least a better life that I envisioned for myself.

I had reached the age where many women have already gone through more than one death in their lives. Parents, grandparents, cousins, close friends, colleagues. Some expected, some sudden. But this, this retirement thing, this was different. It was as if all of these other losses had been put in a bag with a big string around them, and finally in retirement, I had time to lay it all out and take stock of what I had really lost in my life. Now I had time to ask the tough questions. Why had some of these people been taken so young, so purposelessly in the prime of their lives? How could their losses be instructive to me, and how I would move forward in my own life now?

I found myself revisiting and trying to make sense of all the people I had lost in my life and what meaning that had given mine. I tried to think of the blood of my grandmothers that ran through my veins. What would they have done? How would they have handled this enormous change. I thought of them, drawing strength from the pioneering women who buried infant children in the dead of winter when the earth was too frozen to dig a grave. What pain must they have suffered, endured, and yet survived? I felt as if their blood must run in my veins too, and yet I had such trouble finding that strength now.

I walked miles and miles around the mountain where I lived. Some days I wore myself out from the sheer exhaustion of it, just trying to get away from myself. And pretty soon, it dawned on me. I would totally have to start again. Start over. Look again at what I found interesting and exciting. Start with the skills I already had. If I needed new ones, I would have to build those too. It really was high time I stopped feeling so sorry for myself.

I had to let go of what I thought I had lost and look deep inside to what was important that still wanted and needed to come out of me. I needed to matter in my own life. I knew that there was only one person at the center of this whole experience that could really make a difference, and that was me.

I began to read—a lot. Self-help, religion, philosophy, biographies. What had other successful people done? Was there a new way to be successful? How had they handled this winding down? Or maybe a new way of winding up?

Other people looked to me like they were enjoying their retirement. No one talked about hating it like I did. No one looked as unhappy as I felt. I had loved my job, and now it was gone. Retirement made me feel out of control. A life of schedules and deadlines no longer existed. I hated some of that, though at the same time I loved it. It had given my life structure and purpose. And now, I was tired of the floating.

It took another year, at least, for me to find my grounding. I found solace in nature, and I've let go of a lot of the hurt, the shame, the blame, and the pain of it all. I simply had to take the time to let it go. And now I have. So, I'm planning a learning vacation. Something with purpose that fits where I am now in my life. I'm taking up things just because they intrigue me. It no longer is "retirement" for me. It's a different time and place in my life. It's all brand new. It has nothing to do with "re-" anything.

When I think back on it now, I feel foolish and a bit embarrassed about the whole transition. I could have been more plan-full, had a plan for retirement, just like I did for everything else in my life. I had planned my career, planned when to marry, when to have children, what kind of business to build, what kind of staff to hire, what kind of home to buy—a million details in building a life. It felt like there were no more important decisions to be made in my life. But I was entirely wrong about that.

> I needed time to grieve. I needed time to find my spiritual self, the core of who I really was, how to find joy in my life without my business. I needed time to sort out how to stimulate myself. I couldn't depend on other people to do that for me. I had to do that for myself.
>
> My traditional life had certainly changed. Some of it I longed for, but most of it I did not. If anything, "retirement" has been a true transition for me on every front. I'm at that place now, and I must say, it's exciting, and it's freeing. The "worry times" are fewer now. I do make room for them, though, because I know they serve a useful purpose in helping me to navigate yet another course change. It is a rather mysterious adventure and if I look at it that way it becomes not just tolerable, but a new homeostasis. Living with the mystery of what's next has almost become, dare I say, comfortable. It's a bit like planting a garden blindfolded, so that you can trust that things will grow, you just don't know exactly what or where they will be. I feel pretty confident that I'll map a new course soon, and I'm okay being in this discovery phase a bit longer.

Elizabeth's experience reflects one of the most frequently reported challenges faced by people entering retirement: that of change or loss of identity (McCaw, 2011; Schlossberg, 2009). It is not uncommon today for one's work role to define who they are, and when an individual leaves his or her career this identity may require reevaluation and redefinition (Hovanec and Shilton, 2016; McCaw, 2011; McCoyd and Walter, 2016; Sadler, 2000; Schlossberg, 2004, 2009; Taylor and Mintzer, 2011). While some core components of identity may remain consistent across work and nonwork endeavors (Borrero and Kruger, 2015), retirement is a time when the understanding of self and self-worth, undergo a transition—a process that, for many, is a source of considerable anxiety (e.g., McCoyd, 2016; Schlossberg, 2004, 2009).

Finding meaning and purpose in one's everyday life is an important part of a successful transition between work and 'retirement' (Hovanec and Shilton, 2016; McCaw, 2011; McCoyd, 2016; Price, 2003; Sadler, 2000; Schlossberg, 2004, 2009; Taylor and Mintzer, 2011). A sense of value can come from finding and pursuing one's passions (McCoyd, 2016), volunteering, engaging in recreational activities or travel, spiritual journey, "encore careers" or "bridge jobs" (Farrell, 2014; Sadler, 2000; Taylor and Mintzer, 2011). As well, it's important to change the structure of social relationships and connections to replace those established in one's work role and/or physical workplace (Hovanec and Shilton, 2016; McCoy, 2016; Price, 2003; Ragg, 2013; Sadler, 2000; Schlossberg, 2004, 2009; Taylor and Mintzer, 2011). Especially for women, social connections are central to both identity development and satisfaction in retirement (Borrero and Kruger, 2015).

Critical too for women is their financial status and physical health. Women are living longer, and their retirement funds and good health must last longer with them (see, e.g., Hovanec and Shilton, 2016). And often, given their age, retiring women have lived through traditional roles and have been exposed to, if not lived directly, modern/postmodern roles as well, and they understand clearly what movement between them requires of their emotional, psychological, and spiritual capacities. For high achievers, in particular, it is important that these women stay engaged in activities that give them value and that, in return, they can value as way to sustain them into the next stage of their lives.

In summary, retirement is a process, a journey, which often is accompanied by a sense of loss and grief. As in Elizabeth's case, one can see her experience reflecting phases of numbness, searching and pining, depression, and finally, recovery (Parkes, 1964). She went through a process of redefining her personal identity and may continue to do so as she finds or creates meaningful new relationships and social networks to help sustain her (McCaw, 2011; McCoyd and Walter, 2016; Price, 2003; Schlossberg, 2004). Finding meaning and purpose is central to physical, psychosocial, and spiritual wellbeing. And, without doubt, most important of all at this phase of a woman's life, one must remain open to and awed by the mysteries that continue to surprise and anoint our very souls. Grieving reminds us of the "profundity of the mystery of living an individual life, in which struggles with finiteness, change, uncertainty, and vulnerability recur and persist" (Attig, 2011, p. 15).

Notes

1. D. Cohn and A. Caumont (2016), "10 Demographic Trends That Are Shaping the U.S. and the World," March 31, 2016. http://www/pewresearch.org/author/dcohn/.

2. P. Span (2015), "Income Inequality Grows With Age and Shapes Later Years," *New York Times*, http://www.nytimes.com/2015/10/13/health/income-inequality-grows-with-age-and-shapes-later-years.html.

3. The downside is that there is a trend toward greater inequality in longevity and life expectancy in both men and women. In other words, women with resources are expected to live longer and have a better life than those without resources, and this gap is expected to widen.

4. P. Span (2016), "Of Retirement Age, But Remaining in the Work Force," *New York Times*, http://www.nytimes.com/2016/08/02/health/retirement-working-longer.html?smid=tw-share&_r=0.

CHAPTER TEN

Health Impacts of Grief

Grief—A Significant Public Health Issue

The primary task of the public health community is to promote health and prevent disease. Identifying factors that affect the health and well-being of individuals or populations is necessary to reduce the risk of ill health. This is especially relevant for bereaved individuals who experience significant stress after the loss of someone or something significant in their lives. Epidemiological studies have uncovered a significant correlation between grief and ill health (Doka, 2016), and though pinpointing cause and effect within those relationships has been problematic,[1] research does help us to better understand the health impacts of what is considered "normal grief" and more complex, debilitating grief commonly termed "complicated grief" (Prigerson et al., 2009).[2]

It is important to acknowledge that loss and grief are universal human experiences, with individual reactions expressed through emotions, behaviors, and thought processes. In other words, grief can be experienced emotionally, physically, cognitively, and spiritually (Doka, 2016). Common emotional expressions of grief include sadness, yearning, loneliness, guilt, anger, and possibly shame and isolation. Physical manifestations can include headaches, muscular aches, menstrual irregularities, fatigue, chest pains, tightness in the throat or chest, abdominal pain, shortness of breath, weakness and oversensitivity to stimuli, or sexual dysfunction. Common psychological manifestations of grief can include increased rates of depression and anxiety, but irritability, anger, disorientation, or inability to concentrate can also be evident (Prigerson et al., 1997). Socially, grief can cause mourners to lose interest in daily routines and familiar activities, which may lead to withdrawal from family and friends. Spiritually, grief can cause us to question our belief systems, and at times, shakes the very foundation of our faith.

And yet, there are some discernible patterns in how the bereaved generally respond to grief.

Patterns of Grief Response

Some time ago, Parkes (1998) observed that the moment of death (or hearing that death of a loved one has occurred) typically causes great distress in an individual—but that in Western society that distress is quickly repressed and followed by a kind of emotional numbness that can last hours to several days. Parkes referred to this as the first phase of grieving. Second-phase grieving involves intense feelings of pining accompanied by intense intermittent anxiety. Appetite and weight are lost, concentration and short-term memory are reduced, and the bereaved person often becomes irritable and depressed. This usually gives way to third-phase grieving, marked by disorganization and despair. Weight is usually recovered after 3–4 months, and sexual and social appetites generally return, with overall recovery after about two years.

Other researchers have conceptualized response to grief as ranging from minimal psychological disruption (equated with resilience) (Bonanno and Kaltman, 2001), to acute grief lasting 1–2 years (Mancini and Bonanno, 2006), to severe and debilitating grief (sometimes life threatening) lasting longer than two years. This latter response is referred to as complicated grief (Prigerson et al., 1995) or prolonged grief disorder (PGD) (Prigerson et al., 2009). Another view is that grief response exists on a continuum, where resilient individuals regain psychological equilibrium fairly quickly after a loss (Bonanno and Kaltman, 2001), to somewhere in the middle where moderate distress is experienced in the form of shock, anguish or sadness, but over time the bereaved adapt to the loss. At the far end of the spectrum is protracted grieving, where the bereaved experiences profound separation distress, emotionally disturbing memories of the deceased, emptiness and meaninglessness, and an overall inability to accept the loss (Holland et al., 2009).

Serious Health Impacts and Risk Factors

Unfortunately, complicated grief can lead to serious medical, psychological, and psychiatric impacts[3] (Lichtenthal, Cruess, and Prigerson, 2004). But even "uncomplicated" grief can have serious health impacts. Physiological impacts can include impairment of the immune response system, increased adrenocortical activity, serum prolactin, increased growth hormone, psychosomatic disorders, and increased mortality from heart disease (especially in elderly widowers). Parkes (1998) discovered that about one-quarter of widows (and widowers) experience clinical depression and anxiety during the first year of bereavement. He also found increased rates of cardiovascular disease and impaired immune system, which he believed influenced the onset of disease such as cancer (Parkes, Benjamin, and Fitzgerald, 1969). More recent research has confirmed that widows have poorer physical health and greater weight loss over a three-year period following the death of their spouse (Wilcox et al., 2003) than other women. As well, widows who experience traumatic grief have been found to be at even greater risk of cancer or heart attack (Chen, et al., 1999).

When Prigerson et al. (1997) examined the longer-term health impacts of complicated grief, she found that the presence of traumatic grief symptoms approximately six months after the death of a spouse predicted negative health outcomes such as cancer, heart trouble, high blood pressure, suicidal ideation, and changes in eating habits at 13- or 25-month follow-up. Prigerson concluded that it may not be the stress of bereavement, per se, that puts individuals at risk for long-term mental and physical health impairments and adverse health behaviors, but "it appears that psychiatric sequelae such as traumatic grief are of critical importance in determining which bereaved individuals will be at risk for long-term dysfunction" (1997, p. 616)." Interestingly, Prigerson et al.'s research also identified that certain precipitating factors appeared to be associated with traumatic grief, including compulsive care giving, excessive dependency, and defensive separation (Prigerson et al., 1997).

Other research has confirmed additional risk factors that correlate with complicated grief. They include insecure attachment, negative interpretations of grief reactions, lack of meaning, lack of preparedness for death, a perception that the loved one suffered before death, low social support, care giver burden, and some history of psychopathology (Burke and Neimeyer, 2014). The most predictive factors have been found to be low levels of social support, avoidant/anxious/insecure attachment style, discovering the body (in the case of violent death), being a spouse or a parent of the deceased, high levels of pre-death marital dependency, and high levels of neuroticism. Burke and Neimeyer (2014) concluded that:

> Inasmuch as CG [complicated grief] is conceptualized as an attachment-based disorder, with symptomatology indicative of separation distress and preoccupation with the deceased, it is understanding that mourners who are vulnerable to feeling abandoned and alone,[4] who suffer from excessive

> anxiety or obsession, and who lose a security-enhancing- or care-providing relationship, under conditions of minimal support, and perhaps in circumstances that leave them struggling with post-traumatic imagery, would be especially prone to the development of CG. (p. 15)

It is not surprising that these individuals often turn to consciousness suppressors, such as alcohol and tranquilizers,[5,6] to help them cope with grief. A recent Harvard Medical School report[7] noted a dramatic increase in mental health disorders between 1996 and 2006—doubling among adults age 65 and older. During that same time period, rates of psychotropic medication use also increased by about the same percentage (Novotney, 2009). As DiGiacomo et al. pointed out in 2013, "The feminization of ageing and an increasing number of older women living alone with multiple chronic conditions represent significant challenges to health services and societal support systems. Older women's transition to widowhood signals concomitant health transitions and multidimensional support needs." Research confirms that the combination of comorbidities, polypharmacy, and risk behaviors influencing medication management can have a serious and adverse effect on health events.

Conversely, monitoring factors such as social and psychological supports to assist women in their quest to find meaning in the loss they have experienced[8] has been found to help mourners adapt to the life changes that loss causes (Neimeyer, Burke, Mackay, and van Dyke-Stringer, 2009). Bereaved individuals' efforts to make sense of loss appear to be a strong positive predictor of subsequent well-being (e.g., interest, excitement, accomplishment in life).[9]

Addressing Grief in Healthy Ways

Working through grief is not an easy task. It takes courage and it is hard work. Because it is hard work, a woman experiencing grief is usually physically exhausted and vulnerable to disease and illness—the result of insomnia, stress, poor dietary habits, and lack of adequate exercise. She is psychologically drained by the emotions of grief, which include sadness, anger, guilt, and anxiety, resulting in depression and low self-esteem. Social isolation is also a real problem—the necessity of moving away from familiar social settings and friends due to employment or the need to upgrade education, for example. These things can compound the loneliness and hollowness felt when a significant relationship ends.

Successful recovery from loss and grief is best achieved when recovery efforts involve intertwining physical, psychological, and social components into a regular routine associated with the basic activities of daily living. A return to order in one's life is essential, and strict adherence to a healthy routine must encompass proper diet, adequate rest, and exercise.

Diet

Meals should be eaten at regular times every day. The atmosphere at mealtime should be peaceful and relaxed to avoid overstressing the body during digestion. Fast foods, take-outs, and drive-thru dinners are not conducive to healthful living, especially when the high-fat, high-caloric food is opened and digested in front of the television set. Two meals per day are adequate for most individuals, with perhaps one or two healthy snacks such as fresh fruit or low-fat yogurt. Large meals should be avoided because of the lethargic effect, which zaps energy and increases feelings of fatigue, compounding the problem of depression.

Skipping meals should be avoided. The yo-yo effect of high and low levels of blood glucose adds unnecessary stress at this crucial time of recovering from grief. The way to maintain a constant level of glucose and its effect is to eat meals high in complex carbohydrates (whole grain cereals, potatoes, pasta, rice, and beans). An added advantage of eating complex carbohydrates is that these foods also contain dietary fiber, which assures intestinal health and efficient elimination. It also may prevent colon cancer and can aid in lowering blood cholesterol levels essential in the prevention of cardiovascular disease. (As mentioned, these diseases have been associated with grief distress [Parkes and Prigerson, 1989].) Protein consumption is also important in a balanced diet, but the amount should be limited to low-fat varieties such as chicken; fish; or, if vegetarian, beans. Red meat should be avoided due to its high fat content. Some fat in the diet is necessary, but required amounts are far lower than the typical American diet includes. For some women, loss of appetite and weight loss occurs during bereavement. For others, the stress associated with grief's emotions lead to overeating and weight gain. Therefore, caloric intake should be individually calculated in conjunction with an exercise plan.

Exercise

It is well known that the death of a loved one can cause the stress level in a bereaved person to be extremely high, and without proper care this can lead to serious health problems. Anxiety and stress related to finances, housing, loneliness, guilt, children's education, and a myriad of other issues surface quickly after a death, and the bereaved person needs to focus on relieving stressful feelings in order to successfully cope with his or her loss. Unfortunately, this can be a long process for many, and it can be a never-ending one for others.

Tranquilizers are a common method used by physicians to relieve anxiety and stress, but they are not always beneficial to the bereaved because they delay the grieving process. Physicians and mental health professionals alike are beginning to recommend exercise to their patients to improve mood (Hays, 2009). (A positive byproduct is that exercise also helps to reduce weight and lower cholesterol.)

A number of research studies highlight the effectiveness of short-term aerobic exercise to reduce anxiety sensitivity (Broman-Fulks and Storey, 2008; Smits et al., 2008; Strohle et al., 2009). And, participation in a program of strenuous aerobic exercise has been shown to be effective in reducing depression (McCann and Holmes, 1984). This is especially relevant for the bereaved because depression is a natural consequence of loss.

Exercise has also been found to be equally effective to antidepressants for treatment of depression, particularly in older persons (Blumenthal et al., 1999). Greater reductions in anxiety have been reported for exercise groups than for groups receiving other forms of anxiety-reducing treatments (Wipfli, Rethorst, and Landers, 2008). Even in the short term, people who exercise report that they feel better (Weir, 2011).

To reiterate, exercise serves as an antidepressant and offers resistance to physiological and emotional consequences of psychological stressors, including anxiety (Salmon, 2001). Exercise is therapeutic and has many physiological and psychological benefits, including self-mastery and social integration. It is often the first step in lifestyle modification for the prevention and management of chronic disease (Anderson and Shivakumar, 2013), for which the bereaved are at risk because of sedentary lifestyles that depression can precipitate.

In 2002 the U.S. Department of Health and Human Services reported that regular exercise significantly reduces causes of mortality by up to 30 percent for men and women across all age groups and racial/ethnic categories. The Centers for Disease Control and Prevention recommends 30 minutes of moderate- to high-intensity exercise for at least five days a week for all healthy individuals.[10] Several epidemiological studies have shown that exercise improves one's self-esteem and sense of well-being, slows rates of age-related memory and cognitive decline, and reduces signs of depressive and anxiety symptoms. As well, exercise offers a protective factor against the development of mental disorders (van Minnen, Hendriks, and Olff, 2010). Physical exercise can positively impact cognitive functioning and may represent an effective strategy to improve memory in those who have begun to experience cognitive decline (Nagamatsu et al., 2013). These findings are all relevant to the increasing population of widows reflected in the baby boomer bulge.

One type of exercise that has received much attention in enhancing psychological well-being is running (Ekkekakis, 1995). Running has been shown to have a positive effect on depression, nervousness, inability to sleep, and inability to cope with the environment (Griest et al., 1978). Physicians, psychiatrists, and psychologists are beginning to support running as a method of treatment. In his book *The Joy of Running* (2013), psychiatrist Kostrubala, MD, reported that in conversations with runners who run short, long, and medium distances, running done in a particular manner is a natural form of psychotherapy. Kostrubala discussed the occurrence of an "altered state of consciousness" during which runners experience a euphoric "runner's high." Anderson and Shivakumar (2013) reported similar findings linking the positive effects of running on specific psychological and emotional states: depression, anxiety, and self-esteem—all potential problem areas with the bereaved. The consensus among veteran runners is that running is relaxing and reduces tension. It helps to take one's mind off problems by distracting, and the positive effects of running are sustained long after the run is over. What is more, running increases respiratory efficiency, muscle tone, and blood volume, and helps with weight control; moreover, in comparison to other therapies, is inexpensive and time efficient.

Another popular exercise that has been found to be beneficial to the bereaved is yoga. Yoga can improve overall physical fitness, strength, flexibility, and lung capacity while reducing heart rate, blood pressure, and back pain. It also strengthens social attachments, reduces stress, and relieves anxiety, depression, and insomnia. Yoga is being used with post-traumatic stress disorder (Novotney, 2009) and is a proven strategy to benefit mental health. It enhances resilience and improves mind–body awareness and is a natural and readily available approach to maintaining wellness and treating mental health issues (Novotney, 2009). Yoga appears to modulate stress response systems and decrease physiological arousal (reducing heart rate, lowering blood pressure, and easing respiration). As well, there is indication that yoga helps to increase heart rate variability, an indicator of the body's ability to respond to stress more flexibly (Harvard Health Publications, 2009).

Rest

The mind and body require rest. Different individuals participate in various activities that encourage relaxation (including meditation or massage), but sleep is most basic to mind and body relaxation. The amount of sleep needed is an individual requirement, averaging between six and eight hours per night. Setting up a routine of rest and activity means a period of trial and error. The importance of regularity in sleep patterns cannot be overemphasized for the bereaved. Sleeping late in the morning after a late night does not guarantee adequate rest. To function at an optimum level, the mind and body must be maintained with a balance of nutrition, exercise, and rest. Again, exercise, rather than medications, is a preferred choice to support good sleep.

Psychological Well-Being

The importance of psychological well-being cannot be underestimated in the grieving process. The support of a psychiatrist or psychologist may be helpful to listen to and ascertain the level of support appropriate in the bereaved's situation. Widow-to-widow programs and divorce groups, for example, can have a positive effect on the bereaved's grieving process.

One finding that may seem surprising is humor as a wellness strategy for the bereaved. Research indicates that recently widowed women (and men) rated humor and happiness as being very important in their daily lives, and that following the death of their spouse, they were experiencing these emotions at higher levels than they expected (Lund et al., 2008). Being involved in social interactions that create and promote happiness, are enormously beneficial to the bereaved.

Conclusion

Progressing through grief can be a starting point for the bereaved to develop new positive lifestyle habits, a new outlook on life, and active self-realization and self-fulfillment. Controlling factors such as diet, exercise, sleep, and connection or reconnection to family, friends, and community may be the first steps to regaining control of one's life rather than passively accepting the feelings of helplessness and depression that can lead to serious physical, emotional, and psychological problems. Although it is not easy, the bereaved do have an opportunity to lead happy, healthy, and fulfilled lives by drawing on their own inner strengths and resources as well as the support of caring others around them, to learn "how to be and act in a world transformed by loss" (Attig, 2011, p. viii).

Controlling the basic aspects of one's life, such as what we eat, how we spend our free time, and how we look, contribute greatly to our overall sense of self-esteem, which often controls our psychological and emotional well-being. Rather than letting eating habits become destructive or letting physical tension build up, a sensible diet and sustained program of exercise can lead to physical and emotional stability. A person who is in control of her own life on every level is happier and more fulfilled than a person who feels manipulated by a sense of fate. A person who may have been living passively previous to loss may be shocked into having to assume more control over her own life. Although it may seem counterintuitive, loss and grief can be tremendous opportunities for relearning both our world and ourselves.

Notes

1. Establishing causal effect is difficult because of the complexities of human behavior and circumstances of individuals prior to their loss; compounding this difficulty is the difficulty as well of tracking these same individuals over the long term; thus the lack of availability of pre–post data.

2. Prigerson et al. (2009) identified that criteria for prolonged grief disorder (PGD) included in the *DSM-IV* or *ICD-10* can enhance the detection and potential treatment of bereaved individuals at heightened risk of persistent distress and dysfunction.

3. Prolonged grief includes symptoms that have been found to be conceptually linked to depression and several other comorbidities (Schaal, 2015).

4. Other research supports this conclusion. Older adults with long mental health histories, and perhaps multiple previous losses, may also be at considerable risk of complicated grief (Shah and Meeks, 2012).

5. It has been commonly accepted that women who were too socially dependent on their deceased spouses often had greater adjustment problems than women who were not (Lopata, 1973, 1979).

6. In general, grief interventions and treatment targeted for improving depression have been found ineffective in dealing with complicated grief (Shah and Meeks, 2012).

7. Harvard Health Publications (2009), *Health Affairs*, 28(3) May/June, http://www.health.harvard.edu/mentalextra.

8. The concept of widows developing new identities is not a new one (Lopata, 1979) and has been supported in counseling and therapy approaches since the 1980s (e.g., Worden, 1982).

9. Narrative therapies and processes have also been found to offer opportunity for both continuity and change (Romanoff, 2001). Spiritual beliefs in God's existence have also been found to be related to less grief (Easterling et al., 2000).

10. Many organizations across the United States support exercise (e.g., Hospice Caring Project of Santa Cruz County–Center for Grief and Loss, Mayo Clinic).

CHAPTER ELEVEN

Beginnings and Reconciliations

A Painful Reality

Loss is a very real part of human experience that may not occur very frequently but can have profound effects on an individual's life. Loss is something we must learn to accept and cope with. The late anthropologist Margaret Mead said, "When a person is born we rejoice, when they've married we jubilate, but when they die we try to pretend that nothing has happened." This kind of avoidance, a veiling of actual circumstance, has negative consequences for all involved, but especially for those who have experienced the loss.

In our society, it is very difficult to end a relationship after the person has died, and it is difficult to end a relationship that itself has died. The cost of our personal commitment, the "price of love,"[1] is grief, which has negative consequences in the lives of those involved. And yet, loss and grief can also lead to positive change and growth in a person's life.

After we lose someone or something close to us—whether through death, divorce, separation, or retirement—we feel the cost of that commitment. Those costs can be high, and they can be very challenging. Sickness, anxiety, anger, depression, and even death can occur after we suffer a major loss. But this does not necessarily have to be the outcome. What can we do to cope with our loss? How do we center ourselves again, learn to live again, albeit differently and in the absence of the one or thing we loved?

The Journey through Grief—A Review

The process of grief, whether from the loss of someone you love, loss of a job or career, or some other type of loss, entails a similar range of experiences that are not bound to prescribed phases or stages or even time lines. Various approaches and the arguments against them have been outlined in earlier chapters of this book. But grief has a look to it and a certain face that does have some commonality.

There is that first psychological state of shock at hearing the news of the death of a loved one, but also the sudden realization that something has actually ended, and with that a certain numbness and unreality of a life now changed. We seem swallowed in our emotions; our behaviors seem rote and mechanical; and we seem to have limited memory of conversations or discussions that have occurred with other people. This state of shock is normal and generally passes quickly, although the reality of absence soon seeps in. The very strong and very real feelings that come with loss are extremely intense—and more than frightening. The numbness that everyone experiences following a major loss is the mind's way of letting one deal with all of the details that surround the loss. Numbness allows our body and mind to process the details. It gives us a much-needed time-out. How long that lasts is generally up to us. During this time, we may feel distant and disconnected, even from ourselves. And sometimes this leads people to believe that we are under control. In reality, the finality of our loss has not yet been fully felt. The body begins to process loss bit by bit.

After a few weeks, another set of experiences will be triggered by feelings of emptiness and the permanence of loss. Our sense of pain and abandonment can lead to loss of appetite, sleep, and overwhelming depression. These feelings are perfectly normal, and they are vitally necessary to continue to cope. The best thing to do at this time is to loosen inhibitions and emotions to their fullest. Painful as they are, acknowledging their existence is the first step toward alleviating them. It may look like backsliding, but it is not. Persistent weeping, lack of focus, apathy, and black depression are all positive signs at this time, for they show that one is accepting the reality of what has happened—a normal reaction to loss. At this time, belongings of the deceased can be intense painful reminders of the loss. It is not uncommon for the bereaved to want to look at photographs or videos of the deceased. Thinking that one sees or hears the deceased is also common. We may feel like we are going crazy, but we're not. True mental illness is relatively permanent, whereas these grief behaviors are transient, and they will pass as one begins to cope with grief. Feelings of anger may also surface at this time, creating further confusion, but why not? One has been left alone, deserted, without one's most important system support system, especially if the loss has been a spouse. It is logical for the bereaved to feel angry with the one who has departed. And although this anger is natural, and almost inevitable, feeling guilty about one's anger is also natural—but unhealthy, if the guilt persists.

Recognizing and acknowledging our feelings about loss is what distinguishes us as human beings. Our feelings eventually provide us strength to endure and move forward. There is no real time line for this because each person is different precisely because each person's life context is different. Research used to tell us that the degree of attachment to the deceased or the thing lost influenced the duration of our grief, but some now dispute this claim altogether, arguing that an individual's resilience is a much more important factor influencing how one grieves and how one copes (Doka, 2016). Recognizing our own "grief experience," helps us to situate ourselves within this common human experience. It allows us to organize our feelings into coherent and manageable pieces so that, as bereaved, we can feel some control, safety, and a sense that overcoming our grief is an achievable, if not inevitable, process. We understand that it will take some time. We just don't know how much.

For women, who have an innate sense of caregiving and nurturing, this uncertainty is unsettling.

The first signs that a person is dealing successfully with her pain may at first be slight, but any sign, however small, is a major accomplishment, and she should feel good about this success. Again, a day spent without experiencing pain followed by a very painful day does not indicate backsliding, but only the unpredictability associated with the period of recovery. Congratulations for every good hour are well in order, however many hours that may be.

Understanding the different aspects of grief can be instrumental in realizing that one is normal and that it is okay to feel the intense emotions that grief calls forward. What is significant is that although this pain may feel like it exists only in the mind, a very real and present danger exists for the body. The bereaved are under tremendous stress, and the body feels it. Loss of appetite, loss of sleep, and apathy can be very harmful to one's overall well-being.

Grief can affect weight gain and weight loss, and both can cause health problems and an even further lowering of self-esteem. A healthy diet may seem like the last thing that one should be worried about when a significant loss occurs, but one's level of health inevitably reflects on how well and how fast one recovers from loss. Depression, anxiety, anger, guilt, and loneliness all have a severe impact on the eating habits of the bereaved, so a diet rich in protein is important.

Exercise too is a very important aspect of recovery. Muscles that are utilized and healthy circulatory and respiratory systems make people feel better in many ways, and most importantly, exercise supports positive self-esteem. It is not important to run a marathon or lift heavy weights; each individual is different and has different needs. It is only important to remain active physically whether this activity takes the form of running, swimming, or walking the dog. It is very important that one does not cease physical activity when mourning a loss. Being active is part of expressing individuality, and cessation of physical activity can mean a further loss of self-esteem. Survivors need to help themselves through meeting their nutritional and physical needs, even though these may seem the very least important things to attend to at the time of loss.

Loss of sleep is often a sign of depression and a sign that the individual is suffering. Getting enough sleep is critical. Realizing that we are our own most important resource and focusing on health matters helps us to develop a close, intimate relationship with ourselves—especially during the difficult time of loss when it is extremely important to have a well-developed sense of self. Intense introspection is the only thing that can bring the individual survivor of loss to the point of understanding what that loss means in our life, and learning what works to incorporate that loss into our life is what helps us to move forward with self-awareness and self-confidence. These are important milestones in coping with loss and integrating loss into a new life pattern.

The Individuality of a Woman's Grief Experience

In this book, we have focused on building a better understanding of women's grief—not because it is so *completely* different from a man's grief, but because there are social and cultural influences that have made the loss and grief experience for women remarkable in some ways, and it is those experiences that we have tried to illuminate.

In the first two chapters, the social construction of the roles of women (traditional, transitional, modern/postmodern) was explicated in light of a historical look at how grief has been conceptualized and addressed over time. Those insights help us to better understand how women may respond to grief differently, not only because of their age, education level, and financial and social status but because of the critically important sociocultural environment in which the woman was raised and how she functions in her current situation.

A woman's response to loss and grief is influenced by the depth of grief she feels within the context of her life. It is not that grief defines her. It is that she defines her life within—and perhaps in spite of the loss and grief she experiences and the extent to which she integrates that absence into

Table 11.1 What Have Women's Roles Got to Do with Grief Response, Anyway?

	The Traditional Woman (Traditional Societies)	The Transitional Woman (Modern Societies)	The Modern/Postmodern Woman (Postmodern Societies)
Role Characteristics (A Summary)	(Generally over age 40) As primary caretaker, caregiver, and nurturer of the family, the traditional woman's focus is the family and the home. The traditional woman strives to gain approval from parents, family, husband, and church.	The transitional woman weighs the social mores to consider others' opinions, but her own matter as well. She may experience guilt about childcare while being employed outside the home. Men can be supportive (neotraditional) or not, and expect both traditional and modern functions from their spouses/partners (supportive men are generally of a younger generation than traditional men). About three-quarters of women are widowed in middle age (approximately ages 45–65), which causes women to look to roles of their daughters and their mothers simultaneously to determine what may be expected of them. Widowed elderly women are generally resigned to the role they have assumed throughout their life and are ill prepared for independent life.	Modern women will have careers of their own, and will likely raise a family. Their efforts are split among self, partner, family, career, and community, and they sometimes experience conflict in self-definition. The postmodern woman draws on both masculine and feminine traits as required.

(continued)

Table 11.1 *(continued)*

	The Traditional Woman (Traditional Societies)	The Transitional Woman (Modern Societies)	The Modern/Postmodern Woman (Postmodern Societies)
Grief Response (A Summary)	A traditional woman's grief is often severely emotional, internal, and private (or open, depending on her culture). Grief can be prolonged. The traditional woman strongly adheres to social norms and will nurture other bereaved individuals, sometimes setting aside, delaying, or denying her own grief.	The transitional woman receives mixed messages about detaching from her grief, breaking bonds with the deceased, and moving on as quickly as possible. Nevertheless, historically grief has been conceived as something to be "worked through." Grief work takes time, and because love is eternal, a continuing bond with the deceased is encouraged. The transitional woman may openly express her grief, or not, depending on her culture and other factors such as her age and social status.	The modern woman's responses to grief reflect grief norms that are in flux. Her expression may be instrumental or intuitive,[1] or a combination. Rather than seeking out professional help, women may search out support groups or individuals who have shared similar losses and experiences as a way of finding their new place in a changed social context. The modern woman may choose to align with the cultural context in which she finds herself, or she may turn away from it as an independent woman. The duration and intensity of her grief may vary.

[1] The emotional style of grieving is referred to as an "intuitive" pattern, whereby grievers explore and express their emotions, whereas in an "instrumental" pattern, grief is experienced physically (e.g., restlessness or bodily pain) (Doka, 2016).

her continuing life journey. Women's experiences of loss and grief can be very complex, and for many women it is a difficult journey and a difficult story to tell—particularly for women of the baby boomer generation who are now reaching their 60s and 70s. Many of these women were raised in traditional households, where grief was felt and expressed privately and where one just carried on in spite of the lead in one's heart.

For women who have been socialized into a traditional role of caregiving and dependency, a traditional grief response can be expected (Gilligan, 1993; Pipher, 1994). However, because of the growing number of women who are now well educated, with careers of their own (many living independent, single lives and sometimes raising children on their own as well), a grief response that is more reflective of a modern/postmodern woman is becoming more common. As well, women who are younger and who have been raised in modern/postmodern households and societies may experience their partners (usually male) as being more "empathic, egalitarian and sensitive" (Pollack, 1998). These combined factors are changing the complexion of women's grief response—to say nothing of the multicultural influences on both the ways girls and young women are raised and the manner in which they are expected to respond within the boundaries of their particular social and cultural relationships with the males in their lives (i.e., spouses/partners, fathers, brothers, cousins, etc.) and/or significant others of any gender orientation. In short, the culture shaping women's grief is inevitably in transition itself, making any set pattern or expectation of response both unrealistic and ill advised. Nevertheless, for now, and in light of a burgeoning older population of women at hand, the following reference points do provide a way to think about what a woman's experience of loss and grief may look like.

Healthy Expression of Grief

There are varying views on expressions of grief. One view, which we support in this book, is that open expression of grief is much healthier than holding it inside or denying it altogether. Denial is an unconscious psychological defense related to the social norm that individuals always appear "cool, calm, and collected." The reality is that there are many times when human experience is anything but "calm." People are taught to be strong and in control, but often this involves a false sense of strength. The true sign of strength is the ability to express actual feelings, not deny or suppress them. Emotions are not weaknesses. They are not lesser than reason and do not show weak lapses in self-control. They are a legitimate part of experience, just as masculine and feminine traits are a legitimate part of our human characteristics and potentialities.

If sadness is experienced, it is important to cry. If anger is felt, beating on a mattress with a broom, jumping up and down, or yelling aloud are all helpful. Release of extreme emotional tension will help the survivor feel much better.[2] Destructive behavior such as breaking furniture or windows will only create worse feelings later and will destroy any benefits gained.

It is unfortunate in the Western world that showing emotion is perceived as weakness when, in fact, it takes a good deal of strength to let oneself express strong emotions. Probably the most helpful change that could take place to assist survivors of loss would be a change in how our society values masculine and feminine characteristics. Qualities traditionally associated with the masculine, such as aggressiveness, competitiveness, and rigid suppression of anything that is not strictly "rational," have traditionally been valued more highly than have feminine qualities, such as warmth, expressiveness, and caring. That these feminine qualities have been consistently derided and seen as weak is directly related to the difficulty survivors of loss have in progressing through the grieving process. A reevaluation of the masculine and feminine and an increased awareness that these qualities that are indigenous to all human beings, irrespective of biological sex, would be extremely beneficial to both the individual experiencing grief and to societies as a whole—particularly in a world where the masculine ethic of aggression has forced people everywhere through the devastation of two World Wars and now terrorism on a global scale. Both masculine and feminine qualities are valuable and necessary. A widespread acceptance of the integration of the masculine and feminine would help each of us to experience a more healthy grieving process.

Research supports this view. "Intuitive" responses to grief (i.e., through expressing and exploring emotions, commonly ascribed to a feminine response pattern) and "instrumental," or more physical, expression through restlessness or bodily pain, where one "thinks through" or "acts" out grief, commonly ascribed to a more masculine response pattern (Doka, 2016), are both considered effective coping strategies (Doka and Martin, 2010).[3] Importantly, how one grieves and the intensity of the grief response bear no relation to the depth to which one loved the person or the thing lost (Doka, 2016).

Grief as Opportunity for Change and Growth

For survivors to get themselves back into emotional, physical, psychological, and spiritual balance, relying on oneself as their greatest resource can be uplifting and immensely valuable. No one can specify how a person should or should not feel at a particular point in the grieving process, and no one can know exactly what is going on inside the bereaved's mind or heart. One of the most important things a survivor of loss can do, or that anyone else can do to help stabilize and improve the survivor's self-esteem, is to shift the locus of control from others to the self. Accepting the opinions of others as fact can be very damaging and can seriously impede personal progress. Family and friends can be a great help to the survivor of loss, but only those who have experienced grief can truly understand the situation, and these are people to whom a survivor can turn for support. The survivor will have a myriad of questions, which require honest answers, and others who have similar experiences can answer some of them. Survivors should know that they are not alone in their feelings and that their feelings are normal. Culturally and spiritually supportive community support groups can offer specific and directed counseling as required.

The process of grief is not easy and may in fact be the most stressful and painful time in a person's life. However, loss initiates change, and it is up to each individual to decide the form that change will take. Loss can sometimes work as a starting point from which to consciously change many destructive behavioral patterns such as letting the locus of individual self-esteem center on others (as in a traditional role). Loss is never a pleasant experience, but it can form the basis for a way of living through active, conscious choice controlled by the thoughts and actions of the individual herself. Living in the present initiates one into an awareness of the positive within oneself, an awareness which is empowering and which acts as a catalyst for potential growth. For women who survive their spouses (or partners), Naomi Golan (1983) describes recovery as moving from wife to widow, to woman—a kind of metamorphosis in which the change created by the loss initiates a form of search for the self. This search involves a strong will and a personal commitment to accepting change—discovering who and what are happiest being and doing, and consciously moving to sustain this in our lives. Taking active control of our own life and living according to our own decisions is a possible and positive outcome of the grieving process for women that is highly enabling—emotionally, physically, psychologically, and spiritually. We encourage women to seek this growth through their grief, regardless of the sociocultural environment in which they were raised or in which they currently live.

Notes

1. K. Doka (2016), *Grief Is a Journey* (New York: Atria Books). Also, C. Parkes (2015), *The Price of Love: The Selected Works of Colin Murray Parkes* (New York: Routledge).

2. Keeping a journal can assist survivors of loss to understand and come to terms with the various complex and often conflicting emotions accompanying

grief. Recording feelings, along with their strength and frequency, can help survivors to organize their feelings and observe their own progress over time. For example, one might write, "Today I feel terribly empty," and that might be all. Time spent writing is important because it is also time spent thinking, and because loss often engenders confusion, the writing process, itself can help to clarify and sort through. The reflective process often leads the survivor to question their values and society's values as well—perhaps for the first time. Survivors may also question the validity of their religion or their purpose in life, and even the value of life itself. These wonderings are normal, and although answers will not come easily or quickly, it lies within the capacity of each individual to come to terms with these questions in a workable way as part of reframing self-identity.

3. Not displaying emotions such as crying (historically regarded as an inability to grieve) or not dealing with grief, especially in Western world culture, may have been derived from a grief myth that Doka refers to as "an affective bias" in counseling, particularly as it applies to men and grief (i.e., men are perceived to be less likely to show emotion or accept help, and as having more difficulty responding to loss) (Doka, 2016). Coping through open expression is one way (an intuitive pattern), as is physical expression of grief through doing or thinking (an instrumental form of expression).

Appendix: Summary of Feminist Movements

Time Frame	Main Focus
First Wave 1830–1920	
Second Wave 1960s–1970s	**Traditional Feminists** • Includes liberal, radical, and Marxist/socialist schools. • Betty Friedan's book *The Feminine Mystique* is commonly associated with the second wave and tended to reflect the interests and concerns of mainly younger, white, middle-class, articulate women. • Of prime concern were women in the home, division of labor, childcare, reproductive roles, and issues concerning women's sexuality. • Liberal feminists argued that women's oppression lies in their lack of civil rights and poor educational opportunities. • Marxist/socialist feminists believed that women are oppressed by society's structures and that capitalism and patriarchy are the primary causes.
1980s–1990s	**Contemporary Feminists** • Origins in psychoanalytical and postmodernist/ poststructuralist discourses; although there is no unifying definition of feminism, feminism is often associated with a

(continued)

Time Frame	Main Focus
	political label indicating support for the aims of the women's movement and the struggle against all forms of patriarchy and sexism. • Contemporary socialist feminists strive to understand women of color, working-class women, disabled, women, poor women, lesbian women, and old women as well as white, financially privileged, heterosexual women. • Contemporary radical feminists tend to be issues-focused: pornography, family violence, assault, rape, reproductive rights. The primary issue with radical feminism "is not gender difference, but the difference gender makes" (Bernard et al., 2000, p. 11). • Psychoanalytic feminism (also known as cultural feminism) supports a separate women's culture that should be valued and claimed as its own for its own innate qualities (see Gilligan, 1982). • Postmodern and poststructuralist feminists stress plurality (e.g., that even oppression is experienced differently by different women). Poststructuralist feminists wish to deconstruct the ideas, examine them, and reconstruct the elements, albeit with a certain amount of discomfort with the label "postmodern," which would claim that no one identity exists. • Contemporary feminists also criticize Western feminism for having been largely inattentive to race and ethnicity. • Note: The current emphasis on situating women in society is congruent with our approach in this book, that is, of learning about women's experiences of grief—not only young women but older women as well. This is consistent with criticisms meted out by both traditional and contemporary feminists of the failure of psychological models and theories to take into account aging or the experiences of women in mid-life or older women.
Post-1990s	**Post-Feminist Era** • The aging of women has been examined. Although a discussion of women and aging is covered elsewhere (e.g., Bernard et al., 2000), interestingly, Jung (1968) claimed the women in mid-life have become more familiar with

(continued)

Time Frame	Main Focus
	themselves and have easier access to the masculine side of their nature (and become more aggressive) while a parallel occurrence happens with men (they develop more feminine features of gentleness and caring behaviors).
	• Findings from Bernard et al. (2000) indicate that women's experiences of grief were related more to the way in which each woman had developed a sense of self and made sense of her own experience; interestingly, it also found that emotional characteristics drawn from the childhood of each woman gave her an important sense of her life perspectives. Women's experiences do not fit any category nicely; rather, a much more complex process of understanding the world and one's place in it produces a varied response to loss. Bernard's research pointed out that women have a wide range of reactions to bereavement (most of them nonpathological). As well, narrative and story are now seen as important paths to self-discovery and meaning making.

Source: M. Bernard, J. Phillips, L. Machin, and V. Harding Davies, eds., *Women Ageing: Changing Identities, Challenging Myths* (New York: Routledge, 2000).

References

Amato, P. R. (2010). Research on divorce: Continuing trends and new developments. *Journal of Marriage and Family*, 72, 650–666.

Anderson, E., and Shivakumar, G. (2013). Effects of exercise and physical activity on anxiety. doi: 10.3389/fpsyt.2013.00027.

Arnett, J. (2007). Emerging adulthood: What is it, and what is it good for? *Child Development Perspectives*, 1, 68–73.

Attig, T. (1996). *How we grieve: Relearning the world*. New York, NY: Oxford University Press.

Attig, T. (2001). Relearning the world: Making and finding meanings. In R. Neimeyer (ed.), *Meaning reconstruction and the experience of loss* (pp. 33–53). Washington, DC: American Psychological Association.

Attig, T. (2011). *How we grieve: Relearning the world*, rev. ed. New York, NY: Oxford University Press.

Attig, T. (2015). "Seeking wisdom about mortality, dying and bereavement." In J. M. Stillion and T. Attig (eds.), *Death, dying and bereavement: Contemporary perspectives, institutions, and practices* (pp. 1–16). New York, NY: Springer Publishing.

Balk, D., Walker, A., and Baker, A. (2010). Prevalence and severity of college student bereavement examined in a randomly selected sample. *Death Studies*, 34, 459–468.

Barnhill, J., and Jorgenson, J. (2011). *Giving meaning to grief: The role of rituals and stories in coping with sudden family loss*. http://scholarcommons.usf.edu/etd/2996.

Baum, N. (2003). Divorce process variables and the co-parental relationship and parental role fulfillment of divorced parents. *Family Process*, 42(1), 117–131.

Bent, K., and Magilvy, J. (2006). When a partner dies: Lesbian widows. *Issues in Mental Health Nursing*, 27, 447–459.

Berger, P. L., and Luckmann, T. (1967). *The social construction of reality*. Garden City, NY: Anchor.

Blank, J. (2013). *Death of an adult child: A book for and about bereaved parents.* Amityville, New York, NY: Baywood. (Original work published 1998).

Blumenthal, J., Babyak, M., Moore, K., Criaghead, W., Herman, S., Khatri, P., et al. (1999). Effects of exercise training on older patients with major depression. *Archives of Internal Medicine*, 159(19), 2349–2356.

Boerner, K., Wortman, C., and Bonanno, G. (2005). Resilient or at risk? A 4-year study of older adults who initially showed high or low distress following conjugal loss. *Journal of Gerontology*, 60B(2), 67–73.

Bohannon, P. (ed.). (1970). *Divorce and after.* Garden City, NY: Doubleday.

Bonanno, G. (2004). Loss, trauma, and human resilience: Have we underestimated the human capacity to thrive after extremely aversive events? *American Psychologist*, 59(1), 20–28.

Bonanno, G. (2005). "Resilience in the face of potential trauma." *Current Directions in Psychological Science*, 14(3), 135–138.

Bonanno, G. (2009). *The other side of sadness: What the new science of bereavement tells us about life after loss.* New York: Basic Books.

Bonanno, G. A., and Kaltman, S. (2001). The varieties of grief experience. *Clinical Psychology Review*, 21, 705–734.

Bonanno, G., Moskowitz, J., Papa, A., and Folkman, S. (2005). Resilience to loss in bereaved spouses, bereaved parents, and bereaved gay men. *Journal of Personality and Social Psychology*, 88, 827–843.

Bonanno, G., Ray, R., and Gross, J. (2007). Does repressive coping promote resilience? *Journal of Personality and Social Psychology*, 92(4), 745–758.

Bonanno, G., Wortman, C., Lehman, D., Tweed, R., Haring, M., Sonnega, J., et al. (2002). Resilience to loss and chronic grief: A prospective study from preloss to 18-months post-loss. *Journal of Personality and Social Psychology*, 83(5), 150–164.

Borrero, L., and Kruger, T. (2015). The nature and meaning of identity in retired professional women. *Journal of Women Aging*, 27(4), 309–329. doi: 10.1080/08952841.2014.950141.

Boss, P. (2004). Ambiguous loss research, theory and practice: Reflections after 9/11. *Journal of Marriage and the Family*, 66(3), 551–556.

Bowlby, J. (1961). Processes of mourning. *International Journal of Psychoanalysis*, 42, 317–340.

Bowlby, J. (1998). *Attachment and loss: Vol. 3. Loss: Sadness and depression.* London, UK: Pimlico. (Original work published 1980)

Braden, A., Overholser, J., Fisher, J., and Ridley, J. (2015). Life meaning is associated with suicidal ideation among depressed veterans. *Death Studies*, 39, 24–29.

Bramlett, M. D., and W. D. Mosher. (2001). "First Marriage Dissolution, Divorce, and Remarriage: United States." *Advanced Data*, May 31. https://www.cdc.gov/nchs/data/ad/ad323.pdf.

Broman-Fulks, J., and Storey, K. (2008). Evaluation of a brief aerobic exercise intervention for high anxiety sensitivity. *Anxiety Stress Coping*, 21(2), 117–128. doi: 10.1080/10615800701762675.

Brown, J. (2015, March). Grey divorce is all about the math. *Canadian Lawyer.* http://www.canadianlawyermag.com/5490/Grey-divorce-is-all-about-the-math.html.

Buckingham, R. (1983). *The complete hospice guide.* New York: Harper and Rowe.

Buckingham, R. (1990). *Care of the dying child: A practical guide for those who help others.* New York: Continuum.

Burke, L., and Neimeyer, R. (2014). Complicated spiritual grief: Relation to complicated grief symptomatology following violent death bereavement. *Death Studies*, 38(4), 259–267.

Cabot, T., and Wanderer, Z. (1987). *Letting go: A 12-week personal action program to overcome a broken heart.* New York: Putnam.

Cacciatore, J., and Flint, M. (2012). ATTEND: Toward a mindfulness-based bereavement care model. *Death Studies*, 36, 61–82.

Cain, A. (ed.). (1972). *Survivors of suicide.* Springfield, IL: Charles C Thomas.

Carey, I., Shah, S., DeWilde, S., Harris, T., Victor, C., and Cook, D. (2014). Increased risk of acute cardiovascular events after partner bereavement: A matched cohort study. *JAMA Internal Medicine*, 174(4), 598–605.

Carr, D. (2010). New perspectives on the dual process model (DPM): What have we learned? What questions remain? *Omega: Journal of Death and Dying*, 61(4), 371–380.

Charles-Edwards, D. (2005). *Handling death and bereavement at work.* New York: Routledge, Taylor & Francis Group.

Chen, J., Bierhals, A., Prigerson, H., Kasl, S., Mazure, C., and Jacobs, S. (1999). Gender differences in the effects of bereavement-related psychological distress in health outcomes. *Psychological Medicine*, 29, 367–380.

Cherlin, A. (1981). *Marriage, divorce, remarriage.* Cambridge, MA: Harvard University Press.

Christ, G., Siegel, K., and Christ, A. (2002). Adolescent grief: "It never really hit me . . . until it actually happened." *The Journal of the American Medical Association*, 288, 1269–1279.

Clayton, P. J., Halikes, J. A., and Maurice, W. L. (1971). The bereavement of the widowed. *Diseases of the Nervous System*, 32(9): 597–604.

Clayton, P. J., Halikes, J. A., and Maurice, W. L. (1972). The depression of widowhood. *The British Journal of Psychiatry*, 120: 71–77.

Cohn, D., and Caumont, A. (2016). *10 demographic trends that are shaping the U.S. and the world.* http://www.pewresearch.org/fact-tank/2016/03/31/10-demographic-trends-that-are-shaping-the-u-s-and-the-world/.

Coleman, R., and Neimeyer, R. (2010). Measuring meaning: Searching for and making sense of spousal loss in late-life. *Death Studies*, 34, 804–834.

Corden, A., and Hirst, M. (2013). Economic components of grief. *Death Studies*, 37(8), 725–749.

Currier, J., Neimeyer, R., and Berman, J. (2008). The effectiveness of psychotherapeutic interventions for bereaved persons: a comprehensive quantitative review. *Psychology Bulletin*, 134(5), 648–661.

De Beauvoir, S. (1949). *The second sex.* English translation by H. M. Parshley, 1953. Paris: Gallimard.

De Giulio, R. (1989). *Beyond widowhood.* New York: Free Press.

De Groot, M., de Keijser, J., and Neeleman, J. (2006). Grief shortly after suicide and natural death: A comparative study among spouses and first-degree relatives. *Suicide and Life-Threatening Behavior*, 36(4), 418–431.

Deits, B. (2009). *Life after loss: A practical guide to renewing your life after experiencing major loss*, 5th ed. Cambridge, MA: Da Capo/Lifelong.

Deutch, A. (1937). *The mentally ill in America.* New York: Doubleday.

DiGiacomo, M., Lewis, J., Nolan, M., Phillips, J., and Davidson, P. (2013). Health transitions in recently widowed older women: A mixed methods study. *BMC Health Services Research*, 13. http://www.biomedcentral.com/1472–6963/13/143.

Doka, K. (1989). *Disenfranchised grief: Recognizing hidden sorrow.* San Francisco, CA: Jossey-Bass.

Doka, K., (1993). The spiritual crisis of bereavement. In K. J. Doka and J. Morgan (eds.), *Death and spirituality.* Amityville, NY: Baywood.

Doka, K. (ed.). (2002). *Disenfranchised grief: New directions, challenges and strategies for practice.* Champaign, IL: Research Press.

Doka, K. (2016). *Grief is a journey.* New York, NY: Atria Books, Simon & Schuster.

Doka, K. J., and Martin, T. L. (2010). *Grieving beyond gender: Understanding the ways men and women mourn*, 2nd ed. New York, NY: Routledge, Taylor and Francis Group.

Dombrovski, A., Szanto, K., Duberstein, P., Connor, K., Houck, P., and Conwell, Y. (2008). Sex differences in correlates of suicide lethality in late life. *American Journal of Geriatric Psychiatry*, 167(6), 699–707.

Durkheim, E. (1897). *Le suicide.* J. A. Spaulding and G. Simpson, Trans. New York: The Free Press. (Original translation published 1951).

Durkheim, E. (1947). *The division of labour in society.* G. Simpson, Trans. New York: The Free Press.

Easterling, L., Gamino, L., Sewell, K., and Stirman, L. (2000). Spiritual experience, church attendance, and bereavement. *Journal of Pastoral Care*, 54(3), 263–75.

Ekkekakis, P. (1995). Physical activity as a mental health intervention in the era of managed care: A rationale. In Ekkekakis, P., ed. *Routledge handbook of physical activity and mental health.* (Routledge International Handbooks). New York: Routledge.

Erikson, E. (1959). *Childhood and society.* New York: W.W. Norton.

Farrell, C. (2014). *Unretirement: How baby boomers are changing the way we thing about work, community, and the good life.* New York: Bloomsbury.

Forte, A., Hill, M., Pazder, R., and Feudtner, C. (2004). Bereavement care interventions: A systematic review. *BMC Palliative Care*, 3(1): 1–14.

Fox, S. (2008, January). *The divorce rate.* http://survivinggrief.blogspot.ca/2008/01/divorce-rate.html.

Freud, S. (1917). *Mourning and Melancholia. The Standard Edition of the Complete Psychological Works of Sigmund Freud, Vol. XIV (1914–1916): On the History of the Psycho-Analytic Movement, Papers on Metapsychology and Other Works,* 237–258.

Friedan, B. (1997). *The feminine mystique.* New York: W.W. Norton.

Gamino, L., Sewall, K., and Easterling, L. (1998). Scott and White grief study: An empirical test of predictors of intensified mourning. *Death Studies,* 22(7), 333–58.

Gerdes, A., Hoza, B., Arnold, L., Pelham, W., Swanson, J., and Wigal, T. (2007). Maternal depressive symptomatology and parenting behavior: Exploration of possible mediators. *Journal of Abnormal Child Psychology,* 35, 705–14.

Gettleman, S., and Markowitz, J. (1974). *The courage to divorce.* New York: Ballantine Books.

Giddens, A. (1990). *The consequences of modernity.* Stanford, CA: Stanford University Press.

Gilbert, S. M., and Gubar, S. (1979). *The madwoman in the attic: The woman writer and the nineteenth-century literary imagination.* New Haven: Yale University Press.

Gilbert, K., and Horsley, G. (2011). Technology and grief support in the twenty-first century: A multimedia platform. In R. A. Neimeyer, D. L. Harris, H. R. Winokuer, and G.F. Thor (eds.), *Grief and bereavement in contemporary society: Bridging research and practice* (pp. 365–374). New York: Routledge.

Gilligan, C. (1993). *In a different voice: Psychological theory and women's development,* rev. ed. Cambridge, MA: Harvard University Press.

Golan, N. (1983). *Passing through transitions.* New York: The Free Press (A Division of Macmillan).

Goldberg, P. (1968). Are women prejudiced against women? *Transaction,* 4, 28–30.

Gordon, A. (1974). The psychological wisdom of the law. In J. Reimer (ed.), *Jewish reflections on death.* New York: Schocken Books.

Griest, J., Klein, M., Eischens, R., Faris, J., Gurman, A., and Morgan, W. (1978). Running through your mind. *Journal of Psychosomatic Research,* 22, 259–294.

Grollman, E. (1971). *Suicide: Prevention, intervention, postvention.* Boston: Beacon Press.

Habenstein, R., and Lamers, W. (1963). *Funeral customs the world over.* Milwaukee, Wisconsin: Bulfin Printers.

Hagman, G. (2001). Beyond decathexis: Toward a new psychoanalytic understanding and treatment of mourning. In R. Neimeyer (ed.), *Meaning reconstruction and the experience of loss* (pp. 13–31). Washington, DC: American Psychological Association.

Hansson, R., and Stroebe, M. (2007). *Bereavement in late life: Coping, adaptation, and developmental influences.* Washington, DC: American Psychological Association.

Harvard Health Publications (2009a) *Health Affairs,* 28(3) May/June. http://www.health.harvard.edu/mentalextra.

Harvard Health Publications (2009b). "Yoga for anxiety and depression." April 1. http://www.health.harvard.edu/mind-and-mood/yoga-for-anxiety-and-depression.

Hays, K. (2009). *Move your body, tone your mood: The workout therapy workbook.* CA: New Harbinger Publications.

Hekman, S. J. (1990). *Gender and knowledge: Elements of a postmodern feminism.* Boston: Northeastern University Press.

Hepburn, S., and Simon, R. (2006). *Women's roles and statuses the world over.* New York: Rowman and Littlefield Publishers.

Herman, S. (1974). Divorce: A grief process. *Perspectives in Psychiatric Care*, 12(3), 108–112.

Hill, R. (2005). *Positive aging.* New York: Norton.

Holland, J., Neimeyer, R., Boelen, P., and Prigerson, H. (2009). The underlying structure of grief: A taxometric investigation of prolonged and normal reactions to loss. *Journal of Psychopathology and Behavioral Assessment*, 31(3), 190–201.

Hollis, J. (2005). *Finding meaning in the second half of life: How to finally, really grow up.* New York: Avery.

Holmes, T., and Rahe, R. (1967). The social readjustment rating scale. *Journal of Psychosomatic Research*, 11, 213–218.

Hooyman, N., and Kiyak, H. (2007). *Social gerontology.* Boston, MA: Allyn and Bacon.

Hovanec, M., and Shilton, E. (2016). *Redefining retirement: New realities for boomer women.* Toronto, ON, Canada: Second Story Press.

Hughes, M., and Waite, L. (2009). Marital biography and health at mid-life. *Journal of Health and Social Behavior*, 50, 344–358.

Jackson, C. (2013). Something more to say. *Therapy Today*, 24(5), 10–13.

James, J., and Friedman, R. (2009). *The grief recovery handbook: The action program for moving beyond death, divorce, and other losses including health, career, and faith*, 20th anniversary ed. New York: William Morrow.

Junod, H. (1962). *The life of a South African tribe*, Vols. 1–2. New York: University Books.

Kalish, R. A., and Reynolds, D. K. (1976). *Death and ethnicity: A psychocultural study.* Los Angeles: The University of Southern California Press.

Kelly, M. B. (2012). "Divorce cases in civil court, 2010/2011." Statistics Canada. http://statcan.gc.ca/pub/85-002-x/2012001/article/11634-eng.htm#a2.

Keltner, D., and Bonanno, G. (1997). Facial expressions of emotion and the course of conjugal bereavement. *Journal of Abnormal Psychology*, 106(1), 126–137.

Keuls, E. (1985). *The reign of the phallus: Sexual politics in ancient Athens.* Los Angeles: University of California Press.

Klass, D. (2005). The inner representation of the dead child in the psychic and social narratives of bereaved parents. In R. Neimeyer (ed.), *Meaning reconstruction and the experience of loss* (pp. 77–94). Washington, DC: American Psychological Association.

Klass, D., Silverman, P., and Nickman, S. (eds.). (1996). *Continuing bonds: New understandings of grief.* Washington, D.C.: Taylor and Francis.

Kochanek, K. D, S. L. Murphy, X. Jiaquan, and B. Tejada-Vera. (2016) "Deaths: Final Data for 2014." *National Vital Statistics Reports*, 65(4), June, https://www.cdc.gov/nchs/data/nvsr/nvsr65/nvsr65_04.pdf.

Komarovsky, M. (1946). Cultural contradictions and sex roles. *American Journal of Sociology*, 52(3), 184–189.

Konigsberg, R. (2011). *The truth about grief.* New York: Simon and Schuster Paperbacks.

Kostrubala, T. (2013). *The joy of running.* New York: Saint Nicholas.

Kübler-Ross, E. (1969). *On death and dying: What the dying have to teach doctors, nurses, clergy and their own families.* New York: MacMillan.

Kübler-Ross, E. (1974). *Questions and answers on death and dying.* New York: Macmillan.

Lassonde, S. (2002). Family and demography in postwar America: A new hazard of fortunes? In J. C. Agnew and R. Rosenzweig (eds.), *A companion to post-1945 America* (pp. 3–20). Malden, MA: Blackwell.

Lench, H., and Chang, E. (2007). Belief in an unjust world: When beliefs in a just world fail. *Journal of Personality Assessment*, 89(2), 126–135.

Lichtenthal, W., and Cruess, D. (2010). Effects of directed written disclosure on grief and distress symptoms among bereaved individuals. *Death Studies*, 34(6), 475–499.

Lichtenthal, W., Cruess., D., and Prigerson, H. (2004). A case for establishing complicated grief as a distinct mental disorder in DSM-V. *Clinical Psychology Review*, 24, 637–662.

Lindemann, E. (1944). Symptomatology and management of acute grief. *American Journal of Psychiatry*, 101, 141–148.

Lloyd, G., Sailor, J., and Carney, W. (2014). A phenomenological study of postdivorce adjustment in midlife. *Journal of Divorce and Remarriage*, 55(6), 441–450.

Lofland, L. (1985). The social shaping of emotion: The case of grief. *Symbolic Interaction*, 8(2), 171–90. doi: 10.1525/si.1985.8.2.171.

Lopata, H. Z. (1973). *Widowhood in an American city.* Cambridge, MA: Schenkman.

Lopata, H. Z. (1979). *Women as widows: Support systems.* New York: Elsevier.

Love, A. (2007). Progress in understanding grief, complicated grief, and caring for the bereaved. *Contemporary Nurse*, 27, 73–83.

Lund, D., Utz, R., Caserta, M., and de Vries, B. (2008). *Humor, laughter, and happiness in the daily lives of recently bereaved spouses.* Amityville, New York: Baywood.

Maata, K. (2011). The throes and relief of divorce. *Journal of Divorce and Remarriage*, 52, 415–434.

Mancini, A. D., and Bonanno, G. A. (2006). Resilience in the face of potential trauma: clinical practices and illustrations. *Journal of Clinical Psychology*, 62(8), 971–985.

Manor, L., Vincent, M., and Tyano, S. (2004). The wish to die and the wish to commit suicide in the adolescent: Two different matters? *Adolescence*, 39, 279–293.

McCann, I., and Holmes, D. (1984). Influence of aerobic exercise on depression. *Journal of Personality and Social Psychology*, 46(5), 1142–1147.

McCaw, D. (2011). *It's your time: Information and exercises to get you ready for a great retirement*. Toronto, ON, Canada: BPS Books.

McCoyd, J., and Walter, C. (2016). *Grief and loss across the lifespan: A biopsychosocial perspective*, 2nd ed. New York: Springer.

McHale, B. (2008). 1966 nervous breakdown: Or, when did postmodernism begin? *Modern Language Quarterly*, 69(3), 391–413. doi: 10.1215/00267929-2008-004

Mercer, M. (2012, March). What women should know about male grief. http://thegrieftoolbox.com/article/what-women-should-know-about-male-grief.

Miller, C. C. (2014), "The Divorce Surge Is Over, but the Myth Lives On," Upshot, *New York Times* data blog, December 2, http://www.nytimes.com/2014/12/02/upshot/the-divorce-surge-is-over-but-the-myth-lives-on.html?smid=fb-nytimes&smtyp=cur&bicmp=AD&bicmlukp=WT.mc.

Montpetit, M., and Bergeman, C. (2010). The self-concept and conjugal loss: Evidence for structural change. *Death Studies*, 34, 606–624.

Moss, M. S., Moss, S. Z., and Hansson, R. O. (2001). Bereavement and old age. In M. S. Stroebe, R. O. Hansson, W. Stroebe, and H. Schut (eds.), *Handbook of bereavement research: Consequences, coping and care* (pp. 241–260). Washington, DC: American Psychological Association.

Nagamatsu, L. S., Chan, A., Davis, J. C., Battie, B. L., Graf, P., Voss, M. W., et al. (2013). Physical activity improves verbal and spatial memory in older adults with probable mild cognitive impairment: A 6-month randomized controlled trial. *Journal of Aging Research*. doi: 10.1155/2013/861893, 2013

Nagel, A., and Clark, R. (2012). *When your child dies: Tools for mending parents' broken hearts*. Liberty Corner, NJ: New Horizon Press.

Neeld, E. (2003). *Seven choices: Finding daylight after loss shatters your world*. New York: Hachette Book Group.

Neimeyer, R. (2000). Searching for the meaning of meaning: Grief therapy and the process of reconstruction. *Death Studies*, 24(6), 541–558.

Neimeyer, R. (2001). *Meaning reconstruction and the experience of loss*. Washington, DC: The American Psychological Association.

Neimeyer, R., Baldwin, S., and Gillies, J. (2006). Continuing bonds and reconstructing meaning: Mitigating complications in bereavement. *Death Studies*, 30, 715–738.

Neimeyer, R., Burke, L., Mackay, M., and van Dyke-Stringer, J. (2009). Grief therapy and the reconstruction of meaning: From principles to practice. *Journal of Contemporary Psychotherapy*. doi: 10.1007/s10879-009-9135-3.

Neimeyer, R., Klass, D. and Dennis, M. (2014). A social constructionist account of grief: Loss and the narration of meaning. *Death Studies*, 38(8), 485–498.

Noel, B., and Blair, P. (2008). *I wasn't ready to say goodbye.* Illinois: Sourcebooks.

Norris, F., and Murrell, S. (1990). Social support, life events, and stress as modifiers of adjustment to bereavement by older adults. *Psychology and Aging*, 5(3), 429–436.

Novotney, A. (2009, November). Yoga as a practice tool. *Monitor on Psychology*, 40(10). http://www.apa.org/monitor/2009/11/yoga.aspx.

Nugman, G. (2002) "World Divorce Rate," Nugman Gulnar of the Heritage Foundation, 2002, http://www.divorcereform.org/gul.html.

Ortner, S. (1974). Is female to male as nature is to culture? In M. Z. Rosaldo and L. Lamphere (eds.), *Woman, culture, and society* (pp. 68–87). Stanford, CA: Stanford University Press.

Paloma, M., (1972). *Role conflict and the married professional woman.* In C. Safilios-Rothschild (ed.), Toward a sociology of women. Lexington, MA: Xerox.

Pannebaker, J. (1997). Writing about emotional experiences as a therapeutic process. *Psychological Science*, 8(3), 162–166. doi: 10.1111/j.1467-9280.1997.tb00403.

Parkes, C. (1964). The effects of bereavement on physical and mental health: A study of the case records of widows. *British Medical Journal*, 2, 274–279. doi: http://dx.doi.org/10.1136/bmj.2.5404.274.

Parkes, C. (1972). *Bereavement: Studies of grief in adult life.* University of California: International Universities Press.

Parkes, C. (1998). Coping with loss: Bereavement in adult life. *British Medical Journal*, 316, 856–859. doi: 10.1136/bmj.316.7134.856.

Parkes, C. (2015). *The price of love.* New York: Basic Books.

Parkes, C. M., Benjamin, B., and Fitzgerald, R. G. (1969). Broken heart: A statistical study of increased mortality among widowers. *British Medical Journal*, 1, 740–743.

Parkes, C., Laungaini, P., and Young, B. (eds.). (2015). *Death and bereavement across cultures*, 2nd ed. London: Routledge.

Parkes, C., and Prigerson, H. (1989). *Bereavement: Studies of grief in adult life*, 4th ed. New York: Routledge.

Parkes. C. M., and Weiss, R. S. (1983). *Recovery from bereavement.* New York: Basic Books.

Peck, J. H. (1961). *Life with women and how to survive it.* Englewood Cliffs, NJ: Prentice Hall.

Perrig-Chiello, P., Spahni, S., Hopflinger, F., and Carr, D. (2016). Cohort and gender differences in psychosocial adjustment to later-life widowhood. *Journals of Gerontology Series B: Psychological Sciences and Social Sciences*, 71(4), 765–774.

Pipher, M. (1994). *Reviving Ophelia.* New York: Grosset/Putnam.

Pollack, W. (1998). *Real boys: Rescuing our sons from the myths of boyhood.* New York: Henry Holt.

Price, C. A. (2003) Professional women's retirement adjustment: The experience of reestablishing order. *Journal of Aging Studies*, 17, 341–355.

Prigerson, H. (2008). Grief and acceptance as opposite sides of the same coin: Setting a research agenda to study peaceful acceptance of loss. *British Journal of Psychiatry*, 193, 435–443.

Prigerson, H., Bierhals, A., Kasl, S., Reynolds, C., Shear, M., Day, N., et al. (1997). Traumatic grief as a risk factor for mental and physical morbidity. *American Journal of Psychiatry*, 154(5), 616–623.

Prigerson, H. G., Horowitz, M. J., Jacobs, S. C., Parkes, C. M., Aslan, M., Goodkin, K., et al. (2009). Prolonged grief disorder: Psychometric validation of criteria proposed for DSM-V and ICD-11. *PLoS Medicine*, 6(8). doi: 10.1371/journal.pmed.1000121.

Prigerson, H. G., Horowitz, M. J., Jacobs, S. C., Parkes, C. M., Aslan, M., et al. (2013). Erratum: Prolonged grief disorder: Psychometric validation of criteria proposed for DSM-V and ICD-11. *Public Library of Science.* doi: 10.1371/annotation/a1d91e0d-981f-4674-926c-0fbd2463b5ea.

Prigerson, H. G., Mac'lejewskib, P. K., Reynolds, V. F., Bierhals, A. J., Newsomc, J. T., Fasiczkaa, A., et al. (1995). Inventory of complicated grief: A scale to measure maladaptive symptoms of loss. *Psychiatry Research*, 59, 65–79.

Prigerson, H.G., Frank, E., Kasl, S.V., Reynolds, C. F., III, Anderson, B., et al. (1995). "Complicated grief and bereavement-related depression as distinct disorders: preliminary empirical validation in elderly bereaved spouses." *American Journal of Psychiatry*, 152: 22–30.

Prigerson, H. G., Shear, M. K., Frank, E., Beery, L.C., Silberman, R., Prigerson, J., et al. (1997). Traumatic grief: A case for loss-induced trauma. *American Journal of Psychiatry*, 154(7), 1003–1009.

Prigerson, H. G., Vanderwerker, L. C., and Maciejewski, P. K. (2008). A case for the inclusion of prolonged grief disorder in DSM-V. In M. Stroebe, R. Hansson, H. Schut, and W. Stroebe (eds.), *Handbook of bereavement research and practice: 21st-century perspectives* (pp. 165–186). Washington, DC: APA.

Pugh, M. (1993). *Women and the women's movement in Britain 1914–1959.* New York: Paragon House.

Ragg, R. (2013, July). Think men struggle to cope with retirement? For women, it can be even tougher. Mail Online. http://www.dailymail.co.uk/femail/article-2359614/Think-men-struggle-cope-retirement-For-women-tougher.html.

Rando, T. (1986). *Parental loss of a child.* Champaign, IL: Research Press.

Rando, T. (1988). *Grieving: How to go on living when someone you love dies.* Lexington, MA: Lexington Books.

Rando, T. (1993). *Treatment of complicated mourning.* Champaign, IL: Research Press.

Rapoport, R. N., and Rapoport, R. (1972, June). *The working woman and the enabling role of the husband.* Paper presented at the 12th International Family Research Seminar, International Sociological Association, Moscow.

Rask, K., Kaunonen, M., and Paunon-Illomonen, B. (2002). Adolescent coping with grief after the death of a loved one. *International Journal of Nursing Practice*, 8, 137–142.

Rogers, C., Floyd, F., Seltzer, M., Greenberg, J., and Hong, J. (2008). Long-term effects of the death of a child on parents' adjustment in midlife. *Journal of Family Psychology*, 22(2), 203–211.

Romanoff, B. (2001). Research as therapy: The power of narrative to effect change. In R. Neimeyer (ed.), *Meaning reconstruction and the experience of loss* (pp. 245–257). Washington, DC: American Psychological Association.

Rosenblatt, P. C., Walsh, R. P., and Jackson, D. A. (1976). *Grief and mourning in cross-cultural perspective.* New Haven, CT: Human Relations Area Files Press.

Rossi, N., Bisconti, T., and Bergman, D. (2007). The role of dispositional resilience in regaining life satisfaction after the loss of a spouse. *Death Studies*, 31(10), 863–83.

Rueter, M., Holm, K., McGeorge, C., and Conger, R. (2008). Adolescent suicidal ideation subgroups and their association with suicidal plans and attempts in young adulthood. *Suicide and Life-Threatening Behaviors*, 38, 564–575.

Sadler, W. (2000). *The third age: 6 principles of growth and renewal after forty.* Cambridge: Perseus Books.

Sakraida, T. (2005). Divorce transition differences of midlife women. *Mental Health Nursing*, 26(2), 225–249.

Salmon, P. (2001). Effects of physical exercise on anxiety, depression, and sensitivity to stress: A unifying theory. *Clinical Psychology Review*, 21(1), 33–61.

Sanders, C. (1992). *Surviving grief . . . and learning to live again.* New York: John Wiley and Sons.

Sasson, I., and Umberson, D. (2009). Widowhood and depression: New light on gender differences, selection, and psychological adjustment. *Journals of Gerontology, Series B: Psychological and Social Sciences*, 69(1), 135–145.

Scarf, M. (1980). *Unfinished business: Pressure points in the lives of women.* New York: Ballantine Books.

Schaal, S., (2015). Is prolonged grief distinct from depression? *Journal of Loss and Trauma*, 20, 46–55.

Schiff, S. (1977). Personality development and symbiosis. *Transactional Analysis Journal*, 7(4), 310–316.

Schlereth, T. (1991). *Victorian America: Transformations in everyday life, 1876–1915.* New York: Harper-Collins.

Schlossberg, N. (2004). *Retire smart, retire happy: Finding your true path in life.* Washington, DC: American Psychological Association.

Schlossberg, N. (2009). *Revitalizing retirement: Reshaping your identity, relationships, and purpose.* Washington, DC: American Psychological Association.

Schwab, R. (1998). A child's death and divorce: Disspelling the myth. *Death Studies*, 22, 445–468.

Shaffer, S. (1993). Young widows: Rebuilding identity and personal growth following spousal loss. *Dissertation Abstracts International*, 54(1), 94.

Shah, S., and Meeks, S. (2012). Late-life bereavement and complicated grief: A proposed comprehensive framework. *Aging and Mental Health*, 16(1), 35–56. doi: 10.1080/13607863.2011.605054.

Silverman, P. (1981). *Helping women cope with grief.* Beverly Hills, CA: Sage Publications.

Silverman, P. (1986). *Widow to widow.* New York: Springer.

Silverman, P. and Klass, D. (1996). Introduction: What's the problem? In D. Klass, P. Silverman, and S. Nickman (eds.), *Continuing bonds: New understandings of grief* (pp. 3–27). Bristol, PA: Taylor and Francis.

Sisask, M., Kolves, K., and Varnik, A. (2009). Severity of attempted suicide as measured by the Pierce Suicidal Intent Scale. *Crisis*, 30, 136–143.

Sklansky, G. J., and Algazi, L. P. (1981). *Helping women: Counseling girls and women in a decade of change.* South Plainfield, N.J.: Group Work Today, University of Minnesota.

Skucha, F., and Bernard, M. (2000). 'Women's work' and the transition to retirement. In M. Bernard, J. Phillips, L. Machin, and V. Harding Davies (eds.), *Women ageing: Changing identities, challenging myths* (23–39). London: Routledge.

Smits, J., Berry, A., Rosenfield, D., Powers, M., Behar, E., and Otto, M. (2008). Reducing anxiety sensitivity with exercise. *Depression Anxiety*, 25(8), 689–699. doi: 10.1002/da.20411.

Span, P. (2015) "Income inequality grows with age and shapes later years," *New York Times*, http://www.nytimes.com/2015/10/13/health/income-inequality-grows-with-age-and-shapes-later-years.html.

Span, P. (2016) Of Retirement Age, but Remaining in the Work Force. *New York Times*, August 1. http://www.nytimes.com/2016/08/02/health/retirement-working-longer.html?smid=tw-share&_r=0.

Stroebe, M., Gergen, M., Gergen, K., and Stroebe, W. (1992). Broken hearts or broken bonds: Love and death in historical perspective. *American Psychologist*, 47(10), 1205–1212.

Stroebe, M., and Schut, H. (1999). The dual process model of coping with bereavement: Rationale and description. *Death Studies*, 23, 197–224.

Stroebe, M., and Stroebe, W. (1991). Does "grief work" work? *Journal of Consult Clinical Psychology*, 59(3), 479–482.

Strohle, A., Graetz, B., Scheel, M., Wittmann, A., Feller, C., Heinz, A., et al. (2009). The acute antipanic and anxiolytic activity of aerobic exercise in patients with panic disorder and healthy control subjects. *Journal of Psychiatry Research*, 43(12), 1013–1017.

"Suicide." (n.d.) Mental Health America. http://www.mentalhealthamerica.net/suicide.

Taylor, R. and Mintzer, D. (2011) The Couples Retirement Puzzle: 10 Must-Have Conversations for Transitioning to the Second Half of Life. Lincoln Street Press.

van den Berg, G., Lindeboom, M., and Portrait, F. (2011). Conjugal bereavement effects on health and mortality at advanced ages. *Journal of Health Economics*, 30, 774–794.

van Minnen, A., Hendriks, L., and Olff, M. (2010). When do trauma experts choose exposure therapy for PTSD patients? A controlled study of therapist and patient factors. *Behavior Research Therapy*, 48, 312–320. doi: 10.1016/j.brat.2009.12.003.

Walter, C. (2003). *The loss of a life partner: Narratives of the bereaved.* New York, NY: Columbia University Press.

Walter, T. (1996). A new model of grief: Bereavement and biography. *Mortality*, 1(1), 7–25.

Walter, T. (1999). *On bereavement: The culture of grief.* Open University Press.

Walter, T. (2007). Modern grief, postmodern grief. *International Review of Sociology*, 17(1), 123–134.

Waskowic, T., and Chartier, B. (2003). Attachment and the experience of grief following the loss of a spouse. *Omega*, 47(1), 77–91.

Weaver, D. (2010). Widows and social security. *Social Security Bulletin*, 70(3), 89–109.

Weir, K. (2011, December). The exercise effect. *Monitor on Psychology*, 42(11). http://apa.org/monitor/2011/12/exercise.aspx.

Weiss, R. (1975). *Marital separation.* New York: Basic Books.

Wikan, U. (1988). Bereavement and loss in two Muslim communities: Egypt and Bali compared. *Social Science and Medicine*, 27(5), 451–460.

Wilcox, S., Evenson, K., Aragaki, A. Wassertheil-Smoller, S., Mouton, C., and Loevinger, B. (2003). The effects of widowhood on physical and mental health, health behaviors, and health outcomes: The Women's Health Initiative. *Journal of Health Psychology*, 5, 513–522.

Williams, R., and Loeb, M. (1956). The adults' social life space and successful aging: Some suggestions for a conceptual framework. In B. L. Neugarten (ed.), *Middle age and aging: A reader in social psychology.* Chicago: The University of Chicago Press.

Winters, C. (2006). The feminine principle: An evolving idea. *Quest*, 94(5), 206–209, 215.

Wipfli, B., Rethorst, C., and Landers, D. (2008). The anxiolytic effects of exercise: A meta-analysis of randomized trials and dose-response analysis. *Journal of Sport and Exercise Psychology*, 30(4), 392–410.

Wolman, B. (1976). *The therapist's handbook: Treatment methods of mental disorders.* New York: Van Nostrand Reinhold.

Woodman, M. (1985). *The pregnant virgin: A process of psychological transformation.* Toronto, Canada: Inner City Books.

Worden, J. (1982). *Grief counseling and grief therapy: A handbook for the mental health practitioner.* New York: Springer-Verlag.

Worden, J. (2009). *Grief counseling and grief therapy*, 4th ed. New York, NY: Springer.

World Health Organization (2014). *Preventing suicide: A global imperative.* http://www.who.int/mental_health/suicide-prevention/world_report_2014/en/.

Wortman, C., and Silver, R. (1989). The myths of coping with loss. *The Journal of Consulting and Clinical Psychology*, 57(3), 349–357.

Young, D. and Caplan, S. (2010). Online dating and conjugal bereavement. *Death Studies*, 34(7), 575–605. doi: 10.1080/07481181003761542.

Index

About the Authors

Robert W. Buckingham, DrPH, Doctor of Public Health and graduate of Yale School of Medicine, is currently Professor of Public Health at the University of Michigan–Flint. He sits on the Board of Directors of the Association of Schools of Public Health in the European Region (ASPHER) and is the former founding Dean of the School of Public Health at the University of Saskatchewan in Canada. Buckingham is a pioneer in the development of hospice programs in the United States and worldwide. He has established clinics and orphanages in Thailand, Africa, and Honduras. He is the author of 11 books, five of which are on hospice and palliative care. Buckingham received the 2014 Nelson Mandela Award for Academic Leadership presented by Harvard University and the 2006 Ivanosky Prize by the Russian Institute of Health for Humanitarian Medicine for work with people with HIV and AIDS.

Peggy A. Howard holds a PhD in Policy and Administration from the University of Alberta, Canada. Since 1994, she has been a private-sector consultant whose expertise lies in the design and implementation of multiyear, multilevel evaluations in health and social service sectors. She has worked with diverse populations including palliative care patients, HIV clients, survivors of torture and trauma, victims of family violence, Aboriginal and immigrant people. In rural development, Howard has assessed initiatives aimed at improving economic growth and sustainability, community capacity building, improved access to learning and skill building opportunities, and improved access to health services. She also facilitated policy development on elder abuse, and Social Sustainability Plans at municipal government levels. A SSHRC scholar and phenomenologist, Howard's research into the experience of being evaluated has been published in the *Journal of Education Policy, Qualitative Studies in Education*, and *Phenomenology and Pedagogy.*

www.ingramcontent.com/pod-product-compliance
Ingram Content Group UK Ltd.
Pitfield, Milton Keynes, MK11 3LW, UK
UKHW020817290926
15470UKWH00003B/1213

9 781440 857829